COMMON
FLESHY FUNGI

by

CLYDE M. CHRISTENSEN, Ph.D.

Professor of Plant Pathology

Institute of Agriculture

University of Minnesota

**With 200 photographs
by the author**

Burgess Publishing Company

426 South 6th Street • Minneapolis, Minn. 55415

Library of Congress Catalog Card Number 65-11818

CONTENTS

INTRODUCTION   1
  How to Use the Keys   1
  Edible and Poisonous Mushrooms   2

Genera of - WHITE SPORED MUSHROOMS   10
        - YELLOW-BROWN SPORED
          MUSHROOMS   13
        - PINK SPORED MUSHROOMS   14
        - PURPLE-BROWN SPORED
          MUSHROOMS   15
        - BLACK SPORED MUSHROOMS   16

KEYS AND DESCRIPTIONS

WHITE SPORED MUSHROOMS   17
  Amanita   17
  Amanitopsis   22
  Armillaria   23
  Cantharellus   24
  Clitocybe   26
  Collybia   36
  Hygrophorus   43
  Lactarius   48
  Lentinus   55
  Lenzites   58
  Lepiota   60
  Marasmius   66
  Mycena   70
  Omphalia   74
  Panus   75
  Pleurotus   76
  Russula   78
  Schizophyllum   84
  Tricholoma   85
  Trogia   88

YELLOW-BROWN SPORED MUSHROOMS 89
   Bolbitius. 89
   Cortinarius 89
   Crepidotus 94
   Flammula 96
   Galera 98
   Inocybe 99
   Naucoria 102
   Paxillus 103
   Pholiota 105

PINK SPORED MUSHROOMS 113
   Claudopus 113
   Clitopilus 114
   Entoloma 117
   Pluteus 119
   Volvaria 120

PURPLE-BROWN SPORED MUSHROOMS 122
   Agaricus 122
   Hypholoma 126
   Psathyra 127
   Psilocybe 128
   Stropharia 129

BLACK SPORED MUSHROOMS 132
   Coprinus 132
   Panaeolus 136
   Psathyrella 137

POLYPORACEAE - Pore Fungi 141
   Daedalia 142
   Favolus 144
   Fistulina 144
   Fomes 145
   Polyporus 151
   Trametes 169

HYDNACEAE - Tooth Fungi 171
   Hydnum 173

BOLETACEAE - (no common name) 176
   Boletinus 177
   Boletus 178
   Strobilomyces 180

CLAVARIACEAE - Club Fungi 182
  Clavaria 182

THELEPHORACEAE - Smooth Fungi 185
  Aleurodiscus 186
  Corticium 187
  Craterellus 188
  Cryptochaete 188
  Cytidia 189
  Hymenochaete 189
  Laxitextum 190
  Peniophora 191
  Thelephora 191
  Tremellodendron 192
  Stereum 193

GASTROMYCETALES - Puffballs and Relatives . . . 196
  LYCOPERDACEAE 197
    Bovista 197
    Calvatia 198
    Geaster 201
    Lycoperdon 203
  SCLERODERMATACEAE 205
  SECOTIACEAE 206
  NIDULARIACEAE 206
    Crucibulum 206
    Cyathus 207
  PHALLACEAE - Stink Horns 208

TREMELLALES - Jelly Fungi 211

ASCOMYCETES - Cup Fungi and Relatives 213
    Miscellaneous Ascomycetes 214
    Helvella 216
    Morchella 218
    Verpa 220
  PEZIZACEAE 221
    Aleuria and Phaeobulgaria 221
    Patella 222
    Paxina 222
    Peziza 224

References 227
Glossary 229
Index 231

PLATE 1 - AGARICACEAE - Gilled Mushrooms · · ·   3

PLATE 2 - POLYPORACEAE - Pore Fungi;
                BOLETACEAE · · · · · · · · · · · · · ·   4

PLATE 3 - HYDNACEAE - Tooth Fungi;
                CLAVARIACEAE - Club Fungi;
                THELEPHORACEAE - Smooth Fungi · · ·   5

PLATE 4 - GASTROMYCETALES - Puff Balls and
                    Relatives;
                TREMELLALES - Jelly Fungi · · · · · · ·   6

PLATE 5 - ASCOMYCETES - Cup Fungi and
                Relatives · · · · · · · · · · · · · · ·   7

PLATE 6 - Growth and Structure of a Typical
                    Mushroom;
                How to Make a Spore Print · · · · · · · ·   8

PLATE 7 - Attachment of Gills to Stem;
                Shapes of Caps with Descriptive Terms · ·   9

PLATE 8 - Shape and Method of Attachment of
                Pore Fungi · · · · · · · · · · · · · · 139

PLATE 9 - Growth and Structure of Pore Fungi · · · · 140

INTRODUCTION

HOW TO USE THE KEYS

To illustrate the method of using the keys, suppose you find a gill fungus and want to identify it. To find out what group to start off with, turn to the plates on pages 1 to 7. There you see that fungi with gills are taken up on page 9. On page 9 you find that mushrooms with gills are divided into groups according to the color of spores produced.

To make a spore print, remove the cap of the mushroom, or a portion of the cap, and place it on a piece of paper, or better still, on a glass slide or other piece of glass. If the air is dry, cover the cap with a piece of moist paper toweling, and leave it for several hours, by which time usually sufficient spores will have fallen to make a visible print. The virtue of using glass instead of paper is that the glass can be held against a light or dark background and the color of the spores determined more easily. Incidentally, if the spore print is made on a glass microscope slide, it can be kept in a slide box - no covering or coating is necessary to preserve the print in this way, and such prints can be kept for many years, and often serve as a useful reference.

Often mushrooms will have deposited spores on grass, leaves, or the tops of other mushrooms growing beneath them, and will thus have obviated the need for making a spore print. While the making of a spore print entails a certain amount of bother and time, it often is essential for the identification of gill fungi and is useful in the identification of some other fungi.

The spores of the mushroom you found turn out to be purple-brown, and so you start off with the section Purple Brown Spored Mushrooms. There are 2 possibilities given in the key, as follows:

1. Ring present on the stem - - 2
   Ring absent - - 3

The mushroom has a fairly conspicuous ring on the stem, so you go to number 2, which also gives 2 possibilities, as follows:

2. Gills free - - Agaricus
    Gills attached to the stem - - Stropharia

The various types of gills are illustrated in Plate 6, and there you find that "free" gills are those which do not touch the stem. The gills on this specimen definitely are free from the stem, and so the plant unquestionably is Agaricus. To determine the species, turn to the section where the purple-brown spored genera are taken up in detail, and there under the Key to the Genus Agaricus go through the same steps you went through above.

EDIBLE AND POISONOUS MUSHROOMS

There is no general rule or test by which one can determine whether a given mushroom is edible or poisonous. If one intends to eat wild mushrooms, the only safe procedure is to learn to recognize with absolute certainly some of the common, easily identified and almost unmistakable kinds, and to eat only those. Several of the books cited in the Bibliography on page 231 include detailed descriptions of a number of common mushrooms. "Mushroom Collecting for Beginners" by J. Walton Groves, is an excellent and well illustrated bulletin available on request, without cost, from the Division of Botany, Department of Agriculture, Ottawa, Canada. In addition, books such as "Common Edible Mushrooms", for sale by the Charles T. Branford Co., Newton Centre, Mass., and "Edible and Poisonous Mushrooms of Canada" by J. Walton Groves, Dept. Agric., Research Branch, Ottawa, Canada, 1962, will be found useful to those interested in edible wild fungi. Books and bulletins dealing with various groups of the fleshy fungi are listed under the various groups, and also are listed in the References on page 227.

AGARICACEAE
GILLED MUSHROOMS

(see page 10)

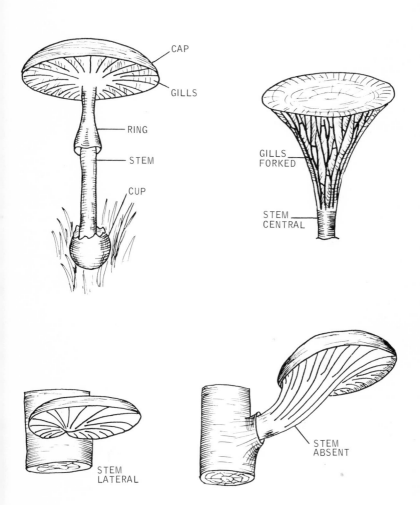

PLATE 1

POLYPORACEAE
PORE FUNGI
(see page 14)

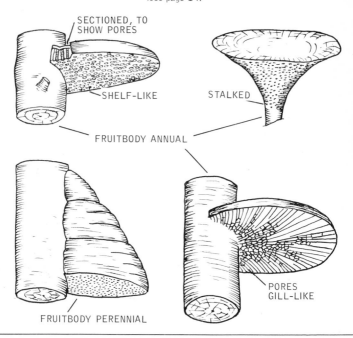

SECTIONED, TO
SHOW PORES

SHELF-LIKE

STALKED

FRUITBODY ANNUAL

FRUITBODY PERENNIAL

PORES
GILL-LIKE

BOLETACEAE
(see page 176)

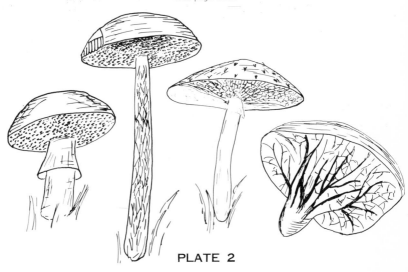

PLATE 2

HYDNACEAE
TOOTH FUNGI

(see page 171)

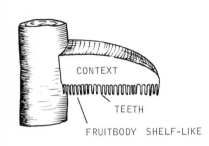
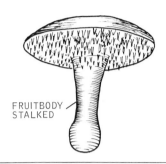

CONTEXT

TEETH

FRUITBODY SHELF-LIKE

FRUITBODY STALKED

CLAVARIACEAE
CLUB FUNGI

(see page 182)

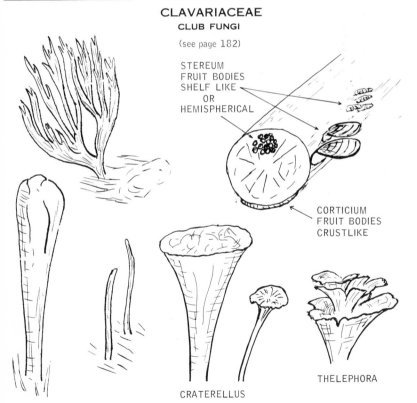

STEREUM
FRUIT BODIES
SHELF LIKE
OR
HEMISPHERICAL

CORTICIUM
FRUIT BODIES
CRUSTLIKE

CRATERELLUS

THELEPHORA

PLATE 3

GASTROMYCETALES
PUFFBALLS AND RELATIVES

(see page 196)

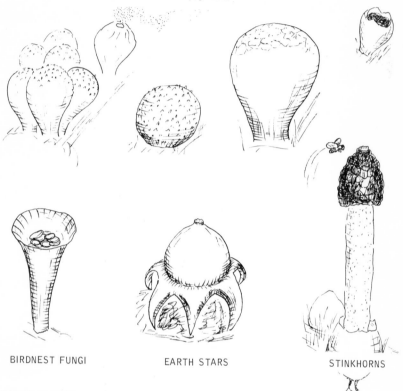

BIRDNEST FUNGI   EARTH STARS   STINKHORNS

TREMELLALES
JELLY FUNGI

(see page 211)

PLATE 4

ASCOMYCETES
CUP FUNGI AND RELATIVES

(see page 213)

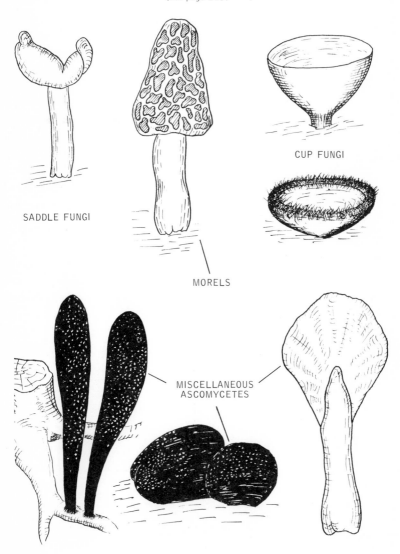

SADDLE FUNGI

MORELS

CUP FUNGI

MISCELLANEOUS
ASCOMYCETES

PLATE 5

A TYPICAL MUSHROOM

(see page 10)

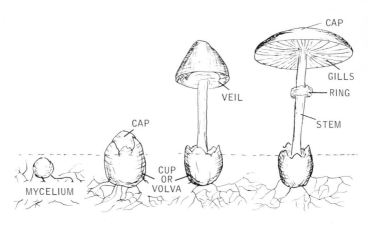

GROWTH AND STRUCTURE OF A TYPICAL MUSHROOM. FOOD AND WATER ARE
TAKEN UP BY THE MYCELIUM, WHICH GROWS THROUGH AND DIGESTS LEAVES,
WOOD AND OTHER PLANT REMAINS IN THE SOIL. THIS MYCELIUM MAY GROW
FOR WEEKS, MONTHS OR EVEN YEARS BEFORE MUSHROOMS ARE PRODUCED.
ONCE ESTABLISHED, THE MYCELIUM MAY PERSIST FOR YEARS OR EVEN
CENTURIES.

HOW TO MAKE A SPORE PRINT

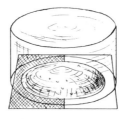

TO MAKE A SPORE PRINT, CUT OFF THE STEM JUST BELOW THE CAP, PLACE
THE CAP ON PAPER, AND COVER IT FOR A FEW HOURS OR OVER NIGHT. A
SPORE PRINT, AS SHOWN AT THE RIGHT ABOVE, CAN BE KEPT INDEFINITELY
IF GENTLY HANDLED.

PLATE 6

ATTACHMENT OF GILLS
TO THE STEM

DECURRENT

SINUATE

ADNATE

ADNEXED

FREE

SHAPES OF CAP

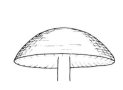

CONVEX

CONICAL

UMBONATE

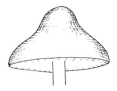

CAMPANULATE
OR BELL SHAPE

UMBILICATE OR
DEPRESSED IN
THE CENTER

FUNNEL
SHAPE

PLATE 7

WHITE SPORED MUSHROOMS

1. Edge of gills prominently and irregularly
    serrate, fruit bodies tough and leathery
    - - Lentinus 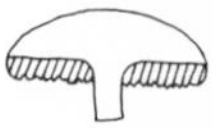
    Edge of gills even - - 2

2. Stem central - - 3

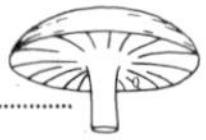

    Stem eccentric or
        lateral - - 14

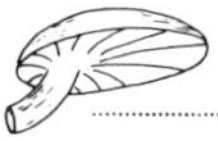

    Stem lacking, fruit body
        shelflike, tough or woody
        in texture, on wood - - 16

3. Flesh of cap exuding white or colored
    juice when broken cap usually depressed
    in the center - - Lactarius
    Flesh of cap not exuding a milky juice - - 4 

4. Stem with both volva
        and ring - - Amanita

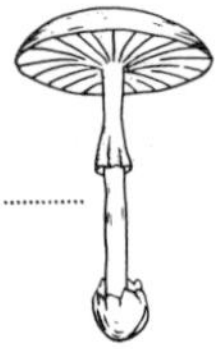

    Stem with volva only
        - - Amanitopsis

    Stem with ring only - - 5

    Stem with neither ring
        nor volva - - 6

5. Gills free, ring prominent,
    stem separating readily
    from the cap - - Lepiota

   Gills adnexed or short
    decurrent, stem not
    separating readily from
    the cap, ring often dis-
    appearing quickly
    - - Armillaria

6. Gills sinuate - - Tricholoma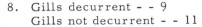
   Gills not sinuate - - 7

7. Gills triangular in cross section, distant,
    usually with veins between them, brittle
    and often of waxy consistency
    - - Hygrophorus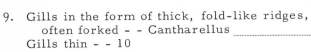
   Gills not noticeably triangular or waxy - - 8

8. Gills decurrent - - 9
   Gills not decurrent - - 11

9. Gills in the form of thick, fold-like ridges,
    often forked - - Cantharellus
   Gills thin - - 10

10. Flesh of cap near stem more than
    1 mm. thick - - Clitocybe
   Flesh of cap near stem 1 mm. or
    less thick, stem 1-2 mm. in
    diameter, tough - - Omphalia

11. Cap and stem tough, withering but not decaying when
    dried, reviving when moistened - - Marasmius
   Not reviving when moistened - - 12

12. Flesh of cap very brittle and almost
    granular, stem stout - - Russula
   Flesh of cap not very brittle, stem
    rather slender - - 13

13. Margin of young cap inrolled,
    mature cap expanded
    - - Collybia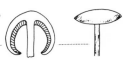

Margin of young cap straight,
    mature cap conical or bell
    shaped - - Mycena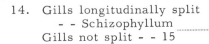

14. Gills longitudinally split
       - - Schizophyllum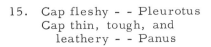
    Gills not split - - 15

15. Cap fleshy - - Pleurotus
    Cap thin, tough, and
       leathery - - Panus

16. Gills vein like, margin of cap lobed
       - - Trogia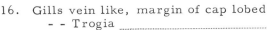

    Gills thin and plate
       like - - Lenzites

YELLOW-BROWN SPORED MUSHROOMS

1. Ring present - - Pholiota ....
    Ring absent - - 2

2. Gills separating easily from
        the cap - - Paxillus ....
    Gills not separating easily
        from the cap - - 3

3. Stem lateral or absent - - Crepidotus ....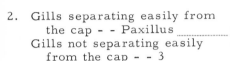
    Stem central - - 4

4. On wood, gills yellow or rusty yellow - - Flammula
    On the ground, gills tan or brown - - 5

5. Cap conical - - 6
    Cap convex or campanulate - - 7

6. Plants very fragile, surface of cap
        smooth or striate - - Bolbitius &
        Galera
    Plants not fragile, surface of cap
        cracked or scaly - - Inocybe ....

7. Stem cartilaginous, brittle - - Naucoria
    Stem fleshy or fibrous - - 8

8. Inner veil of young plants suggesting the
        texture of a cobweb, with each hypha
        composing it distinct and separate
        - - Cortinarius ....
    Inner veil usually absent, when present not cobwebby
        - - 9

9. Surface of cap radially cracked or
        scaly, not sticky - - Inocybe ....
    Surface of cap smooth, often
        sticky - - Hebeloma

PINK SPORED MUSHROOMS

1. Stem lateral or absent, on wood
       - - Claudopus ....
    Stem central - - 2

2. Cup at the base of the stem,
       no ring on the stem
       - - Volvaria ....
    Neither cut nor ring present - - 3

3. Gills free, cap separating easily from
       the stem - - Pluteus
       (P. cervinus often confused with
       yellow-brown spored group) ....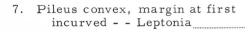
    Gills not free - - 4

4. Stem fleshy or fibrous - - 5
    Stem cartilaginous, slender - - 6

5. Gills sinuate or seceding
       - - Entoloma ....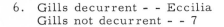
    Gills decurrent or adnate
       - - Clitopilus ....

6. Gills decurrent - - Eccilia
    Gills not decurrent - - 7

7. Pileus convex, margin at first
       incurved - - Leptonia ....

    Pileus bell shaped or conical,
       margin at first straight
       - - Nolanea ....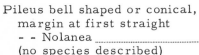
    (no species described)

PURPLE-BROWN SPORED MUSHROOMS

1. Ring present on the stem - - 2
    Ring absent - - 3

2. Gills free - - Agaricus

    Gills attached to the stem
       - - Stropharia

3. Veil present, the remnants of it hanging
        from the margin of the cap
        - - Hypholoma
    Veil absent or evanescent, stem
        slender - - 4

4. Margin of cap at first straight - - Psathyra
    Margin of cap at first incurved - - Psilocybe

BLACK SPORED MUSHROOMS

1. Cap and gills liquifying, beginning
   at the margin and progressing
   toward the center of the cap
   - - Coprinus
   Cap and gills not liquifying - - 2

2. Gills decurrent, waxy,
   cap sticky - - Gomphidius
   (no species described)
   Gills not decurrent - - 3

3. Cap striate or furrowed
   - - Psathyrella

   Cap not furrowed - - Panaeolus

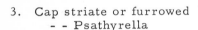

WHITE SPORED MUSHROOMS

Genus AMANITA

The genus is characterized by white spores, free gills, a stem which is easily separated from the cap, and theoretically by the presence of both ring and volva. The ring always is present in newly expanded specimens, but may be inconspicuous in older ones. The volva sometimes is prominent, sometimes is almost hidden in the ground, and in some species consists only of scaly remnants or faint ridges around the swollen base of the stem. This volva or cup is rather conspicuous in some of the more poisonous species of Amanita, and has given rise to the idea that this "death cup" is a sure sign of a poisonous mushroom, an idea which is completely erroneous. Such a cup is present and prominent in some edible species of the genus, and nearly lacking in some of the poisonous species. The writer would feel uneasy about eating any species of Amanita.

Key to Species of Amanita

1. Volva forming a definite, cup shaped, loose sheath around the base of the stem (often beneath the surface of the soil) - - 2
   Volva forming a collar-like ring, broken concentric rings, or scales on the swollen base of the stem - - 3

2. Cap pure white - - A. verna
   Cap tan to brown, at least in the center - - A. phalloides
   Cap yellow to brown, often spotted with wart-like patches - - A. mappa

3. Cap white or pale gray, densely covered with prominent, soft, pyramidal scales - - A. solitaria
   Cap of mature plants dull red, usually with scattered gray or pale reddish warts - - A. rubescens
   Cap yellow to orange, usually with scattered white warts - - 4

4. Margin of cap prominently striate, ring often disappear-
    ing - - A. russuloides
    Margin inconspicuously or not at all striate, ring per-
    sistent - - 5

5. Remains of volva appearing as prominent broken, con-
    centric rings on the base of the stem, diameter of the
    cap usually more than 8 cm. - - A. muscaria
    Volva forming a single, inrolled, collar-like ring, cap
    usually less than 7 cm. wide - - A. frostiana
    Remains of the volva appearing as scattered scales on
    the base of the stem, cap usually less than 7 cm.
    wide - - A. flavoconia

Description of Species of Amanita

1. AMANITA FLAVOCONIA.   Probably poisonous. Cap
                             3 - 8 cm. wide, convex to
flat, often with a small umbo in the center. Surface slightly
sticky, yellow to orange, spotted with soft, pale yellow,
wart-like patches which sometimes disappear with age,
margin not striate. Flesh 3 - 5 mm. thick, white, soft.
Gills 15 - 20 per cm. at the edge of the cap, 3 - 6 mm. wide
free, white, edge usually delicately fringed when seen with
a hand lens. Stem 6 - 10 cm. long, 4 - 8 mm. thick at the
top, tapering slightly upward, enlarged at the base, often
covered with woolly, yellowish scales. Ring thin, yellow.
Volva or cup thin, inconspicuous, quickly disappearing or
remaining only as powdery patches of mycelium on the
swollen base of the stem. Solitary or scattered on the
ground in deciduous and coniferous woods. It resembles A.
frostiana and small specimens of A. muscaria, but the lack
of striations on the margin and the absence of broken concentric rings at the base of the stem make it fairly easy to
distinguish from these.

2. AMANITA FROSTIANA.   Not poisonous, but to be
                           avoided. Cap 3 - 6 cm.
wide, convex or flat, surface slightly sticky when fresh,
yellow to reddish orange, usually with white warty patches
of mycelium, margin inconspicuously ridged. Flesh white,
thin, soft. Gills about 20 per cm., 4 - 6 cm. wide, wider
toward the margin, free, white or pale yellow. Stem 4 - 8
cm. long, 4 - 6 cm. thick at the top, tapering gradually upward, enlarged into a bulb at the base. Ring thin, often
disappearing quickly in dry weather. Volva or cup apparent

only as one or more regular or broken concentric rings or
an inrolled collar like a ring on the enlarged base of the
stem.   Solitary or scattered, on the ground or on very decayed wood, in coniferous and mixed woods.   It resembles
A. muscaria, but is smaller and has spherical spores,
while the spores of A. muscaria are oval.   Because of its
resemblance to both A. muscaria and A. flavoconia, and
the possibility of confusing it with these, it should not be
eaten.

3.   AMANITA MAPPA.   Deadly poisonous.   Cap 4 - 8 cm.
                         wide, convex to flat, surface
white, yellow or brown, often darker in the center, with
prominent soft scales, margin not striate.   Flesh white.
Gills about 20 per cm. , 4 - 8 mm. wide, free but often extending to the stem as faint raised lines or ridges, white,
the edge sometimes fringed when viewed with a lens.   Stem
4 - 8 cm. long, 10 - 15 mm. thick at the top, white or tan,
enlarged abruptly at the base to form a large bulb up to
3 cm. in diameter, which is concave on top.   Ring white or
straw-color, fairly prominent, volva or cup either disappearing quickly or projecting beyond the margin of the bulb.
Scattered on the ground, in coniferous and deciduous woods.

4.   AMANITA MUSCARIA.   Poisonous.   Cap 8 - 24 cm.
                           wide, egg-shaped in young
plants, convex, flat or slightly concave when mature, surface pale yellow to orange-red, usually spotted with numerous white or pale yellow warts which sometimes are in

concentric rings, margin
faintly striate or ridged.
Flesh white, pale yellow
just under the cuticle or
top skin.   Gills about 20
per cm. , 8 - 15 mm. wide,
free or short decurrent in
narrow ridges, white or
pale yellow.   Stem 10 - 20
cm. long, 1 - 2 cm. thick
at the top, tapering upward,
enlarged at the base to form
a bulb, the bulb and lower
part of the stem encircled
by irregular broken rings
or ridges, white or pale
yellow.   Ring or annulus

white, soft, at first prominent but later often drying and becoming inconspicuous. Volva or cup sometimes definite,
but most often becoming inconspicuous as the plants age,
and appearing only as ridges on the lower stem and bulbous
base. Solitary or in groups, sometimes in fairy rings, frequently under spruce trees. It is found in many different
situations, and often is abundant. Several varieties have
been described, all of which apparently are poisonous. It
is said to have been used in regions of Siberia as an intoxi-
cant, small quantities of it inducing symptoms somewhat
resembling those of an overdose of alcohol. Small pieces
of it broken up and placed in water attract house-flies,
which soon are killed by ingesting it, whence the name "fly
agaric."

5. AMANITA PHALLOIDES.   Deadly poisonous. Cap 5
                                                  - 15 cm. wide, flat or with
a small umbo in the center, tan to gray-brown, often paler
toward the margin, surface sticky when moist (dry specimens must be moistened to determine this), sometimes with
a few soft warts or delicate shreds of the volva scattered
over the cap, margin smooth. Flesh white, firm, 3 - 5 mm.
thick. Gills 15 - 20 per cm., 7 - 12 mm. wide, widest
near the margin, free from the stem but often connected to
it by means of fine, raised ridges, white, edge delicately
toothed. Stem 8 - 20 cm. long, 6 - 15 mm. thick at the
top, even or tapering upward, white or light brown, enlarged at the base into a rounded bulb that is below the surface of the ground. Ring white, at first prominent and flaring, striate or ridged on the upper side, later collapsing on
the stem and almost disappearing. The cup or volva surrounding the buried bulb is soft, white and irregularly torn.
Solitary or scattered on the ground or on rotten wood,
usually in deciduous forests and groves. This species is
distinguished from A. verna chiefly by the brown color of
the cap, and some authors consider these two to be merely
different varieties of the same species. Like A. verna, it
often is very abundant, and because of this and of its attractive appearance and odor often has been eaten, and has been
responsible for numerous cases of fatal poisoning.

6. AMANITA RUBESCENS.   Edible, but best avoided.
                                                  Cap 5 - 12 cm. wide, con-
vex, campanulate, or rarely almost flat, surface pale
brown to reddish brown, slightly sticky when fresh and
moist, spotted with white or pale red warts of mycelium,

margin curved downwards, not at all or only faintly striate
or ridged. Flesh white, becoming reddish where bruised.
Gills about 20 per cm. , 8 - 12 mm. wide, white, edge often
slightly fringed when observed with a lens. Stem 8 - 20 cm.
long, 8 - 15 mm. thick at the top, tapering upward, enlarged
gradually at the base into a rounded bulb, pale red, becoming
darker red where bruised. Annulus conspicuous, flaring,
often ridged on the upper side. Volva soon disappearing.
Solitary or scattered in deciduous or mixed woods, occasionally on open ground.

7. AMANITA RUSSULOIDES.   Probably poisonous. Cap
                           6 - 15 cm. wide, conical or
hemispherical when young, flat or depressed in the center
when mature, straw yellow to white, very sticky when moist,
with scattered, prominent white warts that are larger toward the center of the cap, the margin with rather obvious
furrows and ridges 1 - 3 cm. long that become more prominent as the plant matures. Flesh white, soft, 4 - 8 mm.
thick at the center of the cap, disappearing where the furrows begin on the margin. Gills white, free, about 12 - 15
per cm. , 6 - 12 mm. wide. Stem 8 - 18 cm. long, 8 - 12
mm. thick near the top, increasing gradually in thickness
toward the base, often thicker at the top than just below,
white, very brittle. Annulus one-third the way down from
the top of the stem, thin, prominent at first but soon drying
and disappearing.   The cup or volva is a bulb with an inconspicuous margin, sometimes only a bulb with broken rings
on the upper side and tapering to a point below. Solitary or
scattered, usually in deciduous forests, but sometimes on
lawns.

8. AMANITA SOLITARIA.   Edible but best not eaten.
                           Cap 8 - 15 cm. wide, at
first spherical, later flat, surface white or nearly so, when
young covered with large, pyramidal brown warts which become less prominent as the cap expands. Flesh white.
Gills about 20 per cm. , 5 - 10 mm. wide, free, white or
yellowish. Stem 8 - 18 cm. long, 1 - 2 cm. thick at the
top, enlarged rather gradually into a bulb which tapers into
a rootlike base. The bulb of young plants is adorned with
concentric rings of warty tufts similar to those on the cap,
but these become inconspicuous in older specimens. Annulus
or ring thin, small, white or yellowish, collapsing on the
stem and often disappearing. Usually solitary on the ground
in deciduous woods.

9. AMANITA VERNA.   Deadly poisonous. Cap 6 - 15 cm.
                                 wide, first oval, then convex to
flat, surface white, slightly sticky when fresh and moist,
margin not ridged.   Flesh thin, white, soft.   Gills about 20
per cm., 6 - 12 mm. wide, free
or short decurrent in the
form of faint ridges, edge of
gills in old specimens often
faintly serrate. Stem 8 -
20 cm. long, 1 - 2 cm. thick
at the top, tapering upward
gradually, slightly enlarged
at the base to form a bulb
which usually is beneath the
surface of the ground. Ring
white, soft, at first prominent, soon collapsing on the
stem and sometimes dis-
appearing. Volva or cup
white, soft, margin irregularly torn; often the entire
volva is beneath the surface
of the ground, and older
specimens must be exca-
vated with some care to find
it. Solitary or in groups,
usually in hardwood or mixed
forests, but sometimes in
open places.   This mushroom, because of its extreme poi-
sonousness (even a small piece of it apparently is sufficient
to cause death), its wide distribution, abundance, and attractive appearance, probably has been responsible for more
cases of fatal mushroom poisoning than any other species.
Those inclined to eat wild mushrooms gathered at random
and identified only casually should read the detailed and
graphic descriptions of poisoning given in the back of "Mushrooms and Toadstools", by Gussow and Odell.

Genus AMANITOPSIS

This genus differs from Amanita chiefly in that it
lacks a ring on the stem. Only a few species have been
described, and of these A. vaginata is the only one found at
all commonly.

1. AMANITOPSIS VAGINATA. Edible. Cap 5 - 10 cm.
wide, at first oval or con-
vex, later flat, white, gray, or pale orange yellow, surface
smooth and slightly sticky when young and moist, margin
prominently ridged. Flesh thin, white, soft. Gills 12 - 15
per cm., white, free. Stem 9 - 15 cm. long, 6 - 10 mm.
thick at the top, tapering slightly upward, brittle, white,
the base extending 2 - 3 cm. into the ground. Volva or cup
white, clinging closely to the stem, usually apparent only
when the plant is pried carefully out of the ground. Solitary
or scattered in forests and wooded areas, and often very
common.

Genus ARMILLARIA

The name Armillaria is derived from a Latin word
meaning "a ring", referring to the ring or annulus on the
stem, but the name is not too fitting because the ring often
is very inconspicuous and short lived, and frequently is
visible only on young specimens. About 20 species of the
genus have been described, but A. mellea is the only one
known to be common.

1. ARMILLARIA MELLEA. Edible. Cap typically 5 -
13 cm. wide (the writer
has found giant specimens with caps close to 20 cm. wide)
at first spherical and the
margin attached to the stem
by a veil of woolly mycelium
in which the individual
hyphae or threads are visible, convex to plane when
mature, often with an umbo.
The color varies from pale
wood brown, which is typical, to dark brown at one
extreme, and to ochre yellow at the other. The surface usually is covered with
tiny scale-like tufts that
are darker than the cap
surface. The surface of
young, fresh specimens is
very sticky, almost slimy,
but this disappears if the

humidity is at all low, and then the caps must be soaked in
water for some minutes before this stickiness is apparent.
Flesh white, firm, 8 - 20 mm. thick near the stem, usually
becoming abruptly thin and almost disappearing about two-
thirds the way from the stem to the margin, where the margin begins to turn down. Gills usually 18 - 20 per cm., 6 -
11 mm. wide near the stem, narrowing gradually toward the
margin, white or pale yellow, decurrent, often continuing
down the stem as faint ridges as far as the ring. Stem 5 -
20 cm. long, 1 - 2.5 cm. thick, uniform in diameter until
near the base, which may taper downward into a pointed
"root", pale tan to brown, shiny, often becoming brown
where bruised, definitely striate, often twisted, fibrous,
white inside, solid, the outside tough, the inside brittle.
Veil white or pale yellow, at first soft and woolly, thin, with
the individual filaments visible; just after breaking it stands
out from the stem like a collar, but soon it collapses and
often it disappears entirely, making identification somewhat
difficult. The fungus often fruits in abundance around stumps
of trees that have been cut, or that have died, and is very
common both in towns and in the woods. It often has been
blamed as a cause of root rot and death of shade, orchard
and forest trees, but there is good evidence that it follows,
rather than causes, the death of most of these trees.

Genus CANTHARELLUS

The most obvious distinguishing characters of the
genus are the vase or funnel shape of the cap, and the
decurrent, forked gills that in most species are so thick
that they appear more like ridges than true gills. All
species are edible, some are excellent for eating, and
in Europe one or two of them are collected in quantity
for food.

Key to Species of Cantharellus

1. Gills thin, rather crowded, cap and gills golden or
        orange color - - C. aurantiacus
    Gills thick and ridge-like - - 2

2. Top of cap covered with large, prominent scales
        - - C. floccosus
    Cap not scaly - - 3

3. Cap and gills chrome yellow, cap flat or shallow funnel
    shape - - C. cibarius
    Cap tan to brown, gills tan, the depression in the center
    of the cap often extending into the hollow stem - - C.
    infundibuliformis

Description of Species of Cantharellus

1. CANTHARELLUS AURANTIACUS.   Edible.   Cap 5 - 9
                                             cm. in diameter,
at first convex, later shallow funnel shape, golden or orange
yellow, darker in the center, margin curved down or elevated, when elevated usually wavy. Flesh white, 7 - 10 mm.
thick near the stem, soft. Gills 20 - 30 per cm., 3 - 5 mm.
wide, 1/4 - 1/2 mm. thick, thicker at the stem, frequently
forked, short decurrent, colored like the cap. Stem 1.5 -
3 cm. long, 1 - 1.5 cm. thick at the top, tapering upward,
reddish brown. Singly or in clumps of two or three on the
ground or decayed wood.

2. CANTHARELLUS CIBARIUS.   Edible. Cap 3 - 12 cm.
                                        wide, first convex, then
flat, later shallow funnel shape, margin first curved in,
later curved down to upraised, often wavy. Flesh 1 - 2 cm.
thick at the stem, white, fibrous. Gills 15 per cm., 2 - 4
mm. wide, edges blunt, often anastomosing or growing together near the margin, decurrent on the stem, chrome or
pale yellow. Stem 3 - 6 cm. long, 6 - 15 mm. thick at the
top, tapering downward or uniform in diameter, base enlarged, same color as gills or paler. Scattered or in fairly
dense groups, on the ground in both hardwood and coniferous forests.

3. CANTHARELLUS FLOC-
   COSUS.

Edible. Cap 5 - 8 cm. wide,
at first conical or almost
cylindrical with a flat top,
later shallow funnel shape,
scaly, yellow to pale orange,
margin curved downward or
rolled inward. Flesh white,
firm. Gills 8 - 12 per cm.,
1 - 2 mm. wide, 1 mm.

thick, ridge like, long decurrent but ending rather abruptly
on the stem, frequently forked and joined, yellow to reddish
yellow. Stem 3 - 6 cm. long, 1 - 2 cm. thick, uniform in
diameter, solid, pale yellow, often with white mycelium at
the base. Solitary to scattered, on the ground in upland
hardwood and conifer forests.

4. CANTHARELLUS INFUNDIBULIFORMIS.   Edible but
                                     too small to
be interesting for eating. Cap 1.5 - 5 cm. wide, funnel
shape or depressed in the center, the depression often continuing down into the interior
of the stem, yellow to brown,
smooth, the margin curved
down, usually wavy and often
lobed. Flesh 1 - 3 mm.
thick, pliable. Gills 8 - 10
per cm., 2 - 4 mm. wide,
1 mm. thick, edge blunt,
frequently forked, tan, decurrent. Stem 3 - 8 cm.
long, 3 - 8 mm. thick, tan
to yellow, hollow, often
irregularly flattened. Scattered or in groups on the
ground in swamps in conifer
and hardwood forests.

Genus CLITOCYBE

Clitocybe means "sloping head", descriptive of the
decidedly funnel shape cap of several of the common species.
The genus is characterized by white spores, decurrent or
adnate gills, and the rather tough stem that is not separable
from the cap. Kauffman, in "Agaricaceae of Michigan" describes 42 species, and there doubtless are a number of
others, not yet adequately known. Many of the species vary
considerably and grade into one another, and thus are difficult to identify with certainty, but a number of them can
be identified with relative ease.

Key to the Genus Clitocybe

1. Growing on wood - - 2
    Growing on the ground - - 4

2. Cap 1-3 cm. wide - - C. truncicola
    Cap 3-8 cm. wide - - 3

3. Cap not scaly, pale watersoaked gray when moist,
       white when dry - - C. eccentrica
    Cap covered with tiny dark scales, tan or reddish
       brown - - C. ectypoides

4. Gills bright yellow, orange, salmon, or purple brown
       - - 5
    Gills white, pale gray, pale tan, or pale yellow - - 6

5. Cap bright yellow or orange, gills yellow to orange
       red - - C. illudens
    Cap and gills pale watery red, salmon, or purple, gills
       thick, waxy, distant, with prominent veins between
       them - - C. laccata
    Cap and gills purple brown when moist, grayish when
       dry - - C. ochropurpurea

6. Cap funnel shaped or depressed in the center - - 7
    Cap convex or plane - - 11

7. Cap of mature plants over 10 cm. in diameter - - 8
    Cap of mature plants less than 8 cm. in diameter - - 9

8. Stem with enlarged, bulbous base - C. maxima
    Stem not enlarged at base - C. candida and C. gigantea

9. Cap reddish brown, darker in the center - - C. sinopica
    Cap watery tan to dirty white, narrow funnel shaped - -
       C. caespitosa
    Cap pale reddish tan to tan, margin usually with forked
       striations - - C. infundibuliformis
    Cap grayish brown, shallow funnel shaped - - C. parilis
    Cap shiny white - - 10

10. Cap 1-4 cm. wide, usually in fields or grassy deciduous
       woods - - C. dealbata
    Cap 3-12 cm. wide, usually in coniferous woods - - C.
       albissima

11. Plants in dense clumps, numerous stems arising from
       a common base - - 12
    Plants solitary, scattered, or near one another, but
       not with numerous stems arising from a common
       base - - 14

12. Gills of mature plants 1-1.5 cm. wide - - C. gigantea
    Gills less than 1 cm. wide - - 13

13.   Cap covered with a tough skin or cuticle that can be
        peeled off - - C. cartilaginea
      Cap without a tough cuticle - - C. multiceps

14.   Cap grayish brown, plants scattered - - C. parilis
      Cap shiny white, usually numerous plants growing near
        together - - 15

15.   Cap 1-4 cm. wide, usually in fields or grassy deciduous
        woods - - C. dealbata
      Cap 3-12 cm. wide, usually in coniferous woods - - C.
      albissima

Description of Species of Clitocybe

1.   CLITOCYBE ALBISSIMA.   Edibility unknown. Cap
                                    3-12 cm. wide, usually
flat but varying from slightly convex to slightly depressed
in the center; when young the cap often is pale bluish gray
with an inrolled, striate margin, but the bluish color is not
invariably present. When older the cap is watery translucent tan when moist, especially in the center, but uniform
shiny white when dry. The margin remains curved down in
even immature specimens. Flesh 5-10 mm. thick at the
stem, tapering sharply to 0.5 mm. near the margin, white,
spongy to firm. Gills 25-30 per cm., at the margin of the
cap, 3-6 mm. wide, first white, yellowish in old specimens, short decurrent or often extending down the stem for
5-10 mm. as faint ridges, sometimes growing together on
or near the stem, separable from the flesh of the cap, edge
serrate in age. Stem 4-7 cm. long, 6-12 mm. thick, white
to pale yellow, uniform in diameter, the lower part covered
with white mycelium and often curved, the rind cartilaginous or brittle, the interior fibrous. Often several stems
are joined at the base. The species usually has a slight
fragrant odor suggestive of licorice. Scattered or in
groups, usually in conifer woods, sometimes in partial
rings near stumps and trees.

        The gills descending the stem in lines, and some-
times anastomosing on the stem, are supposed to be characters peculiar to C. piceina, a somewhat larger species.
However, all the specimens collected by the writer at
numerous times throughout a period of more than 10 years
in northern Minnesota had minutely echinulate spores,
described by Kauffman as unique for C. albissima. The

spores usually contained a large oil droplet, as those of C.
piceina are supposed to do. It is quite possible that the two
species grade into one another and comprise a series of in-
distinguishable forms.

2. CLITOCYBE CAESPITOSA.   Edibility unknown, but
                                    probably edible. Cap
2-6 cm. wide, deep funnel shape with a decurved margin,
often irregular from contact with adjacent specimens, watery tan when moist, almost
white when dry. Flesh watery tan, 1-2 mm. thick at
the stem, at most 1 mm.
thick at the margin. Gills
20-25 per cm., 1-2 mm.
wide, decurrent, white.
Stem 1.5-3.0 cm. long, 4-
8 mm. thick, rind tough-
brittle, white and fibrous
inside, covered with dense
white mycelium at the base.
Usually in dense clumps,
sometimes scattered, on
the ground in woods or on
compost heaps, rarely on
very rotten wood.

3. CLITOCYBE CANDIDA.   Edible. Cap first convex,
                                 later broad funnel shape, 10-
30 cm. wide, white or very pale tan, smooth and shining.
Flesh 1-2.5 cm. thick at the stem, white, firm; successive
layers of flesh can be peeled off readily. Gills 4-7 mm.
wide, 30-40 per cm., pointed at both ends, first rounded at
the stem or almost sinuate, later short decurrent, first
white, later pale yellow. Stem 1.5-4 cm. thick, 6-10 cm.
long, white or pale yellow, solid, tough, fleshy-fibrous.
In groups or dense clumps on the ground in conifer and
mixed woods. This is considered by some to be a variety
of C. gigantea.

4. CLITOCYBE CARTILAGINEA.   Edible. Cap 4-8 cm.
                                      wide, flat or with a
low, broad umbo, tan or brown in the center, becoming
paler or almost white toward the margin. The texture of
the surface sometimes suggests scales because the brown
fibers separate somewhat. The surface near the margin

of fresh specimens often is slightly translucent and is rough
or radially ridged, and the margins of young caps are definitely curved in. The cap is covered by a tough skin that
can be peeled off. Flesh white, firm, slightly tough, 7-10
mm. thick near the stem, disappearing about 5-10 mm.
from the margin, where the
gills are covered only by
the tough skin of the cap.
Gills 20-30 per cm. at the
margin, 3-5 mm. wide,
short decurrent, adnate, or
sinuate, white. Stem 3-6
cm. long, 8-20 mm. thick
at the top, uniform in diameter or tapering slightly
upward, sometimes enlarged
toward the base, usually a
number of stems arising
from a common base. Scat-
tered or in dense clumps and
and fairy rings on grassy
ground under trees.

5. CLITOCYBE DEALBATA.   Edibility unknown. Cap
                         1-4 cm. wide, convex when
young, at maturity the margin raised and the center depressed, surface shiny white, the margin wavy. Flesh
white, thin. Gills adnate in unexpanded caps, later short
decurrent, white, narrow, crowded. Stem 2-5 cm. long,
2-3 mm. thick, sometimes flattened, tough, the base
covered with woolly mycelium. In groups of 2 to 5 on leaf
mold in deciduous woods and sometimes in lawns and pastures.

6. CLITOCYBE ECCENTRICA.   Probably edible, but
                           not tested. Cap 2-6
cm. wide, flat, very shallow funnel shape or slightly convex, the margin sometimes curved down slightly; the surface watersoaked gray and quite smooth when moist, white
when dry and appearing silky when viewed with a lens.
Flesh 2-4 mm. thick at the stem, gradually becoming
thinner toward the margin, gray when moist, white when
dry, slightly fibrous but brittle. Gills 35 per cm. at the
margin, 3-4 mm. wide where widest, tapering to a point
at both ends, short decurrent. Stem 2-4 cm. long, 4-6
mm. thick, often attached to the cap in an eccentric

fashion, that is, off the
center, uniform in diam-
eter, rather tough and
fibrous, pale tan or nearly
white, the base or often
the entire lower half covered with white woolly mycelium. White, branched
strands of mycelium up to
about a mm. thick run out
from the base of the stem
through the decayed wood
or sawdust on which the
plants grow. Scattered or
in groups of a few on very
decayed food.

7. CLITOCYBE ECTYPOIDES.   Edibility unknown. Cap
                                         6-8 cm. wide, broad
funnel shape with a narrow central depression and down
curved margin; surface reddish brown when moist, yellowish tan when dry, darker
toward the margin, with
darker radial streaks and
many tiny dark scales.
Flesh 2 mm. thick, tan,
watery, firm. Gills 15-
20 per cm. at the margin,
many short and narrow
gills, the largest 3-4 mm.
wide, pale tan, decurrent
and ending abruptly on the
stem, pointed at both ends,
occasionally forked. Stem
3-5 cm. long, 4-6 mm.
thick, tan above, the base
or the entire lower half
covered with white myce-
lium, hollow, fibrous.
Scattered on decaying conifer logs.

8. CLITOCYBE GIGANTEA.   Edible. Cap 4-20 cm. in
                                      diameter, first convex
with the margin inrolled, later flat or shallow funnel shape,
surface ivory white to light tan when young, tan when old,

shiny when dry, the margin often wavy. Flesh white, fibrous, 0.5-2.5 cm. thick at the stem, 1 mm. thick at the

margin. Gills white to pale
tan, occasionally forked,
sometimes fusing with one
another at the stem, decurrent to sinuate, 1-1.5 cm.
wide in mature specimens,
15-20 per cm. at the mar-
gin, easily separated from
the cap. Stem 1.5-5 cm.
in diameter at the top, uniform in diameter, or sometimes narrowed toward the
base and the very base
slightly enlarged, often
curved toward the base,
solid and fibrous, frequently

with 2 to 10 stems joined at the base. Usually in groups and
clusters in grassy woods, sometimes covering several square
yards.

9. CLITOCYBE ILLUDENS.   Poisonous. Cap 6-15 cm.
                                   wide, at first convex with
the margin curved down or inrolled, but at maturity becoming flat or shallow funnel shape, often with a small
round or pointed umbo in the center, bright yellow or
orange yellow, with a dull silky sheen when dry, the margin sometimes lobed or wavy. Flesh 4-6 mm. thick near
the stem, becoming gradually thinner outward and almost
disappearing toward the margin, pale yellow, firm, rather
dry, peeling readily in layers. Gills about 20 per cm. at
the margin, 3-5 mm. wide, bright yellow or orange yellow,
running down the stem 1-2 cm. Stem 12-20 cm. long, 8-15
mm. thick at the top, uniform in diameter to near the base,
where it tapers to a point, pale yellow outside and in, solid,
very fibrous, usually curved. Ordinarily growing in dense
clumps on stumps or logs, with the stems of 5 to 20 fruit
bodies joined into a common base.

     The fruit bodies, and especially the gills, are lumi-
nescent, sometimes strongly so, and because of this the
fungus has been given the name of "jack o' lantern". A
number of different mushrooms share this property of lu-
minescence.

10. CLITOCYBE INFUNDIBULIFORMIS.   Edible. Cap
                                     3-5 cm. wide,
at first convex with a slightly raised center, later depressed
in the center and shallow to deep funnel shape, surface dry
and silky, reddish when
young, later reddish tan to
tan, the margin first in-
rolled, later curved downward, in young specimens
with net-like ridges extending in 5-10 mm. from the
margin. Flesh white, 5-8
mm. thick at the stem, 1
mm. at the margin. Gills
20-25 per cm. at the mar-
gin, 2-3 mm. wide, white
or pale cream color, de-
current, many short gills
between the long ones, some

wavy and with the edges split in a toothed fashion as the cap
expands. Stem 2-6 cm. long, 5-8 mm. thick, uniform in
diameter or tapering slightly either upward or downward,
spongy inside, the base often slightly enlarged and covered
with white mycelium. Single, scattered or in dense groups
on the ground in upland forests.

11. CLITOCYBE LACCATA.   Edible. Cap 1.5-4 cm.
                                     wide, first convex then flat
or shallow funnel shape, surface often with a slightly mealy
texture, when moist pale tan, watery red, salmon color,
mauve or purple, but paler when dry. Gills at the margin
10 per cm. or less, 3-7 mm. wide, up to 1 mm. thick,
colored like the cap, often waxy in texture, decurrent to
adnate, often with rather prominent veins between the gills
on the under side of the cap. Stem 3-8 cm. long, 2-7 mm.
thick, colored like the cap or paler, tough and fibrous,
often twisted. Solitary, scattered or in clumps on ground
or very rotten wood, from swamps to uplands. This species is unusual in several ways, one of which is that it has
spherical, definitely spiny spores; it has been placed in
several different genera, and it does not fit particularly
well in any of them. It is very common and exceedingly
variable in size, shape and color, and might well form a
good subject for some interesting studies on genetics in
relation to classification of higher fungi and to taxonomy in
general. Certainly it offers interesting difficulties to those

who consider that all living things can be separated into
neatly compartmented pigeonholes.

12. CLITOCYBE MAXIMA.   Edible. Cap 10-20 cm. wide,
                         first convex, later flat to
shallow funnel shape, surface pale tan when young, later
darker and with flat scales.   Margin first inrolled and covered with fine hairs, later
curved down, flat or up-
raised. Flesh 1.5-3 cm.
thick at the stem, rapidly
thinner toward the margin,
white, spongy. Gills 20-25
per cm. at the margin, 4-
10 mm. wide, first sinuate,
then short decurrent, white
when young, soon pale yellow, easily separated from
the flesh of the cap. Stem
6-12 cm. long, 2.5-6 cm.
thick at the top, base enlarged to form an oval or

spherical bulb, slightly fuzzy, white or pale tan. Solitary,
scattered or in groups on the ground in upland forests,
sometimes in partial rings.

13. CLITOCYBE MULTICEPS.   Edible. Cap 3-8 cm.
                            wide, convex, surface
white or watery gray, margin first inrolled, later curved
down. Flesh white. Gills 20-25 per cm. at the margin,
adnate, sinuate, or decurrent. Stem 5-10 cm. long, 6-12
mm. thick, colored like the cap, a number of stems joined
into a firm clump at the base. In dense clumps on the
ground beside roads, in pastures and in open deciduous
woods.

14. CLITOCYBE OCHROPURPUREA.   Cap 5-20 cm.
                                wide, at first al-
most hemispherical, later convex to plane or shallow funnel shape, surface purple brown when moist, grayish when
dry, margin often wavy. Flesh slightly paler than the cap,
tough. Gills distant from one another, thick, wide, adnate
to decurrent, colored like the cap. Stem 5-20 cm. long,
1-2 cm. thick, often irregular in thickness, tough and fibrous, sometimes curved and twisted, colored like the cap
or paler. Scattered or in groups on the ground in open
places or deciduous woods.

15. CLITOCYBE PARILIS.   Cap 1.5-3.5 cm. wide, convex when young, shallow fun-
nel shape when mature, surface grayish brown, smooth and
shining to the naked eye, but minutely scaly when viewed
with a lens; margin curved
down or flat. Flesh white,
2-3 mm. thick near the
stem, soft. Gills at first
pale gray, later pale yellow, long decurrent, 1-2
mm. wide, about 30 per
cm. at the margin, many
small gills at the margin
visible only with a lens.
Stem 2-3 cm. long, 2-4
mm. thick at the top, uniform in diameter or tapering downward slightly,
white or pale gray, the

base often covered with white mycelium. Scattered or in
groups on the ground in coniferous or mixed woods.

16. CLITOCYBE SINOPICA.   Cap 3-5 cm. wide, depressed in the center, sur-
face reddish brown, darker in the center, sometimes with
minute, crowded, appressed or flat scales toward the center, margin curved down and wavy. Flesh 2-3 mm. thick
near the stem, 1 mm. thick at the margin, white or pale
tan. Gills 20-25 per cm. at the margin, 3-4 mm. wide,
decurrent, occasionally forked, rather thick and with veins
connecting adjacent gills, first white, then pale yellow or
tan. Stem 3-6 cm. long, 5-8 mm. thick at the top, tapering downward slightly, same color as the cap or paler,
solid, white and fibrous inside, brittle outside. Odor and
taste rather strong and reminiscent of whole wheat meal.
Usually scattered or in dense but small clumps on or near
very decayed wood in swamps and moist situations.

17. CLITOCYBE TRUNCICOLA.   Cap 1-3 cm. wide,
obtuse or flat, some-
times shallow funnel shape, surface white, smooth and
dull or shiny. Flesh 2-3 mm. thick near the stem, 1 mm.
or less at the margin, pale gray and watersoaked in wet
weather, white when dry. Gills white, about 50 per cm. at
the margin, 1-2 mm. wide, pointed at both ends, short decurrent. Stem 2-4 mm. wide at the top, 1-3 cm. long,

white, uniform in diameter
or tapering slightly downward, fibrous, often cur-
ved (as when fruit bodies
are growing on the side of
a log), sometimes slightly
off center. Scattered or in
groups on fallen logs which
still retain their bark, and
sometimes on more thor-
oughly decayed wood.

Genus COLLYBIA

The genus is characterized by white spores, gills
which are not decurrent but which vary from almost free to
adnexed, a somewhat tough stem, and the inrolled margin
of the cap of young specimens. The cap of mature specimens
of most species is flat to convex, often with the margin
turned down.

Key to Species of Collybia

1. Growing on decayed wood - - 2
   Growing on the ground - - 7

2. Gills purple - - C. myriadophylla
   Gills not purple - - 3

3. Stem white - - 4
   Stem tan to reddish brown, paler toward the cap - - 5

4. Densely caespitose in groups of 20-100, cap 1-3 cm.
      wide, gills narrow and almost free - - C. familia
   Usually solitary, cap 6-15 cm. wide, gills 1-2 cm.
      wide, distant from each other and intervenose - -
      C. platyphylla

5. Cap shining as if waxed, stem and cap tan - - C. buty-
      racea
   Cap not shining - - 6

6. Lower half of stem densely covered with reddish brown
      hairs - - C. velutipes
   Stem covered with white woolly mycelium at the base,
      otherwise naked, plants in dense clumps of 20 to 150
      - - C. abundans

7. Stem with a definite, tapering, rootlike extension be-
    neath the surface of the ground - - 8
    Stem without a tapering root - - 9

8. Root 2-6 cm. long, extending straight down - - C. rad-
    icata
    Root up to 25 cm. long, usually horizontal - - C. long-
    ipes

9. Cap and stem white, with rust colored spots - - maculata
    Cap and stem tan to reddish brown - - 10

10. Top of cap shining as if waxed or buttered - - C. butyracea
    Top of cap not shiny - - 11

11. Cap 6-12 mm. wide, stem 0.5 mm. thick - - C. stipitaria
    Cap wider and stem thicker - - 12

12. Gills yellowish brown, cap reddish brown when moist,
    yellow or tan when dry - - C. aquosa
    Gills white or very pale tan - - 13

13. Stem hairy only at the very base - - C. dryophila
    Stem covered with woolly white hairs that become
    sparse toward the top - - 14

14. Stem white, odor of crushed plants sharp and unpleasant
    - - C. hariolorum
    Stem brown, odor of crushed plants not sharp and un-
    pleasant - - C. confluens

Descriptions of Species of Collybia

1. COLLYBIA ABUNDANS.   Cap 1-3.5 cm. wide, convex
                         to almost plane, with a small
umbo, light brown or tan, darker in the center, surface
covered with a delicate fuzz, margin often split in several
places. Gills pale tan, adnate, narrow, 20-25 per cm. at
the margin. Stem 3-12 cm. long, 2-5 cm. thick, at first
pale tan, later dark brown, lighter near the top, covered
with white mycelium at the base. In dense clumps on decaying logs, with sometimes more than 100 specimens in a
clump.

2. COLLYBIA AQUOSA.   Cap 2-4 cm. wide, at first
                       convex or umbonate, later
plane or depressed in the center, watery brown when moist,
yellow or yellowish brown when dry, the margin faintly
striate for 2-3 mm. when moist. Flesh 2-3 mm. thick near

the stem, brown when moist, pale yellow when dry. Gills
25-30 per cm. at the margin, 3-4 mm. wide, narrowly adnexed or free, yellowish tan. Stem 3-5 cm. long, 2-5 mm.
thick, yellowish at the top, usually reddish brown toward
the base, externally glabrous, sometimes flattened, fibrous
inside and solid. In groups on the ground under conifers.

3. COLLYBIA BUTYRACEA.

Cap 2-5 cm. wide, con-
vex to flat, sometimes
umbonate, translucent brown and shining as if waxed when
moist, tan to almost white when dry. Flesh 2-4 mm. thick,

tan when moist, white when
dry. Gills 30-35 per cm.
at the margin, 2-4 mm.
wide, almost free, white,
edge finely toothed when observed with a lens. Stem
3-6 cm. long, 2-6 mm.
thick at the top, tapering
slightly downward to a bulbous base which may be
covered with white myce-
lium and surrounded by a
closely held clump of dirt
or decomposed wood, brown
toward the base and pale
tan or almost white toward

the top. Solitary, in groups, or in clumps of up to 10
specimens, on the ground or on very rotten wood.

4. COLLYBIA CONFLUENS.

Edible. Cap 2-5 cm.
wide, convex or flat, in
old specimens with the margin turned up slightly, with or
without an umbo, surface tan or watery brown when moist,

darker in the center, pale
tan when dry. Flesh 2-3
mm. thick at the stem,
thinning gradually toward
the margin, watery tan when
moist, almost white when
dry. Gills 40-50 per cm.
at the margin, 1-2 mm.
wide, rounded at both ends,
free or rarely adnexed,

pale tan. Stem 4-8 cm. long, 2-5 mm. thick, reddish brown, covered with short woolly white hairs which give it a frosty bloom, hairs less dense toward the top of the stem. The stem often is flat, the outer rind tough and fibrous, the interior first filled with fibrous mycelium, later hollow. In groups or dense clumps on the ground in woods. This species resembles Marasmius in that the fruit bodies shrivel somewhat in dry weather, but do not die and decay readily, and in moist weather revive again.

5. COLLYBIA DRYOPHILA.   Edible. Cap 3-5 cm. wide, at first hemispherical, with a flat center, later convex to flat with the center depressed, tan to reddish brown. Flesh light tan, 2-4 mm.

thick at the stem, becoming gradually thinner toward the margin, soft. Gills about 25 per cm. at the margin, 2-4 mm. wide, adnexed, adnate, or almost free. Stem 3-8 cm. long, 2-5 mm. thick at the top, tapering upward slightly, tough, hollow, at first light tan, later reddish brown, the base enlarged and covered with white mycelium. In groups of several to many specimens on the ground in forests. Sometimes irregular, convoluted, pale yellow growths that bear basidiospores are formed on the stem or the cap. These once were thought to be caused by a parasitic fungus, and were named Tremella mycetophylla, but Buller and others have good evidence that they are only abnormal growths of C. dryophilia, the cause of the abnormality being still unknown.

6. COLLYBIA FAMILIA.

Edible. Cap 1-3 cm. wide, at first hemispherical, later convex to almost plane, usually with a small umbo, surface watersoaked pale tan when moist, almost white when dry, shiny, silky with fine

radial fibers. Flesh white, thin. Gills 20-30 per cm. at
the margin, 2-3 mm. wide, almost free, white. Stem 3-15
cm. long, 2-3 mm. thick, white, brittle, hollow, covered
with white mycelium at the base. In dense clumps of 40 to
60 fruit bodies on rotten wood, frequently with several
clumps appearing near one another simultaneously.

7. COLLYBIA HARIOLARUM.   Cap 3-6 cm. wide, convex
to flat, surface pure white
with a tan center or brown to reddish brown in the center
and paler toward the margin, glabrous or delicately pubescent, becoming very limp in
wet weather or when moi-
stened. Flesh 2-4 mm. thick
near the stem, practically
absent at the margin, soft
and spongy, with definite unpleasant odor when crushed.
Gills 25-35 per cm. at the
margin, 2-3 mm. wide, fairly
uniform in width from the
stem to near the margin, ending in a point at the margin,
white, free or nearly so.
Stem 3-5 cm. long, (when

growing out of cracks in rotten logs some stems may be 10
cm. or more long, but this is abnormal) 3-6 mm. thick,
tapering upward slightly, white to pale reddish tan, tough
to brittle, covered toward the base with velvety or woolly
white hair which toward the top is short and inconspicuous
but dense. Scattered, in groups or dense clumps on the
ground or very rotten wood.

8. COLLYBIA LONGIPES.   Cap 3-8 cm. wide, convex
to nearly flat, with a slight
umbo, surface velvety from a dense covering of short
hairs, brown in the center, paler toward the margin, with
radial wrinkles in the center, margin at first inrolled,
later curved down. Flesh thin, white. Gills 12-15 per cm.
at the margin, 4-8 mm. wide, white, the sides often veined,
the edge fringed when seen with a lens. Stem 6-15 cm.
long, 4-5 mm. thick at the top, tapering upward gradually
from the ground, white, covered with tiny brown flat scales,
the base of the stem extending as a tapering, curved, rootlike growth as much as 25 cm. long down into the soil or
decayed wood on which it grows. The rootlike extension of

the stem must be excavated to be seen, since if the plants
are merely pulled up sharply it will break off. Occurring
usually as individual or widely scattered specimens.

9. COLLYBIA MACULATA.   Edible. Cap 5-13 cm. wide,
                                    convex to flat, white with
obvious rusty red spots, becoming reddish where bruised,
margin curved down and sometimes wavy. Flesh white, 1-
1. 5 cm. thick at the stem,
disappearing at the margin,
fibrous spongy. Gills 25-
30 per cm. at the margin
2-4 mm. wide, white, al-
most free, adnexed, or short
decurrent. Stem 10-18 cm.
long, 1-2 cm. thick at the
top, uniform in diameter or
tapering downward, usually
with one or more bends or
crooks, the rind brittle, the
interior fibrous and in age
hollow, the base extending

into the soil for 5-8 cm. , but without a definite root. Usually
in groups of 5 to 10 on the ground in woods.

10. COLLYBIA MYRIADOPHYLLA.   Cap 1.5-3.5 cm.
                                        wide, first convex,
later flat or depressed in the center, surface at first lilac
to purple, later brown when moist and grayish tan or with
a tinge of lilac when dry, margin of old specimens wavy.
Flesh 1-2 mm. thick in the center, very thin at the margin.
Gills about 50 per cm. at the margin, 2 mm. wide, adnexed,
lilac or deep purple. Stem 3-6 cm. long, 2-3 mm. wide at
the top, even or tapering either upward or downward, often
flat, hollow, brittle, lilac or pale brown, often covered toward the base with coarse woolly lilac colored hair. Scattered or in groups on rotten conifer logs. The bright lilac
or deep purple color of the gills make it a striking plant.

11. COLLYBIA PLATYPHYLLA.   Edible. Cap 6-15 cm.
                                        wide, at first oval to
campanulate, later convex, then flat or with the margin upraised, surface grayish brown in the center, paler toward
the margin, streaked with delicate, dark, radial fibers,
often radially cracked toward the margin, margin often
wavy. Flesh 2-4 mm. thick, white or yellowish, brittle.

Gills 5-10 per cm. 1-2 cm.
wide, white to pale yellow, adnexed, often splitting in older
plants, frequently with prominent veins between the gills
where they are attached to
the under surface of the cap.
Stem 6-15 cm. long, 1-2 cm.
thick at the top, white or tan,
often twisted, even in diameter or tapering downward,
solid, base rounded and sometimes bulbous. Usually solitary, especially growing
from the interior of hollow,
rotten stumps, but sometimes
scattered or in groups of a
few specimens on rotten logs.

12. COLLYBIA RADICATA.   Edible. Cap 3-12 cm. wide,
                         campanulate, flat, or with
the margin raised slightly, usually with an umbo, surface
white or pale tan, the umbo darker, or the entire cap dark
tan and with slight or prom-
inent radial furrows, dry to
very sticky. Flesh thin,
white. Gills 10 per cm. at
the margin, 5-15 mm. wide,
short decurrent to adnexed,
white, thick rather prominently veined on the sides
where they are attached to
the under side of the cap.
Stem 6-15 cm. long, enlarged
at the ground line and tapering
into a root-like extension 2-4
cm. long, 0.3-1.6 cm. thick
at the cap, tapering upward,

fibrous, straight or twisted, white or pale tan. Scattered
or in groups on the ground around hardwood stumps and
trees. There may be great differences between individuals
of the same clump - the cap of one may be dark tan, very
sticky and have prominent radial furrows, while that of the
one next to it is white, almost dry, and has inconspicuous
furrows on the cap.

13. COLLYBIA STIPITARIA.   Cap 6-12 mm. wide, slightly
convex or flat, with a small
definitely outlined depression in the center, surface dark
brown to black in the center, otherwise pale brown with radial ridges composed of
brown hairs, almost white
between the ridges. Flesh
very thin, tough. Gills
white, about 3 per mm., 1-
1.5 mm. wide, adnate to
free. Stem 4-7 cm. long,
0.5 mm. thick, brown, tough,
covered with pale brown hair.
In groups, attached to twigs
and leaves in coniferous and
mixed woods.

14. COLLYBIA VELUTIPES.   Edible. Cap 2-6 cm. wide,
convex to flat, sometimes
the center depressed, surface tan to reddish brown, paler
toward the margin, at first sticky, margin curved down.
Flesh pale tan to white, thin.
Gills 20-25 per cm., adnexed
or toothed near the stem,
white to pale tan, edge
fringed when seen with a lens.
Stem 3-10 cm. long, 3-10
mm. thick, curved, pale yellow when young, later the
upper part pale tan, the lower
portion covered with dense,
velvety, reddish brown hairs,
usually a number of stems
arising from a common short-
rooting structure. In clumps
on living hardwood trees and
on logs and stumps.

Genus HYGROPHORUS

The genus is supposed to be characterized by "waxy"
gills, an ambiguous term. The gills of most species are
rather translucent, thickened toward the base so that in
section they appear more triangular than those of most
other fungi, usually they are somewhat far apart, connected

with one another by veins where they are attached to the
cap, and brittle in texture. In old specimens the surface of
the gills sometimes becomes gelatinous and can be rubbed
off easily. The stem is hollow at maturity, often twisted,
and splits lengthwise readily. No species are known to be
poisonous.

Key to Species of Hygrophorus

1. Gills white - - 2
    Gills colored (yellow, green, orange, red, or brown)
        - - 5

2. Cap white - - H. eburneus
    Cap not white - - 3

3. Cap conical, yellow or red - - H. conicus
    Cap convex - - 4

4. Cap pale pink to red - - H. russula
    Cap tan, sometimes with a tinge of pink - - H. pudorinus
    Cap pale yellow in the center, covered with minute yel-
        low dots near the margin - - H. chrysodon

5. Cap not sticky (dry specimens must be moistened thor-
        oughly to determine this) - - 6
    Cap sticky - - 7

6. Cap 1-4 cm. wide, red or orange - - H. miniatus
    Cap 3-9 cm. wide, reddish brown or tan - - H. pratensis

7. Cap conical, yellow or red - - H. conicus
    Cap not conical - - 8

8. Cap 3-10 cm. wide, bright red when young, pale red
        when old - - H. puniceus
    Cap 1-4 cm. wide - - 9

9. Cap green when young, later dull red, brown or yellow
        - - H. psitticinus
    Cap yellow or golden orange - - H. cerasius

Description of Species of Hygrophorus

1. HYGROPHORUS CERASIUS.   Cap 1-2 cm. wide, con-
                                vex, surface smooth,
yellow to golden orange, sticky, translucent toward the
margin where the gills show through as striations. Flesh

1-2 mm. thick, yellow or orange, the translucent surface layer easily seen when the cap is split. Gills about 20 per cm. at the margin, 2-4 mm. wide, widest midway between margin and stem, adnate or short decurrent, yellow, edge delicately toothed. Stem 2-3 cm. long, 4-6 mm. thick, flat, hollow, yellow, fibrous, easily split lengthwise, very pale yellow inside. Scattered on grassy ground.

2. HYGROPHORUS CHRYSODON. Edible. Cap 3-7 cm. wide, first almost hemispherical, later convex to flat, margin inrolled when young, the surface white with a light yellow center, covered with minute yellow dots that are more numerous near the margin, very sticky when moist. Flesh white. Gills 8-10 per cm., 4-8 mm. wide, decurrent, white, prominent veins between them. Stem 5-10 cm. long, 5-10 mm. thick, white, dotted with yellow like the cap. Solitary or scattered on the ground in open stands of hardwood trees.

3. HYGROPHORUS CONICUS. Cap 2-4 cm. wide, at first acutely conical, later conical to campanulate or the margin upturned, often split from the margin to the stem, surface golden yellow, orange, or red, often becoming black in overmature specimens or where bruised, sticky when young and fresh. Gills 10-15 per cm., 5-15 mm. wide, pale to bright yellow, triangular in cross section, close, almost free. Stem 3-10 cm. long, 4-8 mm. thick, uniform in diameter, prominently ridged and twisted, pale to bright yellow, black in age or where bruised, fibrous, brittle. Solitary or scattered, often in large numbers, on the ground in woods.

4. HYGROPHORUS EBURNEUS. Cap 4-9 cm. wide, umbonate when young, flat or shallow funnel shape when mature, white or ivory color, sticky when young and fresh. The surface of old, dry specimens becomes mucilaginous when moistened, and this mucilaginous cuticle can be peeled off in patches. Flesh white, 6-10 mm. thick near the stem, almost disappearing

half the way to the margin,
fibrous. Gills 10-15 per
cm. at the margin, 6-10
mm. wide at the widest
place, decurrent, thick,
sometimes forked, white
or pale yellow, with veins
between them where they
are attached to the cap.
Stem 1-2 cm. thick at the
top, 5-10 cm. long, tapering downward, for a centi-

meter or two below the gills it is covered with little white
tufts, and from there down it is pale yellow and sticky. The
interior of the stem is fibrous and white or pale yellow.
Scattered or in groups of 2 or 3 on the ground in deciduous
woods.

5. HYGROPHORUS MINIATUS.

Cap 1-4 cm. wide, slightly
convex or flat, sometimes
with a hollow in the center
extending down into the stem,
vermilion to orange, not
sticky, pubescent or delicately scaly, margin often
regularly cracked and somewhat wavy. Flesh pale, thin.
Gills 10-12 per cm., 3-6 mm.

wide, adnate or short decurrent, colored like the cap or
paler. Stem 2-7 cm. long, 2-5 mm. thick, colored like the
cap or yellow. Solitary or in groups on the ground or on
very rotten wood, occasionally on old white pine stumps.

6. HYGROPHORUS PRATENSIS.

Edible. Cap 3-9 cm. wide,
convex to flat, sometimes
with a broad, high umbo,
reddish brown when young,
fading to pale tan, translucent and watersoaked
when moist, not sticky.
Flesh pale tan. Gills 8-12
per cm., 4-10 mm. wide,

decurrent, colored like the cap or paler. Stem 3-7 cm.
long, 8-15 mm. thick, usually tapering downward, colored
like the cap or almost white. Solitary or in groups or
clumps, sometimes in rings, on the ground in open deciduous woods and meadows.

7. HYGROPHORUS PSITTICINUS.   Cap 2-4 cm. wide,
                               campanulate when
young later flat, depressed in the center, sticky when moist,
surface first rather bright green, often changing to dull red,
brown, or yellow, delicately striate. Gills 8-12 per cm.,
3-6 cm. wide, adnate, dull green to red or yellow. Stem
4-7 cm. long, 2-5 mm. wide, green toward the top, red to
yellow below, sticky, tough. Scattered or in groups on the
ground in low swampy woods or open places.

8. HYGROPHORUS PUDORINUS.   Edible. Cap 4-12
                             cm. wide, convex or
campanulate, surface sticky when moist, pale tan or slightly
darker, often tinged with pink, margin at first inrolled and
covered with delicate down. Flesh white or very pale pink.
Gills 10-12 per cm. at the margin, 3-8 mm. wide, short
decurrent, occasionally forked, intervenose, white. Stem
3-8 cm. long, 0.5-2 cm. thick, often tapering downward,
white to tan, sometimes with a tinge of pink, slightly hairy,
roughened toward the top. Scattered or in groups on the
ground in coniferous woods.

9. HYGROPHORUS PUNICEUS.   Edible. Cap 3-10 cm.
                           wide, campanulate to
convex when young, flat to depressed in the center when
old, sticky when moist, bright scarlet, fading in age to pale
red or orange, the margin lobed or wavy. Gills 10-12 per
cm. at the margin, 5-12 mm. wide, narrowly adnexed to
decurrent, scarlet or yellow, prominent veins between the
gills where they are attached to the cap. Stem 5-8 cm.
long, 5-20 mm. wide, reddish yellow toward the top, the
base white, fibrous, striate, hollow. Solitary or scattered
on the ground in woods and open places.

10. HYGROPHORUS RUSSULA.   Edible. Cap 6-12 cm.
                           wide, convex when
young, becoming broad and shallow funnel shape, surface
pale pink to red, sticky when moist, often spotted with
minute scales, margin first inrolled, then raised and lobed
or wavy. Gills 8-12 per cm., 5-14 mm. wide, adnexed to

short decurrent, white when young, irregularly spotted
with red when old. Stem 3-7 cm. long, 1.5-2.5 cm. thick
at the top, tapering downward, white, covered with downy
mycelium. Solitary or caespitose, often in large groups on
the ground in deciduous woods.

Genus LACTARIUS

The genus is characterized by white spores, gills
adnate or short decurrent, flesh of cap and stem very
brittle like that of Russula, to which it is closely related.
The flesh and gills of fresh specimens when broken exude a
white or colored juice, which is the single critical distinguishing character of the genus; the quantity of this juice
varies according to the species and the weather, and sometimes is so scanty that it can be detected only with the aid
of a lens, but ordinarily it is sufficiently obvious to be seen
readily. Gussow and Odell in "Mushrooms and Toadstools"
report that several species previously considered poisonous
because of their unpleasant taste when fresh actually are
edible and delicious, the objectionable flavor disappearing
when the mushrooms are cooked.

Key to Species of Lactarius

1. Milk and entire plant indigo blue - - L. indigo
    Milk first white, soon becoming violet - - L. uvidus
    Milk first white, soon pale yellow, then fading to white
        - - L. cilicioides
    Milk first white, soon becoming sulphur yellow and re-
        maining so - - L. chrysorheus
    Milk yellow or orange - - 2
    Milk white and remaining so - - 3

2. Milk orange - - L. deliciosus
    Milk cream colored to yellow - - L. trivialis

3. Entire plant abortive and very irregular in shape,
        bright orange red, gills only partially formed, cap
        and gills white inside - - Hypomyces lactifluorum
    Cap normal, surface sticky when moist - - 4
    Cap normal, surface not sticky - - 8

4. Gills pale pink - - L. controversus
    Gills not pink - - 5

5. Margin hairy, cap tan to reddish tan, often zoned - -
        L. torminosus
    Margin not hairy - - 6

6. Surface with concentric bands of orange to copper
        color - - L. insulsus
    Surface without concentric bands of color - - 7

7. Surface pale gray to grayish brown, sometimes with a
        violet tinge - - L. trivialis
    Surface pale yellow to pale orange - - L. affinis

8. Entire surface densely covered with short hair - -
        L. vellerius
    Only the margin hairy - - L. deceptivus
    Surface glabrous - - 9

9. Surface white - - L. piperatus
    Surface brown - - 10

10. Cap 2-5 cm. wide - - L. subdulcis
    Cap 5-12 cm. wide - - L. volemus

Description of Species of Lactarius

1. LACTARIUS AFFINIS.   Cap 6-12 cm. wide, first
                               convex with a central de-
pression and the margin inrolled, later broad funnel shape
and the margin curved down; surface yellowish tan to pale
orange, without zones, sticky when moist. Flesh 8-12 mm.
thick near the stem, white, firm, exuding a very bitter
white juice when broken. Gills about 15 per cm., 6-8

mm. wide midway between
the stem and the margin,
tapering to points at both
ends, short decurrent, pale
yellow or cream colored,
many gills branched at the
very base. Stem 8-12 cm.
long, 1.5-2.5 cm. thick at
the top, tapering gradually
up or down or quite cylindrical, the base covered
with white mycelium, solid
until eaten out by larvae.
Solitary or scattered on the
ground in mixed conifer and
hardwoods.

2. LACTARIUS CILICIOIDES.   Cap 7-14 cm. wide, de-
                                             pressed in the center,
the margin first inrolled, later upraised, surface white or
tan and white, sticky, covered with matted hairs, especially
on the margin, or sometimes only the margin hairy.   Flesh
white, 8-10 mm. thick near the stem, becoming pale yellow
almost at once and in a few minutes becoming colorless
again, slightly bitter or tasteless.   Gills 12-18 per cm. ,
3-5 mm. wide, white, exuding juice more copiously than
the flesh, the yellow color of the juice often being most apparent just at the junction of gills and cap, short decurrent,
occasionally forked near the stem, many gills near the
margin 1 cm. or less in length.   Stem 3-5 cm. long, 1. 5-
3 cm. thick, white.   Solitary or scattered on the ground,
chiefly in coniferous woods.

3. LACTARIUS CHRYSORHEUS.   Said to be poisonous.
Cap 4-10 cm. wide, convex with a broad depression in the
center, or wide funnel shape, margin first inrolled, later
elevated; surface pale yellow, pale orange or pale red,
often with concentric zones of alternate yellow and orange,
dry or slightly sticky, margin pubescent.   Flesh at first
white, later pale yellow; juice white, changing to sulphur
yellow, abundant, very bitter.   Gills 20-25 per cm. , 3-5
mm. wide, adnate to short decurrent, infrequently forked
near the stem, white when young, later yellow.   Stem 4-6
cm. long, 1-1. 5 cm. thick, hollow when mature, white or
colored like the cap, sometimes spotted, often pubescent.
Gregarious or in small clumps, on the ground in deciduous
woods.

4. LACTARIUS CONTROVERSUS.   Cap 8-16 cm. wide,
                                            broad funnel shape,
surface white when dry, when moist watersoaked pale tan
and very sticky, usually with several narrow zones near

the margin, often with
numerous reddish brown
blotches although these
are not invariably present;
margin at first inrolled,
later upraised.   Flesh 8-
15 mm. thick, white,
firm, of uniform thickness
almost to the margin.
Gills 15-20 per cm. at the
margin, 3-5 mm. wide,
narrowed to a point at the

stem, short decurrent in old specimens, white when young,
soon pink. Juice white, opaque, fairly abundant in moist
weather, peppery a short time after tasting. Stem 2-4 cm.
long, 1-3 cm. thick at the top, usually tapering downward
and frequently with a lateral "root" at the base made up of
soil and mycelium. On a dry day the cap is not sticky, but
leaves and other debris adhering to it are evidence that it
was sticky when it emerged.

5. LACTARIUS DECEPTIVUS.   Edible. Cap 8-15 cm.
                             wide, flat with a de-
pressed center or broad funnel shape, margin first inrolled,
later upraised; surface dry, white or grayish tan, often
with irregular brown spots, glabrous except the margin
which is covered with dense short hair. Flesh white. Juice
white, not changing color, bitter. Gills 12-15 per cm. , 6-
12 mm. wide, adnate to short decurrent, white or pale yellow, rarely forked. Stem 3-8 cm. long, 1-4 cm. thick,
solid, often tapering downward, delicately hairy, white.
Scattered or gregarious on the ground in conifer or hardwoods.

6. LACTARIUS DELICIOSUS.   Edible. Cap 6-12 cm.
                             wide, convex with a cen-
tral depression and incurved margin when young, later
broad funnel shape and the margin upraised; surface pale
orange when young, fading to grayish orange or pale tan,
usually with alternate lighter and darker zones of color although these may be indistinct or lacking, becoming green
where bruised. Flesh white to orange, tinged green near
the stem, 8-10 mm. thick at the stem. Juice yellow to
orange. Gills 15-20 per cm. at the margin, 5-8 mm. wide,
adnate or short decurrent, occasionally forked, inconspicuous veins between the gills where the gills join the cap,
reddish orange, becoming green when bruised or in age.
Stem 4-8 cm. long, 1-2. 5 cm. thick, cylindrical, delicately
pubescent when young, orange or with orange spots, becoming green where bruised or in age, hollow when mature.
Scattered on the ground in forests.

7. LACTARIUS INDIGO.   Edible. Cap 5-15 cm. wide,
                         convex with a central depres-
sion or broad funnel shape, margin curved down; surface
indigo blue with a silvery sheen, with alternate lighter and
darker blue zones. Flesh indigo blue, 1-2 cm. thick near
the stem. Juice usually abundant, blue, mild in taste.

Gills 15 per cm. , 5-10 mm. wide, adnate to short decurrent, occasionally forked, blue-green to pale green. Stem
2-6 cm. long, 1-3 cm. thick, equal in diameter or tapering
toward the base, blue, hollow at maturity. Solitary or
scattered on the ground in mixed woods.

8. LACTARIUS INSULSUS.   Cap 5-10 cm. wide, first
                           convex with a central de-
pression, later broad funnel shape, margin inrolled when
young, decurved to upraised when old; surface copper colored to orange, with alternate zones of lighter and darker
color, sticky when moist. Flesh white. Juice white, very
bitter. Gills 20 per cm. , 4-8 mm. wide, adnate when
young, later short decurrent, occasionally forked near the
base, white or grayish white. Stem 2-5 cm. long, 8-15 mm.
thick, cylindrical or tapering slightly downward, paler than
the cap, hollow at maturity. Scattered in groups or in
clumps on the ground in open deciduous woods.

9. LACTARIUS PIPERATUS.   Edible. Cap 6-12 cm.
                            wide, plane with a de-
pressed center or broad funnel shape, margin first incurved, later elevated; surface white, without zones, dry,
glabrous. Juice white, abundant, very peppery. Gills 20-
25 per cm. at the margin, 3-6 mm. wide, adnate or short
decurrent, repeatedly forked, white or pale yellow. Stem
2-6 cm. long, 1-3 cm. thick, often tapering downward,
white, sometimes finely pubescent. Scattered or gregarious on the ground in deciduous woods. Gussow and Odell,
in "Mushrooms and Toadstools" describe a variety, per-
gamenus, in which the gills are 15 per cm. and seldom
forked and with the stem more slender, and another variety
has been described in which the juice changes to pale yellow.

10. LACTARIUS SUBDULCIS.   Edible. Cap 2-5 cm.
                            wide, convex or flat when
young, depressed in the center when mature, margin of
young plants not inrolled; surface tan to reddish brown,
without zones, dry. Flesh pale tan. Juice scanty in dry
weather, abundant in moist weather, white, tasteless or
slightly bitter. Gills 15-20 per cm. , 2-5 mm. wide, adnate or short decurrent, occasionally forked, somewhat
paler than the cap, often stained reddish. Stem 4-7 cm.
long, 3-8 mm. thick, colored like the cap or paler, sometimes hairy toward the base, hollow when mature.

Scattered or in groups on the ground in deciduous woods and grassy fields.

11. LACTARIUS TORMINOSUS.   Edible. Cap 5-10 cm. wide, broad funnel shape, margin first inrolled, later decurved; surface pale reddish tan, often with alternate zones of tan and reddish tan, sticky when moist, hairy on the margin. Flesh white or pale red. Juice white, very bitter. Gills 20 per cm., 3-6 mm. wide, short decurrent, some forked near the stem, white or pale yellow when young, later with a reddish tinge. Stem 3-6 cm. long, 1.5-2 cm. thick, sometimes tapering downward, pale red to almost white, often spotted. Scattered or in groups on the ground in deciduous and mixed forests. Kauffman's "Agaricaceae of Michigan" lists this species as poisonous, but Gussow and Odell, in "Mushrooms and Toadstools" state: "To our personal knowledge the species has been eaten and enjoyed without causing any trouble."

12. LACTARIUS TRIVIALIS.   Edibility doubtful. Cap 7-15 cm. wide, first convex, later almost flat with a slight depression in the center, margin inrolled when young and remaining so or at least curved downward; surface pale or dark gray, grayish brown or with a tinge of violet or pink, without zones, glabrous, sticky when moist. Flesh 6-15 mm. thick, soft and fragile, white or pale gray, grayish brown near the surface of the cap. Juice abundant, white to pale yellow, very bitter 20-30 seconds after tasting, although this bitterness may be lacking in old specimens. Gills about 20 per cm. at the margin, 5-10 mm. wide, adnate or short decurrent, often forked near the stem, white or pale tan, sometimes with a greenish tinge where bruised. Stem 4-10 cm. long, 1-2 cm. thick, cylindrical, white or pale gray, glabrous, hollow when mature. Scattered or gregarious on the ground in deciduous and coniferous woods.

13. LACTARIUS UVIDUS.   Said to be poisonous. Cap 4-8 cm. wide, first obtuse with inrolled margin, later flat, at maturity with a shallow depression in the center and decurved margin; surface pale brown or watersoaked tan with a tinge of lavender, sticky. Flesh 8-12 mm. thick at the stem, 1 mm. at the margin, white when freshly cut or broken, soon becoming violet. Gills 12-15 per cm., the larger ones 6-8 mm. wide, many

short gills only 1 mm. or less wide and a few mm. long,
the larger ones tapered toward both ends, white, pale purple where bruised, short decurrent, sometimes forked near
the stem. Juice white, soon becoming violet, abundant in
young specimens. Stem 4-5 cm. long, 1-2 cm. thick at the
top, tapering slightly downward, with a narrow hollow up
the center, both inside and outside becoming purple where
cut or bruised. In groups on the ground in swampy woods.

14. LACTARIUS VELLERIUS.   Edible. Cap 6-12 cm.
                                        wide, convex with the
center depressed, margin first inrolled, later upraised;
surface white or gray, covered with dense short hair which
in young specimens may be matted together. Flesh 4-8 mm.
thick near the stem, white. Juice abundant in moist
weather, scanty to lacking entirely in dry weather, white,
very peppery. Gills 10-15 per cm. at the margin, 4-8 mm.
wide, adnate or short decurrent, white to pale yellow, sometimes becoming brown where bruised, occasionally forked.
Stem 2-4 cm. long, 1-2 cm. thick, often tapering downward,
white, solid, densely covered with short hair or glabrous.
Scattered to gregarious on the ground in deciduous or mixed
woods. Kauffman states that this species is suspected of
being poisonous, but Gussow and Odell in "Mushrooms and
Toadstools" consider it edible.

15. LACTARIUS VOLEMUS.   Edible. Cap 5-12 cm. wide,
                                    convex to flat or depressed
in the center, margin first inrolled, then decurved or flat;
surface golden brown or darker, without zones, glabrous,
often wrinkled. Flesh white or pale tan. Juice usually
abundant, white, mild in taste. Gills about 20 per cm.,
5-10 mm. wide, adnate or short decurrent, occasionally
forked, white or pale brown, darker in age or where bruised.
Stem 3-10 cm. long, 1-2 cm. thick, colored like the cap or
paler, usually solid, cylindrical. Scattered or in groups on
the ground in deciduous woods and open spaces.

16. HYPOMYCES LACTIFLUORUM.   Not poisonous, but
                                          not recommended
for eating. This plant is a combination of two different
fungi; Hypomyces lactifluorum is an Ascomycete which
grows as a parasite on gilled fungi. In some regions of the
country the gilled fungus that serves as a host is Lactarius
piperatus, described above. The writer, however, has
found it in northern Minnesota and Wisconsin almost only

on Russula delica. Both of these host fungi, Lactarius piperatus and Russula delica, are edible, but the parasite Hypomyces lactifluorum may grow on still other gilled fungi, and since the host on which it grows ordinarily is distorted and unidentifiable with certainty, one probably should avoid eating the plants.

The writer and others have eaten these plants at Itasca Park in Minnesota, and while none of us were poisoned we all had rather pronounced intestinal symptoms within the next 12 hours, and the flavor of the plants was not such as to recommend them highly. The plants vary greatly in shape and size, and therefore only a general description can be given - however, the bright orange red color and the aborted gills on the under side of the cap usually serve to identify them.

Cap 5-12 cm. wide, irregularly globose, flat, convex, with margin downcurved or upraised, entire plant orange or orange red in color. This bright color is restricted to a thin layer on the outside, the interior of the plant being white, the texture of the flesh of cap and stem usually firm and brittle. Where the gills ordinarily would be, on the under side of the cap, there may be only suggestions of gills, but if the cap is broken to expose a section of this surface, hints of gills usually can be seen. Stem 2-4 cm. thick, 4-10 cm. long, or the cap merely tapering to a thick stem-like base.

Genus LENTINUS

The genus is characterized by white spores, and by the rather prominently toothed lower edges of the gills. The flesh of the cap is tough, and the fruit bodies endure for a week or more, shrinking in dry weather and reviving with rain. All of the four species here described are found

on wood.   In habit and appearance Lentinus and Panus are
rather similar and some authorities have included them in
a single genus.

Key to Species of Lentinus

1. Stem absent, caps attached laterally, usually imbricate
    - - L. vulpinus
    Stem present, central or eccentric - - 2

2. Caespitose, with many stems joined near the base, cap
    funnel shaped - - L. cochleatus
    Scattered or in groups, stems of adjacent plants not
    joined - - 3

3. Cap 4-12 cm. wide, obtuse to flat, pale yellow or tan,
    scaly - - L. lepideus
    Cap 2-5 cm. wide, flat or depressed in the center, cen-
    ter covered with dark brown, hairy scales - - L.
    tigrinus

Description of Species of Lentinus

1. LENTINUS COCHLEATUS.   Edible. Cap 3-7 cm.
                                       wide, narrow to broad
funnel shape, margin lobed and very irregular in outline,
often distorted from mutual pressure, curved down; surface tan to reddish brown, almost glabrous or covered with
short erect scales, often radially cracked or furrowed.
Gills 15-20 per cm. at the margin, 4-8 mm. wide, long
decurrent, tough, edge saw-toothed, white or pale flesh
color. Stem 3-7 cm. long, 5-10 mm. in diameter, central
to eccentric, tough, solid, tapering downward, irregularly
furrowed, many stems joined near the base, flesh colored
at the top, reddish brown at the base. In dense clumps on
stumps and decaying logs of deciduous trees.

2. LENTINUS LEPIDEUS.   Edible. Cap 4-12 cm. wide,
                                     first convex, later almost
flat, surface white to pale brown, toward the center covered
with coarse brown flat scales, often with conspicuous cracks
extending in from the margin through the entire flesh of the
cap. Flesh white, tough, up to 2 cm. thick. Gills about 20
per cm. at the margin, 5-12 mm. wide, sinuate or decurrent, white or yellow, conspicuously and irregularly

sawtoothed on the lower
edge. Stem 2-7 cm. long,
1-2 cm. thick at the top,
usually rough and scaly,
white or pale yellow,
tough, solid. Singly or 2
to 3 fruit bodies together
on decaying conifer logs,
posts, stumps, railroad
ties, dock and bridge timbers, etc. A veil is present in young specimens,
and sometimes this re-

mains near the top of the stem as a ring. The plant has a
definite odor suggestive of licorice.

3. LENTINUS TIGRINUS. Cap 2-5 cm. wide, first convex, later flat, with a nar-
row depression in the center, tough and leathery; surface
covered with dark brown or black hairy scales; in overmature specimens the margin may be wavy or upraised and
split. Flesh white, 2-3 mm. thick, tough. Gills 20 per
cm. at the margin, 2-4 mm. wide, decurrent, white, edge
toothed. Stem 1-3 cm. long, 3-5 mm. thick, solid, white
or tan, often covered with small scales. Sometimes an
annulus or ring is present, but usually disappears quickly.
Kauffman in "Agaricaceae of Michigan" describes a "mon-
strous" form in which the gills do not develop, and which
he says is fairly common.

4. LENTINUS VULPINUS.

Cap 4-10 cm. wide, ranging
from almost circular to semicircular or irregular at the
margin, tapering to a stemlike base, often numerous
caps arising from a common
point of attachment on the
under side of a log; surface
pale tan, coarsely hairy near
the point of attachment,
slightly or prominently radially furrowed toward the margin; margin curved down or
inrolled. Flesh 1-2 mm.

thick near the base, thinner at the margin, tough, white.
Gills 20 per cm. at the margin, white to pale tan, edge
coarsely sawtoothed, radiating from the stemlike base.
Usually in clusters of several to many fruit bodies arising
from the same point. It has a very peppery taste when
chewed. On logs and stumps of hardwood trees.

Genus LENZITES

The genus is distinguished by white spores, and tough
and stemless fruit bodies that have a broad base of attachment like many of the Polypores. The fruit bodies do not
decay readily but persist for some time, and it is not unusual to find, in the spring and early summer of one year,
fruit bodies that were formed the previous year. Lenzites
appears to form a connecting link between the gill fungi and
the pore fungi, and the genus commonly is placed in both
the Agaricaceae, or gill fungi, and the Polyporaceae, or
pore fungi. The 3 species here described, all of which are
almost world wide in distribution and all of which are common on decaying wood, are the major species in the genus.

1. LENZITES BETULINA.   Fruit body 3-6 cm. wide,
                             projecting from the base 2-4
cm., sessile or effuse reflexed, circular and resupinate
when growing on the under side of a log, typically semicircular when growing from the side of a log, flat; the surface woolly when fresh, with many narrow concentric
ridges and bands of color, alternating pale gray, yellow,
and brownish orange when fresh, fading to dirty gray, margin usually thin. Flesh or context white, corky, firm but
somewhat flexible when dry, 1-3 mm. thick. Gills at first
white, weathering to dirty gray, about 10 per cm. at the
margin, up to 2 mm. thick, firm, leathery or tough. In
groups and clumps on decaying branches, logs and stumps
of birch.

2. LENZITES SEPIARIA.   Cap or pileus 2-7 cm. wide,
                             projecting from the wood
1-4 cm. usually shelflike, sometimes with a stemlike base;
surface at first woolly and yellowish or reddish brown, or
alternate bands of dark and lighter reddish brown; often the
most recent zone of growth of a fresh specimen is yellowish brown, while the older portion is darker; often the surface has concentric ridges, and in fresh specimens the

surface has a hairy covering but this disappears with weathering. Context brown, tough and pliable when fresh, corky when old or dry, 1-5 mm. thick. Gills 10-15 per cm. at the margin, 3-8 mm. wide, thick, the edges of fresh specimens often yellowish with darker mycelium below, so that the slightest bruise or scratch exposes the darker mycelium.

Solitary or scattered on decaying conifer logs and conifer wood. This fungus is a common cause of decay in coniferous construction timber of all kinds, from railroad ties and bridge timbers to boats and buildings, where the wood is occasionally moist and has not been protected by a preservative.

3. LENZITES TRABEA.   Fruit bodies sometimes solitary, usually in groups of 2 to 5, shelflike, each shelf approximately semicircular in outline, 1-2 cm. wide, extending out from the wood 0.5-3 cm., 5-10 mm. thick at the base, margin thin and sharp; upper surface cinnamon brown to gray brown when dry, chocolate brown when moist, when young and fresh covered with woolly matted mycelium which soon disappears leaving the surface smooth, often with several indistinct ridges. Context or flesh 2-3 mm. thick, colored like the upper surface, firm. Pores 10-20 per cm. in a tangential

direction, often radially elongate, especially near the margin. Single pores that are much longer than others in a radial direction are irregularly distributed among the other pores of more or less uniform size. The pores are 2-3 mm. long, the walls and lower ends gray when dry, the lower ends brown when fresh and moist. Singly, scattered and in groups on dead hardwoods and conifers, especially

on posts and poles. It is one of the principal causes of
"shell-rot" of telephone poles and of decay of wood in many
kinds of construction.

Genus LEPIOTA

The genus is characterized by white spores, free gills,
a ring on the stem, and the stem separating readily from
the cap, such definite characters that ordinarily this is one
of the easiest genera to recognize. Most of the species that
have been tested are edible, but the edibility of some is not
known. One species, L. morgani, is poisonous, causing
mild to serious illness but rarely death; it is especially
dangerous because it closely resembles and can easily be
mistaken for some of the edible kinds.

Key to Species of Lepiota

1. Surface of mature cap smooth - - 2
    Surface of mature cap scaly - - 5

2. Cap white - - 3
    Cap tan to dark reddish brown - - 4

3. Ring prominent, cap 4-10 cm. wide - - L. naucina
    Ring soon disappearing, plants growing in dense clumps
        - - L. cepaestipes

4. Cap dark reddish brown, very sticky when young and
        fresh (old dry specimens must be kept wet for some
        time to determine this) - - L. glioderma
    Cap pale tan to pale brown, dry and wrinkled - -
        L. granulosa

5. Spores and gills of mature plant green - - L. morgani
    Spores and gills of mature plant white - - 6

6. Flesh becoming red in old plants or when bruised - -
        L. americana
    Flesh not becoming red - - 7

7. Scales on mature cap erect and pointed - - 8
    Scales on mature cap flat or nearly so - - 9

8. Cap 5-12 cm. wide - - L. acutesquamosa
    Cap 3-5 cm. wide - - L. asperula

9. Ring prominent and persistent - - 10
    Ring soon disappearing - - 12

10. Edge of cap and ring red - - L. rubrotincta
     Edge of cap and ring not red - - 11

11. Stem 15-30 cm. long, ring usually can be moved up and
        down - - L. procera
     Stem 8-20 cm. long, ring not movable - - L. rachodes
        (see also L. morgani)

12. Stem smooth and shiny - - L. cristata
     Stem covered with shreds of mycelium or fluffy scales
        - - 13

13. Growing in dense clumps on manured ground - -
        L. cepaestipes
     Scattered or in groups of 2 or 3 in the forest - -
        L. clypeolaria

Description of Species of Lepiota

1. LEPIOTA ACUTESQUAMOSA.   Cap 5-12 cm. wide,
                                first hemispherical,
later convex to flat; surface at first densely and uniformly
covered with pale brown hairs which as the cap expands form
erect pointed brown scales that are more crowded near the
center; the margin radially cracked and extending beyond
the end of the gills. Flesh white. Gills 20-25 per cm., 4-
7 mm. wide, free, white or pale gray, edge delicately serrate. Stem 6-12 cm. long, 6-12 mm. thick at the top, tapering upward, the base enlarged or bulbous, with few
scattered brown scales below the annulus. Annulus rather
delicate and often disappearing quickly. Scattered or in
groups on the ground and on very rotten wood, sometimes
in yards and gardens.

2. LEPIOTA AMERICANA.   Cap 8-20 cm. wide, oval or
                            bell shaped when young,
later convex or campanulate; margin first incurved, sometimes slightly striate in age; surface of young plants covered
with a continuous reddish brown skin which, as the cap expands, breaks up first into irregular rings, then forms large
scales. Flesh 1-2 cm. thick at the stem, very thin at the
margin, white when young, turning pale red in age or when
bruised; in young specimens this red color is very deep and
appears within a few seconds after the flesh is broken, but
in older specimens the color is rather pale and appears
slowly. Gills 15 per cm. at the margin, 6-12 mm. wide,
free, white, becoming red when bruised. Stem 10-25 cm.

long, 8-20 mm. thick at the top, enlarged at the base or enlarged just above the ground line and tapering both up and
down from there, solid when young, hollow at maturity, becoming reddish brown in age or when bruised. Ring large,
white, soft and pendulous, occasionally movable, sometimes
disappearing quickly. Solitary or in clumps on the ground
in pastures and in woods.

3. LEPIOTA ASPERULA.   Cap 3-5 cm. wide, convex,
                         first uniformly reddish brown
or orange brown but as the cap expands the cuticle breaks
up into very numerous, small, erect scales that are very

dense toward the center;
surface between the scales
pale yellowish brown. Small
white fragments of the veil
hang from the margin of the
cap as it expands but these
soon disappear. Flesh white
or pale tan, 4-7 mm. thick
near the stem, spongy,
brittle. Gills 35-45 per cm.
at the margin, 3-5 mm. wide,
free, first white, soon pale
yellow. Stem 2-6 cm. long,
4-8 mm. thick, solid, fibrous,
scaly like the cap up to the ring, pale yellow or pale reddish brown above the ring; ring soon disappearing. Solitary or in groups of a few.

4. LEPIOTA CEPAESTIPES.

Cap 2-4 cm. wide, oval when
young, broad conical when
mature, white, at first covered with loose, mealy mycelium most of which wears
off. Flesh about 2 mm. thick
near the stem, very soft and
limp. Gills 3-5 mm. wide,
20-25 per cm. at the mar-
gin, white, free. Stem 5-8
cm. long, 2-4 mm. thick at
the top, increasing in diameter toward the base, the

base enlarged in a peculiar way like the bulb of a young
onion, covered below the ring with a layer of mealy white
mycelium that rubs off easily. The ring is thin and soon
dries up and disappears. In dense clumps, with 5 to 15
fruit bodies in each clump, sometimes in partial fairy rings,
on rich soil or freshly manured ground.

5. LEPIOTA CYLPEOLARIA. Cap 3-8 cm. wide, campanulate or flat with an umbo,
surface pale reddish brown and breaking up into numerous
small scales except at the umbo, which is darker, often

radially striate or cracked
near the margin. Pieces
of the veil remain attached
to the margin as the cap expands. Flesh white, thin.
Gills 12-18 per cm. at the
margin, 3-6 mm. wide,
free, white, edge fringed
when viewed with a lens.
Stem 4-10 cm. long, 3-7
mm. thick at the top, tapering gradually upward, covered with loose, pale brown
scales up to the ring, white
above the ring, hollow. Ring thin, delicate and soon disappearing. Solitary or scattered on the ground in conifer or
mixed woods.

6. LEPIOTA CRISTATA. Edible. Cap 2-4 cm. wide,
convex to campanulate, or
flat with an umbo, surface at first dull red or reddish brown,
breaking into concentrically arranged small scales as the

cap expands, umbo remain-
ing tan to brown. The scales
are small or entirely absent
toward the margin. Flesh
thin, white. Gills about 20
per cm. at the margin, 2-4
mm. wide, free, white,
sometimes forked near the
stem, edge delicately wavy.
Stem 3-5 cm. long, 2-5 mm.
thick, usually white when
young, often tinged pale pink
or reddish brown when old,

smooth or covered with loose silky mycelium up to the annulus, hollow or the interior spongy. Annulus small, inconspicuous, white, soon disappearing. Scattered or in groups on the ground in grassy places and forests.

7. LEPIOTA GLIODERMA.   Cap 4-8 cm. wide, convex to flat, reddish brown, very gelatinous sticky when moist, smooth and shiny when dry, the skin removable, margin usually curved down. Flesh

3-5 mm. thick at the stem, pale tan, usually reddish where bruised, spongy. Gills white, pale yellow in age, 20-25 per cm. at the margin, 4-7 mm. wide, narrowly adnexed or free, the edge often irregularly sawtoothed. Stem 6-9 cm. long, 5-8 mm. thick, uniform in diameter, above the ring pale yellowish red and smooth, below the ring covered with irregular streaks and partial rings of reddish mycelium. Veil white or pale yellow each hypha separate and distinct to give a sort of cobweb texture; the ring disappearing almost at once or evident only as a red line around the upper portion of the stem. Single or in groups of 2 or 3 on the ground in conifer and mixed woods.

8. LEPIOTA GRANULOSA.   Cap 3-6 cm. wide, convex or flat with a low umbo, surface light brown to reddish brown, having a somewhat granular texture and whitish sheen, often with radial wrinkles. Flesh thin, white or tinged red. Gills about 20 per cm. at the margin, 4-6 mm. wide, adnexed to almost free, rounded at the stem, white. Stem 2-5 cm. long, 4-8 mm. thick at the top, even or tapering upward, pale red and granular or scaly up to the ring, white above. Ring delicate, quickly disappearing. In groups and dense clumps on the ground in deciduous woods.

9. LEPIOTA MORGANI.   Poisonous. Cap 10-30 cm. wide, at first oval or globose, later convex to flat; surface first covered with a continuous tan or brown cuticle which breaks up, as the

cap expands, to form large irregular patchy scales. Flesh
thick, white. Gills about 15 per cm. at the margin, 8-15
mm. wide, free and sometimes 4-5 mm. from the stem,
white when young, usually becoming green in mature specimens. Stem 10-20 cm. long, 1-2 cm. thick at the top,
tapering gradually upward from an enlarged base, white or
pale tan, solid. Ring or annulus prominent, tough but soft,
and in older specimens it can be moved up and down the
stem. The spore print is dull green. In groups, often in
large fairy rings on the ground in pastures and open woods.
It is said to be eaten by some people without harm, but it
is known to cause vomiting and even serious illness in
others. It can be distinguished from some of the edible
kinds only by making a spore print, and since it sometimes
grows with the edible kinds, even in the same fairy rings,
one can see the need for making a spore print, for positive
identification, of every single specimen that is to be eaten.

10. LEPIOTA NAUCINA.   Edible. Cap 4-8 cm. wide,
                        oval or globose when young,
later convex to almost flat; surface smooth, white or light
tan, sometimes irregularly and inconspicuously cracked
but never scaly. Flesh white, thick, firm. Gills 15 per
cm. at the margin, 5-10 mm. wide, free, white when
young, slowly becoming pinkish, then light brown, edge
delicately fringed. Stem 5-10 cm. long, 6-12 mm. thick
at the top, tapering gradually upward from a bulbous base,
white, hollow when mature. Ring prominent, firm, stick-
ing straight out from the stem, sometimes loose so that it
can be moved up and down the stem. Scattered or in groups
on the ground in pastures, fields, parks and open woods.

11. LEPIOTA PROCERA.   Edible. Cap 5-12 cm. wide,
                        oval when young, later cam-
panulate to convex or flat with an umbo; surface at first
uniform reddish brown but as the cap expands breaking up
into prominent concentrically arranged brown scales except
on the umbo, sometimes with small white woolly scales between the large brown ones. Flesh thick, white. Gills
about 15 per cm., 6-12 mm. wide, narrow toward the stem
and wider toward the middle, free and rather distant from
the stem, white when young, pale brown when old, edge
delicately fringed. Stem 15-30 cm. long, 6-12 mm. thick
at the top, tapering upward from a bulbous base, delicately
scaly, usually hollow. Ring thick, prominent, white above,
brown scales on the under side, capable of being moved up

down. Singly or scattered on the ground in pastures or open deciduous woods.

12. LEPIOTA RACHODES.   Edible. Cap 9-16 cm. wide, at first nearly spherical, later convex to flat; surface layer at first brown, breaking up into concentrically arranged flat scales. Flesh 1-2 cm. thick near the stem, tapering gradually to the margin, soft and spongy, white, often becoming reddish brown where broken or bruised. Gills 14-16 per cm. at the margin, 8-12 mm. wide, at first white, later tinged yellow to pale brown, edge delicately toothed and sometimes definitely brown. Stem 8-18 cm. long, 12-20 mm. thick at the top, gradually increasing in diameter toward the base which is enlarged and almost spherical. In groups and fairy rings on the ground in pastures and open deciduous woods.

13. LEPIOTA RUBROTINCTA.   Cap 3-8 cm. wide, obtuse to campanulate, at first uniform reddish brown or rust colored, later the colored surface breaking up into flat scales. Gills white, free, 15-20 per cm. at the margin, 4-8 mm. wide, edge fringed when viewed with a lens. Stem 7-14 cm. long, 5-15 mm. thick at the top, tapering upward, rind cartilaginous, interior fibrous. Ring rather prominent, part of it attached to the stem like a collar, the remainder flaring out either above or below this collar, the edge rusty red. Singly or in groups on the ground in open hardwood forests.

Genus MARASMIUS

The genus is distinguished by white spores a rather tough texture, and the so-called "reviving" habit; that is, the plants shrivel and shrink in dry weather, but when moistened revive again and continue to shed spores. Some of them persist for a surprising length of time, at least for weeks and sometimes perhaps for several months.

Key to Species of Marasmius

1. Stem white or pale tan - - 2
    Stem reddish brown toward the base or entirely so - - 3

2. Gills attached to a collar, cap radially striate or furrowed - - M. olneyi

Gills adnate to free, cap not striate - - M. oreades
Gills decurrent, interveined near stem - - M. resinosus

3. Cap white or pale tan - - 4
Cap brown - - 5

4. Cap 5-12 mm. wide, hemispherical, with prominent ra-
dial furrows - - M. rotula
Cap 1-2.5 cm. wide, nearly flat, margin striate - -
M. delectans

5. Cap with distinct radial furrows from the margin to the
center - - M. siccus
Cap without radial furrows - - 6

6. Entire stem densely covered with short white hair - -
M. urens
Stem hairy only at the very base - - M. cohaerens

Descriptions of Species of Marasmius

1. MARASMIUS COHAERENS.   Cap 1-2.5 cm. wide,
                                 convex to flat, some-
times with an umbo, margin in old specimens often turned
up and wavy; surface brown or reddish brown, fading to tan
in age. Flesh 1-3 mm. thick near the stem, same color as
the surface. Gills 15-20 per cm. at the margin, 1.5-3 mm.
wide, adnate or sinuate, pale brown when young, reddish
brown when mature, sometimes with inconspicuous veins
between them. Stem 5-12 cm. long, 4-6 mm. thick, reddish brown, shiny, hollow, the cap enlarged and paler, the
base dark brown and covered with dense white hairs, several stems often joined near the base, the fused portion
covered with white mycelium. Singly or in groups and
clumps on the ground or on very rotten wood in deciduous
woods.

2. MARASMIUS DELECTANS.   Cap 1-4 cm. wide, al-
                                 most flat, curved down a
little at the margin; surface pale ivory when moist, white
when dry, slightly or prominently furrowed from the margin almost to the center. Flesh white, about 1 mm. thick
in the center of the cap but consisting of only a skin over
the rest of the cap. Gills white, adnexed, 8-10 per cm. at
the margin, 3-5 mm. wide at the widest place, usually with
prominent veins connecting adjacent gills where they are

attached to the cap. Stem
3-5 cm. long, 2-4 mm.
thick at top, tapering downward, top white for 1/2 to
1 cm. below the cap then becoming gradually dark brown,
the very base covered with
white mycelium, hollow,
rather fragile. In groups on
leaves in deciduous forests,
the leaves often being bound
together by mycelium from
which fruit bodies arise.

3. MARASMIUS OLNEYI.   Cap 1-1.5 cm. wide, first
                           convex, later flat or the cen-
ter depressed, surface pale reddish brown, glabrous, radially striate when young and moist, the striations in age
deepening into prominent wrinkles. Flesh thin, tough, same
color as the cap. Gills 10-20 per cm., 1-2 mm. wide, attached to a collar near the stem, white, edge slightly wavy.
Stem 2-4 cm. long, 1 mm. thick, enlarged at the top, hollow, white or pale gray, covered with fine short hair, extending a short distance into the material on which it grows.
Scattered or in groups on fallen leaves and twigs in deciduous woods.

4. MARASMIUS OREADES.   Edible. Cap 1.5-4 cm.
                          wide, at first convex, later
campanulate to flat, tan to nearly white, smooth. Flesh
pale tan to white, fairly thick near the stem. Gills almost
free, white or pale tan,
usually rather distant from
one another, often with veins
between them, the long gills
regularly interspersed with
short ones, and these with
still shorter ones. Stem 4-7
cm. long, 3-5 mm. thick,
white or pale tan, tough,
finely hairy. In groups,
usually in rings or partial
rings on grassy ground. It is
one of the best of the edible
mushrooms and can be pre-
served merely by drying.

5. MARASMIUS RESINOSUS.   Cap 6-12 mm. wide, convex to shallow funnel shape,
the center often depressed, the margin curved down; surface
white, covered with short hair than can be seen only with a
lens.   The entire cap is soft and pliable, but tough.   Flesh
1 mm. or less thick, white, tough.   Gills 8-12 per cm. at
the margin, 2-3 mm. wide, white, decurrent, usually with
veins between adjacent ones where they join the cap.   Stem
2-5 cm. long, about 1 mm. thick, gray, covered with short
hair, tough, the base slightly enlarged.   Usually in groups
on wood and twigs in deciduous woods and groves.

6. MARASMIUS ROTULA.   Cap 5-12 mm. wide, hemispherical, with a small de-
pression in the center of the cap just above the point of attachment of the stem; surface white, with radial furrows
extending from the center to
the margin.   Gills white, relatively distant from one another, attached to a collar or
ring near the stem.   Stem 2-
5 cm. long, 1 mm. thick,
hollow, shiny, dark brown or
black, paler near the top,
glabrous.   Usually in groups
of a few to several dozen
specimens on leaf litter and
on the bark of living hardwood
trees.

7. MARASMIUS SICCUS.   Cap 1-2.5 cm. wide, first
conical, later campanulate;
surface yellowish red to rose brown or rusty brown, darker
in the center, distinct radial furrows extending from the
center to the margin, gla-
brous.   Flesh 1 mm. or less
thick, tough and pliable.
Gills 8-12 per cm. at the
margin, 1-3 mm. wide near
the margin, narrowed toward
the stem, free or narrowly
attached to the stem, white
to pale reddish brown, frequently with inconspicuous
veins on the sides and between
them where they are attached.

to the cap. Stem 4-8 cm. long, 1-2 mm. thick, dark brown, almost white near the top, tough, hollow, base slightly hairy. Scattered or in groups on fallen leaves, twigs and decayed wood under coniferous and deciduous trees.

8. MARASMIUS URENS. Cap 2-5 cm. wide, first hemispherical, later campanulate to convex or flat, margin incurved when young; surface dark tan to reddish brown, first smooth, later wrinkled, glabrous. Flesh 2-4 mm. thick near the stem, white, tough and pliable. Gills 10-12 per cm., 2-4 mm. wide, free, with inconspicuous veins between them where they join the cap, white when young, tan or pale reddish brown in age. Stem 5-8 cm. long, 1-3 mm. thick, uniform in diameter, often curved, pale reddish brown, paler at the top and very dark brown at the base, densely covered with short white hair. Taste very bitter. Scattered or in groups on the ground in grassy places and deciduous woods.

Genus MYCENA

The genus has white spores and a rather characteristic shape of cap as shown in the drawings where the genus is listed. The margin of the cap is straight, not incurved, in young specimens, and the stem usually is fragile, hollow and with a rather brittle rind. Most species are so small that their edibility has not been tested.

Key to Species of Mycena

1. Cap 4-10 mm. wide - - 2
   Cap 1-4 cm. wide - - 3

2. Cap pure white, growing on the ground or on rotten wood - - M. immaculata
   Cap black to grayish brown, on the bark of living trees - - M. corticola
   Cap reddish brown in the center, yellow on the margin, growing on the ground - - M. subincarnata

3. Growing on the ground - - 4
   Growing on wood - - 5

4. Cap brown when moist, gray when dry - - M. atroalba
   Cap pale violet to pale pink - - M. pura

5. Cap, gills, and stem yellow to orange, cap with a sticky
       epidermis that can be peeled off - - M. leajana
    Cap and stem pale reddish brown, margin usually with
       wavy lobes - - M. haematopa
    Cap brown in the center, pale tan toward the margin
       - - M. galericulata

Description of Species of Mycena

1. MYCENA ATROALBA.   Cap 1-2. 5 cm. wide, campan-
                             ulate, or plane with an umbo,
brown when moist, grayish when dry, radial striations extending from margin to umbo.
Gills 10-15 per cm. at the
margin, 2-4 mm. wide, narrowly adnexed, pale gray.
Stem 4-6 cm. long, 1-2 mm.
thick, brown almost to the
cap, paler at the top, fragile,
hollow, covered with white
mycelium at the base. Scattered or in groups on the
ground in forests.

2. MYCENA CORTICOLA.   Cap 4-10 mm. wide, hemi-
                             spherical to convex, often
with a small depression in the center, surface black to
grayish brown, small ridges and furrows from the center
to the margin, covered with
short, fine hair. Flesh less
than 1 mm. thick, tough.
Gills about 1 per mm. at the
margin, 1-2 mm. wide, widest in the center, paler than
the cap. Stem 6-15 mm. long,
1 mm. or less thick, paler
than the cap, curved, glabrous
or delicately hairy. Scattered
or in groups on the bark of
living deciduous trees, especially elm and maple.

3. MYCENA GALERICULATA.   Edible. Cap 2-4 cm.
                             wide, broadly conical
with a definite umbo, surface brown in the center, becoming

tan toward the margin, sometimes gray or silvery in age,
with irregular yellow, purple brown or reddish brown areas,
striate from the margin to the umbo, glabrous. Flesh 2-3
mm. thick, pale tan, tough. Gills 12-15 per cm. at the
margin, 2-4 mm. wide, adnate, sinuate or short decurrent,
white when young, often pale reddish brown when old, often
stained like the cap, edge sometimes slightly wavy, spaces
between the gills veined where gills and cap join. Stem 4-
12 cm. long, 1-3 mm. thick, reddish brown, pale brown or
white near the top, tough, hollow, sometimes twisted, glabrous, the basal portion of several stems often fused and
covered with brown or yellow hair. In dense clumps of a
few to 20 or more specimens on decaying wood of deciduous
and coniferous trees.

4. MYCENA HAEMATOPA.   Cap 1-3 cm. wide, hemi-
                                            spherical, convex, or cam-
panulate with a definite umbo, pale reddish brown on the
margin, becoming darker toward the center, margin striate
and usually scalloped. Flesh white to pale pink, 1 mm.
thick at the stem, disappear-
ing toward the margin so that
the gills are covered only with
a thin skin. Gills 12-18 per
cm. at the margin, 2-4 mm.
wide in the middle, light pink
to whitish, first narrowly adnate, then ascending, edge
minutely fringed when seen
with a lens. Stem 4-10 cm.
long, 1-3 mm. thick, reddish,
hollow, very brittle, when
young and fresh exuding a red
juice when broken, but this
juice is absent or scanty in
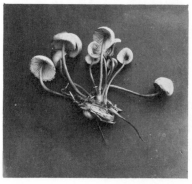
dry weather; base of stem covered with white hairy mycel-
ium. In clumps of several to 20 specimens on very rotten
logs and trees.

5. MYCENA IMMACULATA.   Cap 4-10 mm. wide, con-
                                            ical or almost hemispher-
ical, margin faintly striate, surface pure white. Flesh
less than 1 mm. thick, somewhat tough. Gills about 1 per
mm. at the margin, 1-2 mm. wide, adnate, sinuate or
short decurrent, white. Stem 2-5 cm. long, 0.5-1 mm.
wide, slightly thicker at the top, white, hairy at the base,

fragile. Scattered or in groups on moss, leaf litter or decayed wood in moist places in woods.

6. MYCENA LEAJANA.   Cap 1-2 cm. wide, hemispher-
                     ical to convex, usually with a
broad umbo, bright golden yellow when young, pale yellow
when old, outer skin sticky, tough, easily stripped off the
entire cap in one piece, mar-
gin striate. Flesh white,
about 1 mm. thick at the stem,
disappearing near the margin.
Gills 15-20 per cm. at the
margin, 3-4 mm. wide, ad-
nate to adnexed, yellow, edge
red although this may be evident only when seen with a
lens. Stem 2-6 cm. long, 2-
3 mm. thick, brittle, sticky
when moist, hollow, yellow
throughout or orange red near
the top and yellow elsewhere,
covered with yellow hairs at
the base. In dense clumps of
10 to 50 or more on rotten
logs and dead trees of deciduous species.

7. MYCENA PURA.   Cap 2-4 cm. wide, convex to flat,
                   often with an inconspicuous, rather
broad umbo; surface violet, rose color or rose purple,
glabrous, margin striate. Flesh 1-2 mm. thick, white or
pale red, watery. Gills 15-20 per cm., 2-5 mm. wide, adnate or sinuate, white, pale violet, or rose colored, often
with veins on the sides or between adjacent gills. Stem 5-
10 cm. long, 2-4 mm. thick, colored like the cap or paler,
hollow, tough, the base hairy. Solitary, scattered or in
clumps on rich ground, moss, or very rotten wood in deciduous forests.

8. MYCENA SUBINCARNATA.   Cap 5-10 mm. wide,
                          conical to campanulate,
reddish brown in the center, yellowish on the margin, striate from the margin half way to the center. Gills pale flesh
color, attached to a ring at the stem. Stem 3-4 cm. long,
1 mm. thick, white, base hairy. Scattered or in groups on
the ground in open hardwoods.

Genus OMPHALIA

The genus is distinguished by white spores, a marked depression in the center of the cap, decurrent gills, tough stem and small size.

Key to Species of Omphalia

1. Cap and gills reddish brown to orange brown - - O. campanella
    Cap and gills gray or pale brown - - O. epichysium

Description of Species of Omphalia

1. OMPHALIA CAMPANELLA.   Cap 0.5-3 cm. wide, convex to campanulate with a narrow depression in the center; reddish brown in the center, paler toward the margin, striate from the margin to the center. Flesh less than 1 mm. thick, tough and pliable. Gills 12 per cm. at the margin, 2-3 mm. wide, rather thick, sometimes forked, prominent veins between the gills and extending down the sides of the gills, long decurrent, same color as the cap or slightly paler. Stem 2-4 cm. long, 1-2 mm. thick, uniform in diameter, yellow at the top, dark brown and shiny below, the rind tough, the base thick and usually covered with buff colored mycelium. In dense groups of up to several hundred specimens on decaying stumps and logs of white pine. One such group in which the individual plants were counted by the writer contained 681 specimens.

2. OMPHALIA EPICHYSIUM.   Cap 2-4 cm. wide, convex with a deep depression in the center, gray to gray-brown, translucent, striate, the margin often wavy. Flesh thin, gray. Gills 8-12 per cm., 2-4 mm. wide, short decurrent, same color as

cap. Stem 2-4 cm. long, 1-3 mm. thick, uniform in diameter or tapering downward. Solitary or scattered on decaying hardwood logs.

Genus PANUS

The genus has white spores, eccentric or lateral stem,
tough, leathery texture, gill edges even, not sawtoothed as
in Lentinus, and grow on wood.

Key to Species of Panus

1. Cap 0.5-2.0 cm. wide, tan to brown, not hairy - -
       P. stipticus
    Cap larger, densely covered with hair - - 2

2. Cap 2-5 cm. wide, reddish brown to tan - - P. rudis
    Cap 10-30 cm. wide, white to yellow - - P. strigosus

Description of Species of Panus

1. PANUS RUDIS.   Edible. Cap 2-5 cm. wide, funnel
                    shape with a decurved margin, tan to
reddish brown when fresh, pale brown to pale tan when dry,
densely covered with stiff
woolly hairs. Flesh thin,
tough and pliable when moist,
brittle when dry. Gills decurrent, crowded, narrow,
tan. Stem lateral, eccentric,
or almost lacking, up to 2 cm.
long and 1 cm. wide, very
hairy, same color as the cap.
In dense clumps or scattered
on dead hardwood trees and
logs. It is said to be a good
flavoring for gravies, and
its toughness certainly would
limit its use to that.

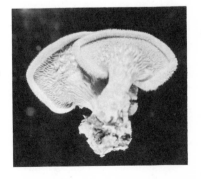

2. PANUS STIPTICUS.   Inedible. Cap 0.5-2 cm. wide,
                       spathulate or tongue shape to
semicircular, convex, the margin often wavy, dark tan
when moist, pale when dry. Flesh very thin and tough.

Gills slightly darker than the cap, narrow, very close together, frequently with veins between them.   Stem lateral, 2-6 mm. long, 2-5 mm. thick, pale tan, pubescent.   In clumps of a few to many specimens on decaying hardwood. The fruit bodies shrivel in dry weather, but revive again with moisture.   The plant has a very bitter, peppery taste, and is said to be a purgative.   Fresh

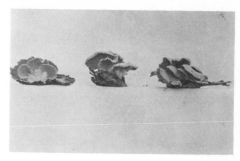

specimens, as well as the wood on which they are growing, are luminescent, sometimes glowing so brightly that they can be seen several yards away, and it is possible to take a picture of a specimen with no other light than that given off by the fungus itself.

3.   PANUS STRIGOSUS.   Edible.   Cap 10-30 cm. wide, funnel shape with a decurved margin, reniform to almost circular; surface nearly white when fresh, soon becoming yellow, densely covered with long coarse hairs.   Gills about 20 per cm. at the margin, 5-15 mm. wide, decurrent, first white, later yellow.   Stem 5-15 cm. long, 2-4 cm. thick, eccentric to lateral, densely hairy, first white and either remaining so or becoming yellow.   Solitary or in clumps of several specimens on living trees or

decaying logs of hardwood species.

Genus PLEUROTUS

The genus is characterized by white spores, an eccentric or lateral stem (although P. ulmarius often has a central stem), fleshy texture, and habit on wood.

Key to Species of Pleurotus

1. Stem central to eccentric, 4-10 cm. long, gills sinuate,
      on living trees - - P. ulmarius
   Stem lateral, 0-3 cm. long, gills decurrent, on logs
      - - 2

2. Spore mass white - - P. ostreatus
   Spore mass pale violet - - P. sapidus

Description of Species of Pleurotus

1. PLEUROTUS OSTREATUS.   Edible. Cap 2-15 cm.
                                        wide, 3-11 cm. long, up-
per surface smooth and white, spathulate to kidney shape,
margin decurved or inrolled, usually with a short stem or
stemlike base, imbricate in
groups of 5-20 or more.
Flesh 5-15 mm. thick at the
stem, soft and spongy. Gills
18-20 per cm. at the margin,
5-15 mm. wide, decurrent,
sometimes uniting to form a
net or porelike pattern on the
stem, white when fresh, yellow when dry. Stem lateral
or eccentric, 1-3 cm. long,
0.5-2 cm. thick, covered with
white mycelium at the base.
Common on hardwood logs,
rarely on living trees.

2. PLEUROTUS SAPIDUS.

Edible. The description given
above for Pleurotus ostreatus
applies to this species also.
They supposedly differ in that
Pleurotus sapidus has pale
purple spores; a rather heavy
spore deposit is necessary to
determine this, and whether
this minor difference is sufficient to justify separation into
a distinct species certainly is
questionable.

3. PLEUROTUS ULMARIUS.   Edible.   Cap 5-15 cm. wide,
                                usually convex, rarely flat,
glabrous or with large flat scales toward the center, white
or pale tan, the scales darker, the top of overmature specimens often with large cracks. Flesh 1-3 cm. thick at the
stem, white, firm or rather tough. Gills about 20-25 per
cm. at the margin, 8-15 mm. wide, first sinuate then adnexed or rounded at the stem. Stem 4-10 cm. long, 1-2 cm.
thick, solid, firm, usually curved, sometimes eccentric,
glabrous or covered with fine hair, white. Usually solitary,
but sometimes 2 to 3 specimens appear in a clump, usually
from old branchstubs of decaying hardwood trees. Often it
is common on street trees in towns.

Genus RUSSULA

The distinguishing characters of the genus are white
spores (with the exception of a few species which have pale
yellow spores), a peculiar brittle texture of the cap, thick
cylindrical stem, and convex to flat or rarely shallow funnel shape cap. It is closely related to Lactarius from
which it differs chiefly in that the flesh does not exude a
juice when broken. Most species are edible, although some
have been given a bad name because of their unpleasant
taste when raw.

Key to Species of Russula

1. Long and short gills alternating (short gills are those
        that reach from the margin of the cap one-half or less
        the distance to the stem) cap funnel-shaped - - 2
    Few or no short gills, cap usually convex or flat - - 3

2. Cap usually white, often with irregular pale brown
        splotches, flesh white - - R. delica
    Cap brown in the center or all over, flesh turning red-
        dish brown, then dark gray several minutes after
        being broken - - R. nigricans

3. Cap red - - 4
    Cap not red - - 8

4. Spores yellow in mass (gills of mature plants yellow)- - 5
    Spores and gills white - - 7

5. Flesh turning red, then black, where bruised - - R.
    rubescens
    Flesh not turning red - - 6

6. Cap scarlet or blood red, 6-13 cm. wide, margin incon-
    spicuously or not at all striate - - R. borealis
    Cap pale red, 3-6 cm. wide, margin prominently striate
    - - R. rosipes

7. Taste very bitter and unpleasant - - R. emetica
    Taste not bitter - - R. atropurpurea

8. Cap green - - 9
    Cap not green - - 10

9. Surface cracking into patches, cuticle not removable
    - - R. virescens
    Surface not cracking into patches, cuticle removable
    from margin - - R. aeruginea

10. Cap tan to yellowish brown, sticky when young, with
    acrid odor - - R. foetans
    Cap dark purple - - R. atropurpurea
    Cap lemon yellow, pale orange yellow or pale reddish
    yellow - - 11

11. Taste of flesh peppery 10-20 seconds after it is chewed,
    cap yellow or pale orange yellow - - R. aurantialutea
    Taste not peppery, cap usually reddish yellow - -
    R. amygdaloides

Description of Species of Russula

1. RUSSULA AERUGINEA.   Cap 5-10 cm. wide, hemi-
                            spherical when young, later
convex to flat, sometimes slightly
depressed in the center, surface
uniform pale green, grayish green,
or dark green, sticky when moist,
margin faintly striate, cuticle removable from the cap from the
margin half way to the center.
Flesh white, firm, brittle, 5-10
mm. thick at the stem. Gills
white, 8-12 per cm. at the margin, 4-7 mm. wide, rounded at
the margin, pointed at the stem,
almost free, frequently forked

at the stem.   Stem 5-8 cm. long, 1-2 cm. thick, even,
white, solid.   Taste mild or none.   Solitary or scattered on
the ground in coniferous or mixed woods.

2.   RUSSULA AMYGDALOIDES.   Cap 6-12 cm. wide, reddish tan to dull yellow,
slightly convex to slightly depressed in the center, broad
funnel shape when old; surface very sticky when moist, mar-

gin prominently striate, the
entire cuticle can be peeled
from the surface.   Flesh
white, brittle, 5-8 mm. thick
near the stem.   Gills white
when young, later yellow,
free or nearly so, few short
gills, few forked, 8-10 per
cm. at the margin, 5-8 mm.
wide.   Stem 1.5-2 cm. thick,
5-8 cm. long, white.   Solitary
or scattered on the ground in
coniferous and mixed woods.

3.   RUSSULA ATROPURPUREA.   Edible.   Cap 5-10 cm.
wide, slightly convex,
flat, or depressed in the center, surface bright or dark red
when young, later becoming dark purple, darker toward the
center, sometimes with pale yellow blotches, slightly sticky
when young, margin often slightly striate, cuticle easily
peeled from the surface.   Flesh red under the cuticle, otherwise white or gray.   Gills 12-15 per cm. at the margin, 4-
8 mm. wide, adnexed, white or pale yellow, spaces between
the gills veined where the gills join the cap, a few gills
forked near the stem.   Stem 4-7 cm. long, 1-3 cm. thick,
even, white, delicately hairy, spongy and brittle.   Solitary
or scattered on the ground or on very rotten wood in coniferous or mixed woods.

4.   RUSSULA AURANTIALUTEA.

Cap 7-14 cm. wide, slightly
convex to flat or slightly depressed in the center; surface
yellow to orange yellow,
sticky when moist, cuticle
easily peeled off half way from
the margin to the center, margin

closely striate. Flesh white, 6-10 mm. thick near the
stem, disappearing near the margin. Gills 6-10 per cm.
at the margin, 5-10 mm. wide, rounded at the margin and
tapering to a point at the stem, white when young, later
yellow, very short decurrent, occasionally forked at the
stem. Stem 1.5-3 cm. thick at the top, 5-8 cm. long,
white, solid. Taste not obvious immediately, but within
half a minute very peppery. Solitary or scattered in conifer woods.

5. RUSSUAL BOREALIS.   Cap 6-13 cm. wide, first
                       nearly spherical, later flat or
depressed in the center, uniform scarlet or blood red, not
sticky, cuticle easily peeled from the surface, margin
smooth or striate for only a few millimeters. Flesh red
beneath the cuticle, otherwise white, 6-10 mm. thick at the
stem, extending out to a few millimeters from the margin.
Gills 5-10 per cm., 7-10 mm. wide, 1-1.5 mm. thick,
pale yellow, prominent veins between adjacent gills where
they join the cap, coming to a point on the stem, rounded
at the margin, sometimes the edges near the stem are pale
red. Stem 6-12 cm. long, 1.5-3 cm. thick at the top, uniform in diameter, usually tinged reddish, sometimes red
only in places, sometimes entirely white, solid. Usually
scattered, sometimes solitary, on the ground in forests.

6. RUSSULA DELICA.   Edible. Cap 10-20 cm. wide, at
                      first with a central depression
and incurved margin, later the margin upraised so that the
cap is broad funnel shape; surface dull white, often with
rusty brown patches, glabrous or delicately hairy.   Flesh
5-12 mm. thick, white, firm.
Gills 8-12 per cm. at the
margin, 4-8 mm. wide, short
decurrent, white, few forked,
short and long gills alternating. Stem 2-5 cm. long, 1-3
cm. thick cylindrical or tapering downward, sometimes with
a narrow pale green or blue
zone just beneath the gills,
glabrous or slightly hairy.
Solitary or in groups of 2 or
3 on the ground in deciduous
or mixed woods. In the writer's experience this is the

fungus most commonly parasitized by the Ascomycete Hypomyces lactifluorum, described on page 55.

7. **RUSSULA EMETICA.**   Edible.   Cap 4-8 cm. wide, convex, flat, or slightly depressed in the center, surface bright red when fresh, fading to pale red when old, cuticle easily peeled off, surface slightly sticky when young, margin prominently striate.

Flesh pale red under the cuticle, otherwise white, 2-4 mm. thick at the stem, disappearing toward the margin. Gills 8-12 per cm. at the margin, 4-8 mm. wide, narrowly adnexed or free, white, spaces between them veined where the gills join the cap, a few forked near the stem. Stem 4-7 cm. long, 1-2 cm. thick, cylindrical or tapering upward, white or tinged red, spongy, solid. Solitary  or scattered on the ground or very rotten wood in swampy places.   When raw it has a very biting taste, but this disappears upon cooking.

8. **RUSSULA FOETANS.**   Cap first spherical and 3-4 cm. in diameter as it appears above the ground, very sticky, on the incurved margin the sticky material is 2-3 mm. thick and transparent; later the cap becomes hemispherical and may remain so or become flat with the margin decurved, yellowish tan to pale brown, coarsely striate for 2-3 cm. in from the margin, cuticle easily peeled off and often dry at maturity although it almost always is sticky when moist. Flesh 5-10 mm. thick at the stem, disappearing half way to the margin, white. Gills white or pale yellow, 8-12 per cm. at the margin, 6-  10 mm. wide, sinuate or short decurrent, often forked at the stem, veins between adjacent gills near the margin,

exuding drops of liquid from the edges when fresh. Stem 6-12 cm. long, 2-4 cm. thick, white, pale brown where bruised, quickly hollowed out by insect larvae. Odor acrid and characteristic when fresh, putrid when old. On the ground under trees in lawns and in woodlots and forests.

9. RUSSULA NIGRICANS.   Edible. Cap 8-13 cm. wide, depressed in the center, the margin decurved when young, upraised in overmature specimens, dirty white at the margin, brown toward the center, when old the center is dark brown, the margin gray, surface sticky when moist, the cuticle easily peeled off. Flesh 1-1.5 cm. thick at the stem, 2-3 mm. thick at the margin, white when first broken, slowly becoming pale reddish brown, then bluish or dark gray. Gills white, adnate, 12-18 per cm. at the margin, 4-5 mm. wide, many short gills alternating with the long ones. Stem 6-10 cm.  long, 1.5-3.5 cm. thick at the top, tapering gradually toward the base, solid, white, becoming grayish brown where handled, interior becoming definitely red where bruised. Scattered on the ground in conifer woods.

10. RUSSULA ROSIPES.   Edible. Cap 3-6 cm. wide, convex, flat, or slightly depressed in the center, surface bright red or sometimes yellowish in the center, sticky when young, the cuticle easily peeled off, margin prominently striate. Flesh thin, white. Gills 15 per cm. at the margin, 3-5 mm. wide, free or slightly adnexed, white when young, soon definitely yellow, spaces between the gills veined where gills and cap meet, few gills forked. Stem 3-5 cm. long, 6-12 mm. thick, cylindrical or tapering gradually upward, pale red, spongy. Solitary or scattered on the ground in coniferous and mixed woods.

11. RUSSULA RUBESCENS.   Edible. Cap 4-10 cm. wide, convex to flat, surface dull red, sometimes with indistinct blotches of yellow or violet, margin faintly striate. Flesh white or nearly so,

when wounded becoming red, then black, when old becoming
gray. Gills 15-20 per cm. at the margin, 4-8 mm. wide,
narrowly adnate, white when young, pale yellow or cream
colored when mature. Stem 3-7 cm. long, 1-2.5 cm. thick,
white to gray, when bruised becoming first red, then gray.
On the ground in woods.

12. RUSSULA VIRESCENS.   Edible. Cap 5-12 cm. wide,
                                convex, flat, or slightly
depressed in the center; surface uniform green when young,
later the superficial green layer breaking up into irregular
patches, especially toward the margin, exposing the white
beneath. Flesh 5-10 mm. thick, white, not changing color.
Gills 8-12 per cm. at the margin, 5-10 mm. wide, usually
free, occasionally forked near the stem, few short gills,
white. Stem 3-7 cm. long, 1-2 cm. thick, often tapered
near the base, white or pale green, solid but spongy. Solitary or scattered on the ground in coniferous and deciduous
woods.

Genus SCHIZOPHYLLUM

        The genus is distinguished by white spores and gills
that are divided along the edge into two halves that in dry
weather curl up, with the spore bearing surface on the inner
side. When a dry fruit body is moistened the gill halves un-
roll slowly and soon begin to produce spores again. A fruit
body will remain viable for at least several months. Only
a single species is common.

1. SCHIZOPHYLLUM COMMUNE.   Cap 1-3 cm. wide,
                                   semicircular or al-
most circular, surface densely hairy, gray when young and
fresh, almost white when
old, margin inrolled or incurved. Context or flesh
1-2 mm. thick, gray, pliable
when moist, brittle when dry.
Gills 10-15 per cm., 2-3
mm. wide, radiating from
the point where the fruit body
is attached, grayish white or
pale tan, split and in dry
weather curled, the exposed
sides of the curled gills

covered with fine gray hair visible with a lens. Usually in
groups or clumps on branches and trunks of recently dead
hardwood trees.

Genus TRICHOLOMA

The distinguishing character of the genus supposedly
is the sinuate attachment of the gills to the stem. Actually
the gills are likely to be adnate in young specimens and
short decurrent in older ones, making the genus somewhat
difficult to separate from Clitocybe. The spores are white
and the plants grow only on the ground. Hard in "The
Mushroom" and Kauffman in "Agaricaceae of Michigan"
each describe 37 species of Tricholoma, and together they
describe 70 species, Hard working mainly in Ohio and
Kauffman in the adjacent state of Michigan. At present
many of the species are very difficult to identify, and only
a few of the more common ones are described here.

Key to Species of Tricholoma

1. Whole plant pale lavender when fresh, fading to grayish
      lavender - - T. personatum
   Whole plant sulphur yellow - - T. sulphureum
   Cap brown or grayish brown - - 2

2. Cap sticky when young and moist, reddish brown, gills
      pale yellow - - T. flavobrunnea
   Cap not sticky (old dry plants must be moistened to
      determine this) - - 3

3. Cap brown when moist, tan and shiny when dry - -
      T. melaleucum
   Cap gray or grayish brown, not becoming paler when
      dry, velvety or delicately scaly - - T. terreum

Description of Species of Tricholoma

1. TRICHOLOMA FLAVOBRUNNEA.   Cap 4-7 cm. wide,
                                 at first almost
hemispherical and with an umbo, later convex then flat;
surface covered with dark brown fine radial fibers, the
umbo darker, entire surface sticky when moist, margin
incurved for a long time, later flat, often wavy. Flesh

1-2 cm. thick near the stem, 1 mm. thick at the margin,
firm, white or pale yellow, becoming reddish brown around
larval tunnels or where wounded, of the same texture as the
stem. Gills adnate to long decurrent in young specimens,
sinuate when mature, yellow,
3-7 mm. wide, 20 per cm. at
the margin, occasionally
forked, becoming reddish
brown slowly where bruised
and also on the edge. Stem
5-9 cm. long 8-12 mm. thick,
fibrous, yellowish brown toward the top, darker toward
the bottom, streaked with
reddish brown when old, often
several stems joined at the
base. Odor of crushed flesh
strong, and reminiscent of
wheat meal. In groups or
clumps on the ground in
swamps and low places.

2. TRICHOLOMA MELALEUCUM. Edible. Cap 2-7 cm.
                                wide, slightly convex
to flat, with a definite umbo in the center, brown and sometimes slightly sticky when moist, gray or grayish brown
when dry, the margin sometimes faintly striate. Flesh 2-7
mm. thick near the stem,
practically disappearing one-
half or two-thirds the way to
the margin, soft, white, easily peeled off in layers. Gills
20-25 per cm. at the margin,
4-7 mm. wide, sinuate or
almost free, many gills of
intermediate length, white at
first, later pale brown. Stem
2-9 cm. long, 4-10 mm.
thick at the top, cylindrical
or tapering either up or down,
pale brown, striate and
usually twisted, the base often
enlarged slightly and sometimes covered with white mycelium that binds the soil or
leaf mold together and thus

causes a little clump of it to be brought up when plants are
picked. Usually in groups of 2 or 3 to a dozen on the ground
in grassy places in lawns and woods.

3. TRICHOLOMA PERSONATUM.   Edible. Cap 5-12 cm.
wide, at first convex
with a strongly incurved margin, later convex to flat; the
margin first covered with fine fuzz, later naked, decurved
and wavy in mature plants;
surface pale watery gray when
young, usually pale lavender
when mature and fading to
dirty white. Flesh 1-2 cm.
thick, pale lavender to pale
gray. Gills sinuate, adnate,
or almost free, close, at
first pale blue, then lavender
or grayish white, easily
peeled from the flesh of the
cap. Stem 3-8 cm. long, 1-3
cm. thick, enlarged at the
base, same color as the cap.

In groups and often dense clumps on the ground in woodlots,
mixed woods and hardwood forests. At times it is so abundant that literally bushels of it can be picked within a short
time.

4. TRICHOLOMA SULPHUREUM.   Cap 3-8 cm. wide,
slightly convex or
flat with an umbo, brownish yellow in the center, sulphur
yellow toward the margin, silky when young, glabrous when
mature. Flesh pale yellow, 5-10 mm. thick near the stem.
Gills yellow, first adnexed, then sinuate, 6-10 mm. wide,
10-15 per cm. at the margin. Stem 5-10 cm. long, 5-10
mm. thick, cylindrical or enlarged toward the base, yellow
or brownish yellow on the surface, yellow within, fibrous,
somewhat brittle. The flesh usually has an unpleasant odor
when crushed, but this is not invariably present. Usually
in groups in deciduous or mixed woods.

5. TRICHOLOMA TERREUM.   Edible. Cap 3-6 cm.
wide, convex to flat, with
a small umbo, surface gray or grayish brown, velvety or
delicately scaly. Flesh 2-4 mm. thick near the stem, almost disappearing about half way to the margin, pale gray,
soft. Gills 12-15 per cm. at the margin, 5-10 mm. wide,

adnate or sinuate, edge often
uneven, white or pale gray,
sometimes with yellow areas.
Stem 3-6 cm. long, 5-10 mm.
thick, cylindrical, often
curved, gray or pale brown,
solid, fibrous and splitting
lengthwise readily. Solitary,
in groups, or in small clusters on the ground in open
coniferous and hardwoods.

Genus TROGIA

The genus is distinguished by white spores, the stemless, shelflike fruit bodies made up of a number of lobes,
and the rounded, ridgelike or veinlike gills. The fruit bodies
are tough and pliable, shrinking and becoming very inconspicuous in dry weather but reviving rapidly when moistened.
Only a single species is known to be common.

1. TROGIA CRISPA.   Cap 1-3 cm. wide, surface covered
                      with fine hair, pale tan when fresh,
brown when old, with varicolored concentric zones, the

margin definitely lobed and
wavy and usually lighter in
color than the rest of the cap.
Flesh 1-2 mm. thick, pale
brown, tough and flexible when
moist, brittle when dry. Gills
white, ridgelike, branched
frequently, wavy, radiating
from the point where the fruit
body is attached to the wood.
In densely imbricate clumps
on old logs and fallen branches
of hardwoods, especially birch.

YELLOW-BROWN SPORED MUSHROOMS

Genus BOLBITIUS

The genus has rusty brown spores, a fragile cap and stem, and gills that become soft and watery in moist weather. Only a single species is described here.

1. BOLBITIUS TENER. Cap of young specimens up to 1 cm. wide and 2 cm. high and narrow conical, when mature broad conical and 3-6 cm. wide, pale yellow to nearly white, slightly sticky when fresh, striate from the margin about 1/3 the way to the center, the margin splitting in several places as the cap expands. Flesh about 1-2 mm. thick in the center, otherwise practically non-existent. Gills 1-3 mm. wide, 20-25 per cm. at the margin, free or nearly so, white when young, soon yellowish brown, then dark brown, in moist weather becoming liquid so that nothing remains of the cap but a few moist shreds. Stem 6-12 cm. long, 2-3 mm. thick at the top, increasing slightly in diameter downward and the base enlarged into a  small bulb that is covered with mycelium. Scattered or in groups on lawns, sometimes in hundreds, usually evident in early morning.

Genus CORTINARIUS

The genus is characterized by rusty brown spores and a veil in which each hypha is distinct and separate.

This delicate veil is visible almost only in young specimens just as the cap is expanding, and it is the chief character by which members of the genus can be recognized. The gills are white or colored when young but become rusty brown in age from the color of the spores. It is one of the larger genera of gilled fungi, and Kauffman in "Agaricaceae of Michigan" includes 153 species; some of these grade into one another, and even with the use of microscopic characters one must have long experience to identify many of these with any degree of certainty. Only those have been included here which in the writer's experience were most common in the areas visited and which seemed identifiable by field characters.

Key to Species of Cortinarius

1. Cap sticky when moist - - 2
    Cap not sticky - - 3

2. Stem encircled by one or more irregular reddish bands
        up to 5 mm. wide - - C. armillatus
    Stem white and very sticky when young, no reddish
        bands on the stem - - C. mucifluus

3. Cap with small scales - - 4
    Cap smooth and silky - - 5

4. Cap tan, gills pale violet when young - - C. deceptivus
    Cap violet, metallic shiny, gills dark violet when young
        - - C. violaceous
    Cap yellow to golden brown, gills pale yellow when
        young - - C. annulatus
    Cap yellowish brown, gills orange red to crimson when
        young - - C. semisanguineus

5. Gills light brown when young, about 10-12 per cm.
        - - C. distans
    Gills violet when young - - 6
    Gills orange red to crimson when young - - 8

6. Gills tan when old - - C. deceptivus
    Gills dark brown when old - - 7

7. Stem pale violet and sticky when young, brown when
        old - - C. cylindripes
    Stem pale violet when young and remaining so, not
        sticky, the base enlarged into a bulb - - C. albovio-
        laceous

8. Cap orange red - - C. cinnabarinus
    Cap yellowish brown - - C. semisanguineous

Description of Species of Cortinarius

1. CORTINARIUS ALBOVIOLACEOUS.   Edible. Cap 3-
                                           10 cm. wide,
convex, often with a broad umbo, shiny with a silky sheen,
pale violet to nearly white, margin incurved. Flesh pale
violet. Gills 15-20 per cm. at the margin, 4-8 mm. wide,
at first adnate, later sinuate or short decurrent, at first
pale violet, later purple, then cinnamon brown, edge
fringed when seen with a lens. Stem 3-8 cm. long, 5-12
mm. thick at the top, the base gradually enlarged into an
oval bulb, solid, spongy, pale violet. Scattered or in
groups on the ground in low, moist woods.

2. CORTINARIUS ANNULATUS.   Cap 4-9 cm. wide, con-
                                    vex to almost flat, yel-
low to golden brown, with a bronze lustre, covered with
very numerous, minute, pointed, erect brown scales.
Flesh thick, pale tan. Gills about 15 per cm. at the margin, 4-8 mm. wide, at first pale yellow, later brown,
usually the edge paler. Stem 4-10 cm. long, 8-15 mm.
thick at the top, increasing gradually in thickness downward,
covered to above the middle by a delicate, silky sheath, pale
brown or yellow, with an indistinct annulus. Scattered or
in groups on moist ground in deciduous or mixed forests.

3. CORTINARIUS ARMILLATUS.   Edible. Cap 5-12 cm.
                                      wide, at first almost
hemispherical, later slightly convex or flat, surface
slightly sticky when fresh or in wet weather, reddish brown,
paler toward the margin, smooth or slightly scaly, margin
sometimes projecting beyond the gills. Flesh pale lavender
to white. Gills about 15-20 per cm. at the margin, 6-12
mm. wide, adnate or sinuate, first nearly white, later
rusty brown. Stem 6-15 cm. long, 1-2 cm. thick at the
top, tapering upward, the base gradually enlarged into a
bulb, reddish tan or brown, often paler toward the top,
often encircled by one or more reddish irregular bands up
to 5 mm. wide, consisting of the remains of the veil. Often
there is a faint ring. Solitary or scattered on soil and very
rotten wood in coniferous forests.

4. CORTINARIUS CINNABARINUS. Cap 3-6 cm. wide, campanulate, convex, or flat with an umbo, surface silky shiny, bright orange red to reddish tan or reddish brown, surface sometimes cracked and the margin split. Flesh pale reddish brown. Gills about 20-30 per cm. at the margin, 6-15 mm. wide, first orange red, later brownish red, first adnate, then emarginate. Stem 2-5 cm. long, 4-8 mm. thick at the top, sometimes tapering upward, orange red or reddish brown, fibrous, hollow when old. Veil orange red. Scattered on the ground in hardwood forests.

5. CORTINARIUS CYLINDRIPES. Cap 3-7 cm. wide, at first oval, later campanulate, violet when young, then yellowish violet and finally brown, margin incurved and delicately striate. Flesh thin, pale violet to white. Gills 15-20 per cm. at the margin, 4-8 mm. wide, first adnate, later sinuate, violet when young, brown when old, the edge paler and fringed or delicately saw-toothed. Stem 8-10 cm. long, 4-10 mm. thick at the top, at first sticky and violet colored, later the sticky material drying and cracking into patches and the stem becoming brown, usually with a faint ring or annulus, pale violet within. Scattered or in groups on low, moist ground in woods.

6. CORTINARIUS DECEPTIVUS. Cap 2-7 cm. wide, at first oval, later campanulate to convex, tan or light brown, at first with a tinge of pale violet which later is not evident, when young covered with minute brown scales, when old usually glabrous and finely wrinkled. Flesh thin, pale violet when young, when old pale tan. Gills about 20 per cm. at the margin, 3-5 mm. wide, first adnate, then sinuate, pale violet when young, later tan. Stem 3-6 cm. long, 4-10 mm. thick at the top, in young plants before the stem elongates the base is gradually enlarged and club shape, but this is not evident in mature plants. When young the stem is covered by fibrous, violet colored remnants of mycelium, but when mature the stem is pale tan or nearly white. Scattered or in groups on the ground in low, moist coniferous or mixed woods.

7. CORTINARIUS DISTANS. Cap 4-9 cm. wide, at first rather conical, later campanulate, or flat with an umbo, the margin decurved and often split, the surface brown and watersoaked in wet

weather, silky when dry. Flesh 4-6 mm. thick, pale brown
or yellow. Gills 6-10 per cm. at the margin, 8-12 mm.
wide, first adnate, later sinuate, light brown when young,
dark reddish brown when old. Stem 4-8 cm. long, 5-12
mm. thick at the top, sometimes tapering downward, often
curved, brown, in dry weather with a white zone near or
below the middle from the remains of the veil. Scattered or
in groups on the ground in grassy open places in deciduous
woods.

8. CORTINARIUS MUCIFLUUS.   Edible. Cap 3-8 cm.
                            wide, first almost glo-
bose, then campanulate with an incurved margin, later flat,
with or without an umbo, surface very sticky as if covered
with a layer of mucilage when moist, pale yellow, orange,
or brown, often with reddish stains, shiny when dry. Flesh
pale yellow to reddish. Gills about 20 per cm. at the margin, 4-8 mm. wide, at first pale gray, then dark tan, later
reddish brown. Stem 6-12 cm. long, 6-12 mm. thick at
the top, cylindrical or tapering slightly downward, at first
whitish and very sticky, the mucilaginous portion drying
and cracking into scaly bands and becoming yellow to brown,
with a faint ring or annulus. Solitary, scattered, or in
groups on low moist ground, often in moss covered areas,
in coniferous and deciduous forests.

9. CORTINARIUS SEMISANGUINEOUS.   Cap 2-6 cm.
                                  wide, at first
conical, later campanulate, or convex with an umbo, yellowish brown, silky or with delicate scales, margin often
split. Flesh pale yellow. Gills about 20 per cm. at the
margin, 2-5 mm. wide, orange red to crimson, first adnate, later short decurrent. Stem 3-8 cm. long, 3-6 mm.
wide at the top, yellow, solid, fibrous. Veil yellowish
brown. Scattered or in groups on the ground in swamps
and low places, and in sphagnum bogs.

10. CORTINARIUS VIOLACEOUS.   Edible. Cap 5-15 cm.
                              wide, convex to al-
most flat with the margin decurved, surface covered with
numerous minute, erect scales, violet, metallic shiny.
Flesh thick, gray to dark violet. Gills about 15 per cm.
at the margin, 6-12 mm. wide, first adnate, later sinuate,
often with veins between adjacent gills where the gills join
the cap, first dark violet, later grayish brown. Stem 8-12
cm. long, 10-15 mm. thick at the top, solid, gradually

enlarged at the base into a thick bulb, dark violet outside
and within. Solitary or scattered on the ground in coniferous
and mixed woods.

Genus CREPIDOTUS

The genus has brown spores and only a short lateral
stem or no stem at all, the shelflike fruit bodies being
attached by their base to wood; the fruit bodies are soft, decay quickly, and usually do not persist more than a few days
at most.

Key to Species of Crepidotus

1. Surface hairy when young - - 2
    Surface not hairy - - 4

2. Surface brown, densely covered with brown hairs when
        young, scaly and tan to yellow when old - - C. fulvo-
        tomentosus
    Surface white or pale tan - - 3

3. Cap 3-8 cm. wide, covered with short hairs - -
        C. putrigenus
    Cap 8-20 mm. wide, covered with fine, long hairs
        - - C. versutus
    Cap 3-10 mm. wide, covered with fine long hairs
        - - C. herbarum

4. Cap 3-10 mm. wide - - C. herbarum
    Cap 1-5 cm. wide - - 5

5. Gills 30-50 per cm. - - C. mollis
    Gills 15-20 per cm. - - 6

6. Surface sticky when moist, margin not striate
        - - C. haerens
    Surface not sticky, margin delicately or prominently
        striate - - C. malachius

Description of Species of Crepidotus

1. CREPIODOTUS FULVOTOMENTOSUS.   Cap 1-5 cm.
                                        wide, semi-
circular to reniform or kidney shape, stem short or absent,
margin incurved when young, surface light brown when

young and with a dense covering of hair, later becoming tan with faint scales. Gills 20 per cm. at the margin, 2-8 mm. wide, radiating from the stemlike base, first white, then brown, the edge delicately fringed with white. Scattered or in clumps on decayed wood.

2. CREPIODOTUS HAERENS. Cap 1-5 cm. wide, convex to flat, semicircular or reniform, margin first inrolled, later decurved, surface sticky when moist, watersoaked brown or gray with delicate striations, almost white when dry, white hairy at the stem-like base. Gills about 20 per cm. at the margin, 1-3 mm. wide, radiating from the stemlike base, first white, later brown. Scattered on decaying wood of deciduous trees.

3. CREPIDOTUS HERBARUM.

Cap 3-10 mm. wide, oval or semicircular, slightly convex, margin decurved to flat when mature, surface white and covered entirely or only at the base with rather long, fine hairs. Gills 12-15 per cm. at the margin, 1 mm. wide, radiating from a common point, first white, later brown. Scattered and in clumps on decaying wood.

4. CREPIDOTUS MALACHIUS.

Cap 1-4 cm. wide, slightly convex, spatulate to reniform, stem short or lacking, watery gray when moist, almost white when dry, margin delicately or prominently striate. Gills 15-20 per cm. at the margin, 2-5 mm. wide, white when young, later light brown. Stem, when present, covered with dense white hair. Scattered or in groups on decaying wood.

5. CREPIDOTUS MOLLIS. Cap 1-5 cm. wide, half oval to reniform, slightly convex to flat, the margin first inrolled, later decurved, surface when moist grayish brown and sometimes slightly sticky,

covered with an elastic cuticle that can be peeled off, pale
tan to white when dry. Flesh 1-2 mm. thick, limp, pale
tan or white. Gills about 30-50 per cm. at the margin, 1-4
mm. wide, radiating from the stemlike base, first white,
then brown. In imbricate clumps with the fruit bodies overlapping one another, on decaying wood.

6. CREPIDOTUS PUTRIGENUS.   Cap 3-8 cm. wide, con-
                              vex, dull white or yel-
lowish white, densely covered with short coarse hair, margin decurved. Flesh 3-7 mm. thick at the base, white when
dry, gray when moist. Gills 20-25 per cm. at the margin,
4-10 mm. wide, radiating from the stemlike base. Odor
and taste disagreeable. Solitary or scattered on decaying
wood.

7. CREPIDOTUS VERSUTUS.   Cap 8-20 mm. wide, half
                           oval or reniform, margin
incurved, surface white, covered with rather fine long hairs.
Flesh 1 mm. or less thick, white. Gills 25-30 per cm. at
the margin, up to 2 mm. wide, radiating from a common
point, first white, later brown. In rather dense clumps on
decaying wood.

Genus FLAMMULA

The genus is characterized by yellow to brown spores,
yellow to orange cap, fibrous stem that is continuous with
the flesh of the cap, absence of a definite ring, and growth
on wood. Most species have a rather bitter taste when raw
and their edibility has not been tested, so far as the writer
knows, probably because they seldom are found in sufficient
quantity to warrant it.

Key to Species of Flammula

1. Cap sticky - - 2
    Cap not sticky - - 3

2. Cap with concentric rows of scales near the margin,
        spores with a faint purple tinge in mass - - F. poly-
        chroa
    Cap without scales, epidermis can be peeled off the
        entire surface of the cap - - F. spumosa

3. Cap dry, golden yellow to yellowish brown, on coniferous
       wood - - F. sapinea
    Cap moist and slippery, bright yellow to reddish brown,
       often with a tinge of green, on the wood of deciduous
       trees - - F. alnicola

Description of Species of Flammula

1. FLAMMULA ALNICOLA.   Cap 5-9 cm. wide, convex
                              to flat, surface slippery,
often delicately scaly, bright yellow when young, reddish
brown or tinged with green when old. Gills about 20 per
cm. on the margin, 4-8 mm. wide, first adnate, later short
decurrent, pale yellow when young, reddish brown when old.
Stem 5-10 cm. long, 6-12 mm. thick, yellow when young,
later brown, curved, tapering downward, with a rootlike
base. In small clusters on stumps and branches of alder,
birch, willow and other hardwoods.

2. FLAMMULA POLYCHROA.   Cap 3-7 cm. wide, first
                              convex, later almost flat
to depressed in the center, surface orange brown to yellow
brown in the center, paler toward the margin, very sticky
when young, with concentric rows of delicate yellow or
brown triangular scales near the margin. Flesh pale yellow. Gills 20-25 per cm. at the margin, 3-6 mm. wide,
tapering toward the margin, first adnate, later sinuate to
short decurrent, tan when young, becoming dark grayish
brown tinged with purple, edge fringed with white. Stem
3-6 cm. long, 3-5 mm. thick, reddish brown and delicately
scaly up to the faint annulus, yellow above the annulus,
curved, tough and fibrous. The spores in mass have a
faint purple tinge. Solitary or in crowded groups on decaying wood of coniferous and deciduous trees.

3. FLAMMULA SAPINEA.

Cap 2-8 cm. wide, at first
conical, later with a broad
umbo and decurved margin,
golden yellow to yellowish
brown, paler toward the margin, covered with minute flat
scales, overmature specimens
often with 1-3 large cracks in

the center. Flesh pale yellow. Gills 20 per cm. at the
margin, 2-6 mm. wide, at first yellow, later brown. Stem
4-9 cm. long, 4-10 mm. thick at the top, cylindrical, silky
and shiny, usually curved, sometimes flattened, yellow like
the cap, often stained brown when bruised, the base frequently covered with woolly white mycelium. Solitary or in
clumps on decaying stumps and logs of coniferous wood.

4. FLAMMULA SPUMOSA.

Cap 3-8 cm. wide, convex
to flat, the margin often definitely decurved, yellow brown
in the center, yellow toward
the margin, with a sticky cuticle that can be stripped off
easily. Flesh 5-8 mm. thick
near the stem, tapering to
1 mm. at the margin, yellow
or greenish yellow. Gills 15-
25 per cm. at the margin, 3-5 mm. wide, adnate when
young, becoming sinuate or short decurrent, at first bright
yellow or yellowish green, later pale reddish brown. Stem
3-8 cm. long, 3-8 mm. thick, reddish brown at the base,
yellow near the top, tough and fibrous. Scattered or in
crowded groups on very rotten coniferous logs.

Genus GALERA

The genus has rusty to rather dark brown spores,
fragile thin caps, slender, fragile and hollow stems, and
is found on mossy or grassy ground, frequently in swamps,
and on manure piles and manured ground. So far as is
known, none of them have been tested for food. Kauffman's
"Agaricaceae of Michigan" includes 12 species, one of
which is unnamed, and several of which apparently were
rarely found. Only 3 species have been commonly found by
the writer.

Key to Species of Galera

1. Growing on moss in swamps - - G. hypnorum
    Growing usually on manure heaps, stem with a hori-
         zontal root 4-8 cm. long - - G. antipus

Growing usually on lawns and in pastures, stem without
a root - - G. tenera

Description of Species of Galera

1. GALERA ANTIPUS.   Cap 1-4 cm. wide, conical, campanulate or almost convex, brown
when moist, pale tan when dry.   Gills 25 per cm. at the
margin, 2-3 mm. wide, narrowly adnate, pale brown when
young, dark brown when old.   Stem 3-6 cm. long, 2-4 mm.
thick above the ground, enlarged at the base and with a
subterranean rootlike part extending 4-8 cm. horizontally.
Scattered or in groups on manure heaps.

2. GALERA HYPNORUM.   Cap 6-20 mm. wide, conical
or campanulate, watery yel-
lowish brown and striate when moist, pale tan when dry.
Gills about 15 per cm. at the margin, 1-4 mm. wide, adnate, brown, edge delicately fringed when seen with a lens.
Stem 3-6 cm. long, 1-3 mm. thick, brown, fragile.   Scattered on moss in swamps.

3. GALERA TENERA.   Cap 1-3 cm. wide, usually conical to campanulate or hemispher-
ical with a rather sharp point, tan when moist, almost
white when dry, margin finely
striate, the top cuticle or
skin easily peeled off, surface
of fresh specimens often covered with minute shiny particles that may be visible only
with the aid of a lens.   Gills
20-25 per cm. at the margin,
1-3 mm. wide, adnate, brown.
Stem 3-8 cm. long, 1-2 mm.
wide, brittle, shiny, light tan
to white.   Scattered on lawns,
and in pastures and grassy
fields.

Genus INOCYBE

The genus has rather light brown spores, a conical
to campanulate cap that is fibrous or scaly, and the gills

vary from short decurrent to free. The spores of many
species are very angular, which is rather unusual among
mushroom spores. Kauffman's "Agaricaceae of Michigan"
includes 31 species, but a considerably larger number have
been described in Europe. Of these, only the 6 species
found most commonly by the writer are included here.

Key to Species of Inocybe

1. Cap white or pale tan - - 2
    Cap brown, scaly or radially cracked - - 3

2. Edge of gills irregular - - I. fibrosa
    Edge of gills regular - - I. geophylla

3. Cap scaly - - 4
    Cap radially cracked - - 5

4. Cap conical when young - - I. calospora
    Cap convex when young - - I. caesariata

5. Cap yellowish white to golden brown - - I. fastigiata
    Cap dark brown - - I. rimosa, I. destricta

Description of Species of Inocybe

1. INOCYBE CAESARIATA.   Cap 2-4 cm. wide, hemi-
                             spherical or convex when
young, flat, umbonate or depressed in the center when old,
yellowish brown, darker in the center; surface covered with
small hairy scales, margin at first connected to the stem
by a thin, pale yellow veil that remains on the margin for a
short time as the cap expands. Flesh pale tan, sometimes
darker and watery just above the gills, 2-3 mm. thick at
the stem, less than 1 mm. at the margin. Gills 20-25 per
cm. at the margin of the cap, 2-3 mm. wide, tan when
young, yellowish brown at maturity, first adnate, later
sinuate, the edge white and delicately fringed when seen
with a lens. Stem 2-3 cm. long, 2-5 mm. thick, paler than
the cap, silky and shiny or delicately scaly, cylindrical or
tapering downward. In groups in the woods.

2. INOCYBE CALOSPORA.   Cap 1-3 cm. wide, conical
                           or narrowly campanulate
when young, later flat with a small pointed umbo, first dark
brown, then yellowish brown toward the margin but the

pointed umbo remaining dark, covered from margin to umbo with small loose or recurved scales. Flesh pale brown. Gills 10-12 per cm. at the margin, 2-3 mm. wide, grayish tan when young, brown when old, edge white. Stem 3-6 cm. long, 1.5-2.5 mm. thick, brown, often curved, sometimes expanded at the base into a small bulb. Scattered or in groups on the ground in low, moist deciduous woods.

3. INOCYBE DESTRICTA. Cap 2.5-4 cm. wide, first conical, then campanulate, later flat with a definite umbo, uniformly dark brown or dark brown on the umbo and paler toward the margin, covered with fine scales that are obvious only when the cap is wet; the surface layer cracks radially from the margin inwards as the cap expands, exposing the lighter colored flesh beneath. Flesh 2-3 mm. thick near the stem, disappearing near the margin, pale tan or white, firm. Gills 15-20 per cm. at the margin, 5-7 mm. wide, sinuate or adnexed, first gray, brown when mature, edge delicately fringed when seen with a lens. Stem 4-6 cm. long, 3-5 mm. in diameter at the top, cylindrical or slightly enlarged at both the top and the bottom, pale brown, striate, often twisted, fibrous, solid, the interior very brittle. In groups on the ground in conifer woods. This species looks much like Inocybe rimosa, and can be distinguished from that species only by the microscopic cystidia, each with a mass of crystals at the top, on the sides of the gills of I. destricta.

4. INOCYBE FASTIGIATA. Cap 3-7 cm. wide, first conical, then campanulate, later almost flat with a prominent umbo, surface yellowish white to golden brown, the surface radially cracked from margin to umbo and exposing the lighter colored flesh beneath, margin often split in age. Flesh 1-3 mm. thick near the stem, pale tan. Gills 12-15 per cm. at the margin of the cap, 4-8 mm. wide, adnexed to sinuate, grayish when young, dark grayish brown when old. Stem 5-9 cm. long, 4-10 mm. thick, usually striate, often twisted, white to pale brown, slightly enlarged at the base. Scattered or in groups on the ground in swampy woods.

5. INOCYBE FIBROSA. Said to be poisonous. Cap 3-6 cm. wide, broad conical to almost flat, with a low umbo, pale cream yellow, with a band of netlike wrinkles between the margin and the center. Flesh 3-5 mm. thick near the stem, gradually thinner

toward the margin, white, firm. Gills about 20 per cm. at
the margin of the cap, 4-7 mm. wide, free, first white,
then grayish tan, the edge white when seen with a lens and
irregular or toothed. Stem 6-10 cm. long, 8-12 mm. thick
at the top, tapering downward, definitely striate, shiny,
nearly white, fibrous and splitting lengthwise easily, hollow.
Scattered or in groups on the ground near deciduous trees.

6. INOCYBE GEOPHYLLA.   Cap 1-3 cm. wide, conical
                                       when young, flat with an
umbo when old, surface white or pale tan, with a silky
sheen. Flesh white. Gills 15-20 per cm. at the cap margin, 3-5 mm. wide, adnexed, white when young, pale grayish brown when old. Stem 2-5 cm. long, 2-3 mm. thick,
white and silky, delicately hairy at the top. Scattered or
in groups on the ground in coniferous and deciduous woods.
Inocybe lilacina, sometimes given as a variety of Inocybe
geophylla, differs only in that the cap and stem are tinged
with violet.

7. INOCYBE RIMOSA.   Cap 2-5 cm. wide, at first con-
                                   ical, later campanulate with a
conical umbo, surface silky, splitting as the cap expands
and forming irregular furrows, tan to brown, the flesh exposed by the split surface lighter in color, margin often

split, sometimes wavy or irregularly scalloped. Gills 15
per cm. at the margin of the
cap, 2-4 mm. wide, almost
free, grayish brown, edge
white. Stem 4-8 cm. long,
3-5 mm. thick, cylindrical,
pale brown or white, sometimes expanded into a flattened bulb at the base. Scattered or in groups on the
ground in coniferous and hardwood swamps.

Genus NAUCORIA

     The genus has brown spores, the margin of the cap
first incurved when young, gills adnate or adnexed, and
the stem tough and fibrous. More than 20 species have
been described in the United States, but the writer has encountered only two commonly.

Key to Species of Naucoria

1. Cap yellow to yellowish brown, stem not flattened
    - - N. semiorbicularis
    Cap dark brown, stem usually flattened - - N. platysperma

Description of Species of Naucoria

1. NAUCORIA PLATYSPERMA.   Cap 2-4 cm. wide, con-
                                vex to almost flat, at
first pale to dark brown, later dirty yellow, slightly sticky
when moist. Flesh 2-4 mm. thick near the stem, pale tan
to white. Gills 20-25 per cm. at the margin of the cap, 3-
7 mm. wide, adnate, tan when young, dark brown when old,
edge often tan. Stem 3-5 cm. long, 2-6 mm. thick, tan to
brown, often flat and twisted, striate toward the top, hollow, tough and pliable. Microscopically, some of the spores
often are somewhat flat and irregular. In groups of several
on manure heaps, manured ground and grassy places.

2. NAUCORIA SEMIORBICULARIS.   Cap 1-4 cm. wide,
                                   convex to almost
flat, surface tan to yellow, darker in the center, slightly
sticky when moist. Flesh 1-3 mm. thick at the stem, very
pale tan. Gills 15-20 per cm. at the cap margin, 2-5 mm.
wide, adnate or almost free, pale tan when young, rusty
brown when old, edge sometimes delicately fringed with
white. Stem 4-6 cm. long, 2-6 mm. thick, yellow to light
brown, with a silky sheen, often striate, tough and pliable.
Scattered or in groups on the ground in lawns and grassy
places. This is one of the most common small mushrooms
in pastures and lawns, often appearing in the same places
in some abundance year after year.

Genus PAXILLUS

     The genus is characterized by brown spores, and by
decurrent gills that may be peeled very easily from the cap.
The genus has only a few species, Kauffman's "Agaricaceae
of Michigan" describing only 5, of which the writer has
found only 3 commonly.

Key to Species of Paxillus

1. Stem densely covered with dark brown hair
    - - P. atrotomentosus
    Stem not hairy - - 2

2. Gills tan, becoming dark brown when bruised
    - - P. involutus
    Gills golden yellow, prominently interveined
    - - P. rhodoxanthus

Description of Species of Paxillus

1. **PAXILLUS ATROTOMENTOSUS.** Edible. Cap 6-12 cm. wide, convex when young, later flat or depressed in the center, surface reddish brown or very dark brown, hairy when young, glabrous when mature; margin of young specimens inrolled, later incurved, often wavy. Flesh white, thick spongy or firm. Gills about 20 per cm. at the cap margin, 4-6 mm. wide, adnate or short decurrent, forked near the stem, sometimes forming a netlike arrangement on the stem, usually with veins between them where they are attached to the cap, tan to brown, separable from the cap. Stem central, eccentric or lateral, 4-10 cm. long, 1-3 cm. thick, covered with short, dark brown hairs. Solitary or in clumps of a few on decayed logs, stumps and fence posts.

2. **PAXILLUS INVOLUTUS.** Edible. Cap 5-11 cm. wide, at first convex, then flat to depressed in the center, silky brown and some areas shiny, the remainder covered with darker flat scales; margin at first strongly inrolled and during dry weather remaining so. Flesh pale yellow, becoming brown where bruised, continuous with the interior flesh of the stem. Gills 20 per cm. at the cap margin, 5-8 mm. wide, tapering toward both ends, decurrent, light brown, becoming dark reddish brown where bruised, occasionally forked into 2, some often forming

netlike connections on the stem, easily separable from the
flesh of the cap. Stem 4-8 cm. long, 1-2.5 cm. in diameter at the top, cylindrical or somewhat irregular, tough,
brown or streaked yellow and brown. Singly or in small
groups of a few specimens on the ground or on very decayed
wood.

3. PAXILLUS RHODOXANTHUS.   Edible. Cap 4-9 cm.
                                          wide, convex when
young and remaining so or becoming flat to depressed in
the center; surface delicately hairy to glabrous, reddish
yellow or reddish brown. Flesh pale yellow, thick, firm.
Gills 12-16 per cm. at the cap margin, 4-7 mm. wide, decurrent, golden yellow, with prominent veins between adjacent gills where they meet the cap, occasionally forked,
sometimes forming a netlike or porelike arrangement on or
near the stem. Stem 4-8 cm. long, 5-10 mm. thick, solid,
reddish yellow toward the top, yellow toward the base,
sometimes covered with minute reddish brown scales. Solitary or scattered on the ground in woods.

Genus PHOLIOTA

The genus is characterized by brown spores and a
ring or annulus on the stem, although the ring is indistinct
in some species, or present only in very young specimens
just when the cap has separated from the veil that connects
it to the stem. Most of the common species grow on wood,
but a few of them grow on the ground. Most of those here
described are edible, and some are considered to be very
delicious, but the edibility of some is unknown.

Key to Species of Pholiota

1. Cap scaly - - 2
    Cap smooth - - 9

2. Edge of gills beaded with white drops 1-2 mm. in diam-
        eter - - P. albocrenulata
    Edge of gills not beaded - - 3

3. Cap sticky when moist (dry specimens must be soaked
        in water 10-15 minutes to determine this) - - 4
    Cap not sticky - - 5

4. Gills 8-12 mm. wide - - P. adiposa
    Gills 3-5 mm. wide - - P. squarrosoides

5. Scales prominent, dense - - 6
    Scales inconspicuous, appressed - - 7

6. Cap 5-10 cm. wide, yellow or reddish brown
        - - P. squarrosa
    Cap 1-3 cm. wide, brown - - P. erinaceela

7. Gills 3-4 mm. wide - - P. confragosa
    Gills 5-10 mm. wide - - 8

8. Scales darker than surface of cap - - P. muricata
    Scales white - - P. destruens

9. Ring soon disappearing - - 10
    Ring persistent - - 11

10. Cap 2-6 cm. wide, white, pale yellow or pale brown,
        on the ground - - P. praecox
    Cap 1.5-3.0 cm. wide, reddish tan in the center, paler
        toward the margin, on logs - - P. marginata

11. Ring striate on the upper side, cap 0.5-3.0 cm. wide
        - - P. rugosa
    Ring not striate - - 12

12. Cap 2-4 cm. wide, ring very narrow - - P. discolor
    Cap 5-10 cm. wide, ring broad and white
        - - P. caperata

Description of Species of Pholiota

1. PHOLIOTA ADIPOSA.   Edible. Cap 3-12 cm. wide,
                                first hemispherical, later
convex to campanulate, or flat with an umbo, chrome yellow to pale yellow, sticky or
slimy when moist, usually
with concentric rows of flat
brown scales, sometimes with
remnants of the veil hanging
from the margin. Flesh pale
yellow, 7-12 mm. thick near
the stem, thinning abruptly to
3-5 mm. at the edge of the
umbo. Gills 15-20 per cm.
at the cap margin, 8-12 mm.
wide, at first pale yellow,

later dark brown, first adnate, then emarginate. Stem 5-
15 cm. long, 8-15 mm. thick at the top, curved, tough and
fibrous, yellow like the cap, scaly up to the annulus.
Annulus thin and disappearing quickly. In dense clumps of
several to a dozen specimens, all arising from the same
point, on branch stubs of living hardwood trees and stumps
and logs of hardwoods.

2. PHOLIOTA ALBOCRENULATA.   Cap 3-12 cm. in
diameter, convex
to campanulate with an umbo, reddish brown in the center
or all over, sometimes paler toward the margin, very
sticky or slimy when moist
and fresh, covered with flat
scales that are dark when
moist and whitish when dry
and which usually are in concentric rows; margin of the
cap extending a little past the
gills when young, and remnants of the veil clinging to it
as the cap expands. Gills 20-
25 per cm. at the cap margin,
10 mm. wide near the stem,
at first adnate, soon sinuate,
grayish to almost white in
young specimens, becoming
reddish brown in mature plants,
beaded with white droplets that
are very obvious in moist
weather but which may require

a lens to detect in dry weather. Stem 6-12 cm. long, 7-10
mm. in diameter at the top, tapering slightly upward, covered with brown scales up to the annulus, white or faintly
hairy above the annulus. Ring or annulus brown, narrow,
inconspicuous, soon disappearing. Solitary or in small
groups of a few specimens on rotten logs or living hardwood
trees.

3. PHOLIOTA CAPERATA.   Cap 5-10 cm. wide, at first
oval, then campanulate;
surface yellow or light brown, conspicuously wrinkled, when
young often covered with delicate white hairs, glabrous
when old. Flesh 4-9 cm. thick at the stem, white. Gills
about 20-25 per cm. at the cap margin, 4-9 mm. wide, adnate or sinuate, first white, later pale brown, edge often

wavy. Stem 7-12 cm. long, 1-2 cm. thick, dingy white, glabrous, solid. Annulus or ring near the middle of the stem, flared downward, white, persistent, tough. Scattered on the ground in coniferous or mixed woods.

4. PHOLIOTA CONFRAGOSA.   Cap 2.5-6 cm. wide, convex or almost flat with a slight depression in the center, watersoaked reddish brown when moist, fading when dry to pale tan, densely covered with very tiny scales that are individually visible and can be rubbed off easily when the cap is moist, but appear as a fine pubescence when the cap is dry; the margin sometimes faintly striate in moist specimens. Flesh 2-3 mm. thick at the stem, colored like the cap, with a peculiar brittle texture like cold paraffin. Gills 20-30 per cm. at the cap margin, 3-4 mm. wide, reddish brown, adnate, broadest at the stem and tapering to a point at the margin. Stem 2-4 cm. long, 4-7 mm. thick at the top, slightly enlarged at the base, when fresh covered with silky white mycelium that can be rubbed off easily and soon disappears, reddish brown beneath this mycelium, hollow, fibrous. Annulus or ring thin, white or pale tan, when the veil first breaks the annulus sticks straight out from the stem like a disc, but

it soon collapses and then is very inconspicuous, apparent only as a ridge about 5-8 mm. from the top of the stem. In groups on very decayed logs.

5. PHOLIOTA DESTRUENS.

Cap 6-12 cm. wide, at first almost spherical with the margin inrolled, later slightly convex to flat, surface brown when watersoaked, yellow when dry, slightly sticky near the margin only, or not sticky at all, with 6 to 9 concentric rows of white, pointed, thin scales that are very flat and

inconspicuous toward the center of the cap but more evident
toward the margin.   Sometimes remnants of the broken veil
hang for a short time from the margin of expanding caps,
but these soon dry up and disappear. Flesh 1-2 cm. thick
near the stem, tapering gradually toward the margin, white
when fresh, pale yellow where broken and dried, firm.
Gills 20-25 per cm. at the cap margin, 5-10 mm. wide,
adnate, in overmature specimens breaking away from the
stem and sometimes appearing to be free from the stem,
widest near the stem and tapering gradually toward the margin, gray when young, dark brown when mature.   Stem 3-15
cm. long, 15-30 mm. thick at the top, enlarged near the
base and then tapering rapidly downward from this enlarge-
ment, at first covered with woolly white mycelium, later
pale brown; solid, interior white or yellow except at the
base, which is watersoaked and brown.   Annulus or ring
thin, soon disappearing. Scattered or in groups on decaying hardwood logs.

6. PHOLIOTA DISCOLOR.   Cap 2-4 cm. wide, when
                             young hemispherical with a
flat top, later almost flat, when moist sticky and dark tan,
becoming lighter in color as it dries and even in moist
weather it may be bright golden yellow; the margin striate.
Gills short decurrent, at first very pale tan, darker with
maturity, the edge wavy when seen with a lens.   Stem 4-6
cm. long, 3-8 mm. thick, pale brown, tough.   Ring or
annulus thin and persistent. Solitary or in groups of a few
on decaying wood.

7. PHOLIOTA ERINACEELLA.   Cap 1-2 cm. wide,
                               hemispherical when
young, later convex, brown, covered with conical or
rounded scales that are very
dense near the center of the
cap and sparse toward the
margin.   Flesh 2-3 mm. thick,
with a thin yellow layer just
beneath the scales and a
thicker, watersoaked, brown
region below, fragile. Gills
about 25 per cm. at the cap
margin, 3-4 mm. wide near
the stem, gradually narrowed
to a point at the margin, pale
brown when young, becoming

darker at maturity, adnexed or adnate. Stem 2-3 cm. long,
2-3 mm. thick at the top, gradually thicker toward the bottom, yellowish brown, often without a ring but smooth from
the top down to where the margin of the cap was attached
and densely covered with conical scales from there to the
base, fibrous, curved, sometimes with a small hollow in
the center. Scattered or in clusters on very rotten wood of
deciduous trees.

8. PHOLIOTA MARGINATA.   Cap 1.5-3.5 cm. wide,
                             first convex with a flat
center, later flat with a small umbo; center shiny reddish
tan, paler toward the margin, surface slightly sticky when
moist, margin faintly striate. Gills adnate, sometimes
separating entirely from the stem in age, at first pale yellow, later reddish tan to brown, 2-4 mm. wide, 25 per cm.
at the cap margin. Stem 4-6 cm. long, 2-4 mm. thick,
first pale tan, later brown, silky, brittle, the base enlarged,
often several stems joined at the base. Annulus or ring
paler than the stem, thin, soon collapsing and disappearing.
Scattered or in groups on rotten logs.

9. PHOLIOTA MURICATA.   Cap 3-5 cm. wide, convex
                           to almost flat, covered with
flat pointed scales, yellowish tan to brown, darker in the
center and the scales darker than the rest of the surface.
Gills 20-25 per cm. at the
cap margin, 5-7 mm. wide,
adnate to decurrent, first yellow, later rusty brown. Stem
2-5 cm. long, 3-5 mm. thick,
curved, first solid, later hollow, hairy up to the annulus,
light brown, sometimes eccentric. Annulus or ring
quickly disappearing or remaining only as a ragged line
around the stem. Solitary or
in clumps of 2-5 on decaying
hardwood logs.

10. PHOLIOTA PRAECOX.   Edible. Cap 2-6 cm. wide,
                           convex to flat, pale brown
to white, slightly sticky when moist, smooth and glabrous.
Flesh 3-8 mm. thick near the stem, white, soft. Gills
15-20 per cm. at the cap margin, 3-8 mm. wide, adnate or

sinuate, first white, then gray,
later grayish brown, edge
white and delicately wavy when
seen with a lens. Stem 4-8
cm. long, 3-7 mm. thick,
cylindrical or tapering slightly
downward, white or pale gray,
slightly hairy near the top,
solid, fibrous and silky shining within. Veil sometimes
forming a fragile ring near the
top of the stem, but this quickly
disappears. Solitary or in
groups on lawns, around cultivated plants, in pastures and
open woods.

11. PHOLIOTA RUGOSA. Cap 0.5-3 cm. wide, broadly
conical when young, later flat
with an umbo, surface yellowish brown when moist, yellow
or pale tan when dry, margin slightly striate when moist,
entire surface conspicuously wrinkled when dry. Flesh 1-2
mm. thick, colored like the cap. Gills 15-20 per cm. at
the cap margin, 2-3 mm. wide, adnexed, pale yellow when
young, later rusty brown, the edge white. Stem 3-5 cm.
long, 1-3 mm. thick, sometimes slightly enlarged at the
base, pale tan or yellowish, white mealy above the ring or
annulus, covered with small scales below the ring, hollow.
Ring or annulus just above the middle of the stem, tough,
pale tan, striate on the upper side, dingy white beneath.
Solitary or in groups on very rotten wood and moist ground
in deciduous and mixed woods.

12. PHOLIOTA SQUARROSA.

Edible. Cap 5-10 cm. wide,
almost spherical when young,
later convex to flat, yellow to
reddish brown, covered with
prominent, erect, pointed
scales that usually are in concentric circles. Flesh 5-10
mm. thick near the stem,
pale yellow. Gills 25 per cm.
at the cap margin, 2-3 mm.
wide, at first colored pale

olive, later yellow, then rusty brown, adnexed to sinuate or
slightly decurrent. Stem 5-15 cm. long, 5-15 mm. thick,
tapering downward slightly, colored like the cap and covered
with scales like those on the cap, as far up as the annulus,
pale yellow to white and smooth above the annulus. Annulus
or ring fairly heavy, soft, persistent, often parts of it hanging from the margin of the expanded cap. Usually in dense
clumps of several to more than a dozen specimens arising
from a common point on decaying hardwood trees, stumps
and logs. It has a strong and somewhat unpleasant odor.

13. PHOLIOTA SQUARROSOIDES.   Cap 4-7 cm. wide,
                                          hemispherical and
with inrolled margin when young, later campanulate, pale
yellow to pale reddish brown, sticky when moist, covered
with small, pointed, erect,
reddish brown scales that are
smaller and more dense toward the center of the cap.
Flesh 5-8 mm. thick near the
stem, becoming abruptly thin
about 2/3 the way to the margin, white, firm. Gills 25-30
per cm. at the cap margin,
3-5 mm. wide, pale olive or
pale yellow when young, pale
brown when mature, sinuate
or short decurrent. Stem 7-
11 cm. long, 8-12 mm. thick
at the top, yellow to reddish
brown and covered with rough,
projecting scales up to the
annulus, smooth and white
above the annulus. Annulus

prominent, persistent, near the top of the stem. In dense
clumps of 10 to 30 specimens, all arising from a common
point, on decaying hardwood logs.

PINK SPORED MUSHROOMS

Genus CLAUDOPUS

The genus has pink spores and either a lateral stem or no stem, resembling the genus PLEUROTUS of the white spored group, and CREPIDOTUS of the brown spored group.

Key to Species of Claudopus

1. Cap and gills yellow, odor pungent and disagreeable
   - - C. nidulans
   Cap white, gills pink to reddish, without any obvious odor - - C. variabilis

Description of Species of Claudopus

1. CLAUDOPUS NIDULANS.   Cap 3-8 cm. wide, spatulate to reniform, narrowed to a stemlike base at the place of attachment, one cap often sub-divided into several others, surface golden yellow to tan, covered with dense coarse hair, margin inrolled. Flesh thin, tough, pale yellow to white. Gills 25-30 per cm. at the cap margin, 2-4 cm. wide, decurrent to adnate, often branched near the base, golden yellow. The stemlike base usually is covered with white mycelium from where the gills end to the place of attach-ment to the wood on which it grows. It has a strong, pun-gent and disagreeable odor. In imbricate clumps on decay-ing hardwood.

2. CLAUDOPUS VARIABILIS.   Cap 1-3 cm. wide, flat,
                                    irregularly circular or
oval, surface hairy, white, margin inrolled. Flesh white,
thin. Gills 10-15 per cm. , 1-2 mm. wide, pink or reddish,
radiating from the stemlike base. In small clumps on decaying wood.

Genus CLITOPILUS

The genus is characterized by pale pink spores, decurrent or adnate gills, fleshy or fleshy-fibrous stem, and
growth on the ground.

Key to Species of Clitopilus

1. Cap slightly sticky when moistened - - C. orcella
    Cap not sticky - - 2

2. Cap 1-2 cm. wide - - C. micropus
    Cap 3 cm. or more wide - - 3

3. Gills long decurrent - - 4
    Gills short decurrent - - 5

4. Cap depressed in the center or funnel shaped, taste very
        bitter - - C. novaboracensis
    Cap convex to flat, taste not bitter - - C. prunulus

5. Cap grayish brown or dark watersoaked brown
        - - C. subvilis
    Cap white or nearly so - - 6

6. Usually caespitose, rare - C. caespitosa
    Solitary or scattered, often aborted, common
        - - C. abortivus

Description of Species of Clitopilus

1. CLITOPILUS ABORTIVUS.   Edible. Cap 3-12 cm.
                                    wide, at first hemispher-
ical or convex with the margin inrolled, later convex, flat
or shallow funnel shape, surface gray to tan, silky. Flesh
6-10 mm. thick near the stem rapidly becoming thinner
toward the margin and usually disappearing where the margin begins to curve down, white, rather firm. The flesh
has a definite and rather sharp odor suggestive of freshly
ground wheat meal. Gills 5-8 mm. wide, 25-30 per cm.

at the cap margin, decurrent for a few mm., gray when
young, pale rose colored when mature.   Stem 5-10 cm.
long, 6-12 mm. thick at the
top, gray and often delicately
hairy at the upper end for 1
or 2 cm., white toward the
base, the upper portion often
striate, the interior white and
definitely fibrous. Aborted
specimens common and con-
sisting of irregular to almost
spherical clumps, usually
mixed in among the normal
specimens; these aborted
specimens are malformed because they have been attacked

by another fungus, but this does not affect their edibility.
Scattered or in groups on the ground, usually under hardwood trees.

2. CLITOPILUS CAESPITOSUS.   Cap 5-15 cm. wide,
                                  convex when young,
later flat or depressed in the center, margin first inrolled,
later curved upward and split, surface white or pale gray
when young, often pale tan when old, watersoaked in wet
weather, with a silky sheen when dry. Flesh pale gray,
thin. Gills 30 or more per cm. at cap margin, 2-5 mm.
wide, short decurrent, white when young, pale pink when
old, sometimes the edge delicately fringed. Stem 3-7 cm.
long, 5-12 mm. thick, sometimes tapering slightly downward, pale gray or white. Usually in clumps, on the
ground. The spore print on white paper, or on glass, appears pale pink, but on black paper it appears white, and
the fungus thus could be confused with a Clitocybe.

3. CLITOPILUS MICROPUS.   Cap 1-2 cm. wide, de-
                             pressed in the center,
the margin curved down, white to gray, silky, a few faint
concentric zones on the margin. Gills 25-30 per cm. at
cap margin, up to 2 mm. wide, very short decurrent, narrowed to a point at both ends. Stem 1-2 cm. long, 2-3 mm.
thick, delicately hairy, rather tough, pale gray with woolly
white mycelium at the base. Scattered or in dense groups,
on the ground in open or sparsely wooded places.

4. CLITOPILUS NOVABORACENSIS.   Cap 3-6 cm. wide,
                                    slightly convex,
flat, or funnel shape, ivory white to pale bluish or brownish gray, shiny when dry, with fine concentric wrinkles,
margin inrolled, sometimes
faintly zoned. Flesh up to 1
cm. thick at the stem, tapering gradually toward the margin, white, pliable. Gills 30
per cm. at the cap margin,
1-2 mm. wide, rather long
decurrent, often forming a
netlike arrangement on the
stem, white to gray, becoming bluish gray where bruised,
easily peeled from the cap.
Stem 4-6 cm. long, 3-8 mm.
thick, white to grayish tan,

glabrous or finely hairy, the outside tough, the interior
spongy, base covered with woolly white mycelium. The
taste is very bitter and disagreeable. The spores are so
pale pink that a rather heavy deposit of them is needed,
preferably on white paper or on glass, to make sure of
their color. Usually in groups, sometimes of hundreds of
specimens, on the ground under conifer trees.

5. CLITOPILUS ORCELLA.   Edible. Cap 4-12 cm.
                          wide, convex when young,
flat or depressed in the center when old, surface white to
pale yellow, sticky when moist, margin often wavy and
lobed. Flesh white. Gills 25-30 per cm., 1-4 mm. wide,
long decurrent, white when young, pink when old. Stem
2-6 cm. long, 4-10 mm. wide, covered with minute hairs,
sometimes slightly eccentric. This species resembles
Clitopilus prunulus except for the sticky cap, but in dry
weather the cap must be moistened to detect this. On the
ground or on moss in moist places in deciduous woods.

6. CLITOPILUS PRUNULUS.   Edible. Cap 5-12 cm.
                          wide, first convex, later
almost flat, surface white to gray, not sticky when moist,
margin decurved and often somewhat wavy. Flesh white.
Gills about 20 per cm. at the cap margin, 1-4 mm. wide,
long decurrent, white when young, later pink. Stem 3-8
cm. long, 5-15 mm. thick at the top, tapering upward,
striate, often slightly woolly at the base. Scattered on the
ground in open deciduous woods.

7. CLITOPILUS SUBVILIS.   Cap 2.5-4 cm. wide,
                                slightly convex, with either
a low umbo or a shallow depression in the center, watersoaked brown when moist, translucent so that the gills can
be seen from above as dark lines, grayish brown and with
a silky sheen when dry. Flesh 1-2 mm. thick at the stem,
colored like the cap surface. Gills 12-16 per cm., 4-7 mm.
wide, widest near the stem, first adnate, later decurrent,
gray when young, then tinged red from the spores, which in
mass are rather dark red. In groups on the ground in conifer and mixed woods.

Genus ENTOLOMA

        The genus is characterized by definitely pink spores,
adnexed or sinuate gills, and a fleshy stem that does not
separate from the cap. Several of the species are reputed
to be poisonous, and the edibility of most of the others has
not been adequately tested; since most of the species are
relatively difficult to identify with certainty it probably is
wiser to avoid eating any of them.

Key to Species of Entoloma

1. Gills 3-5 mm. wide - - E. sericatum
    Gills 4-12 mm. wide - - 2

2. Edge of gills not fringed - - E. rhodopolium
    Edge of gills delicately fringed - - E. clypeatum

Description of Species of Entoloma

1. ENTOLOMA CLYPEATUM.   Edible. Cap 3-10 cm.
                              wide, campanulate,
dark brown when moist, grayish brown to almost white
when dry, often streaked with darker fibers, margin often
wavy. Flesh thin, white. Gills 15-20 per cm., 4-10 mm.
wide, first adnexed, later sinuate, the edge delicately serrate, white when young, pale rose when mature. Stem 4-6
cm. long, 6-12 mm. thick, sometimes irregularly flat,
brittle, white, delicately hairy near the top. Scattered or
in clumps on low ground in deciduous woods and around
stumps in lawns.

2.   ENTOLOMA RHODOPOLIUM.   Cap 4-10 cm. wide,
                                   campanulate to flat;
surface when wet pale watery brown, translucent toward
the margin, and slightly sticky, when dry it is glabrous and
shiny; margin first incurved, later decurved, wavy.   Flesh
watery white, 4-7 mm.
thick at the stem. Gills
12-18 per cm. at the cap
margin, 7-12 mm. wide,
widest near the stem,
first adnate, later sin-
uate, almost white when
young, later deep pink.
Stem 4-10 cm. long,
6-12 mm. thick, white
or pale gray, striate,
fibrous, brittle, tapering
gradually either up or
down, hollow at maturity,
the interior wall of the
hollow portion covered
with recurved scales. The

odor of the crushed flesh often is decidedly like fresh wheat
meal, the taste slightly so or sometimes unpleasant.   Solitary or in groups or clumps on the ground in deciduous or
mixed woods.

3.   ENTOLOMA SERICATUM.   Cap 3-8 cm. wide, cam-
                                panulate when young,
later flat with a low umbo, sometimes depressed in the
center; surface grayish brown
when moist, pale tan and shiny
when dry, margin faintly
striate because the flesh there
is thin and, when wet, translucent so that the gills can be
seen as faint dark lines.
Flesh thin, pale tan. Gills
25-30 per cm. at the cap margin, 3-5 mm. wide, gradually
narrowed toward the margin,
first adnexed, adnate, or short
decurrent, later sinuate, white
when young, pale pink when
mature. Stem 5-10 cm. long,
5-10 mm. thick, even or

tapering slightly downward, curved, white and shiny, fibrous,
brittle, hollow at maturity, the inner walls of the hollow
covered with small recurved shreds. Odor of crushed flesh
like that of fresh wheat meal. Scattered or in groups on the
ground in woods.

Genus PLUTEUS

The genus is characterized by pink or pinkish tan
spores, free gills, and the stem easily separable from the
cap. Most of the species are distinguished from one another
by microscopic characters of the cystidia on the gills, but
those here included can be separated with certainty from
one another, if not from certain other species in the genus,
on the basis of microscopic characters.

Key to Species of Pluteus

1. Cap pale tan to brown silky shining, rarely faintly
        scaly, common - - P. cervinus
    Cap white, covered with fine hairs or tufts of hair
        - - P. tomentosulus
    Cap dark brown, with radial ridges in the center
        - - P. nanus
    Cap bright lemon yellow - - P. leoninus

Description of Species of Pluteus

1. PLUTEUS CERVINUS.

Edible. Cap 5-14 cm. wide,
campanulate, convex or flat,
sometimes with a broad umbo,
in overmature specimens the
margin upraised; surface
silky fibrous, white, tan, or
brown, cuticle easily peeled
off. Flesh 5-10 mm. thick at
the stem, becoming gradually
thinner, white, soft. Gills
10-15 per cm. at cap margin,
1-2.5 cm. wide, free, first
white and remaining so for

some time, later flesh color to tan. Stem 6-15 cm. long,
0. 6-2. 5 cm. thick at the top, tapering slightly either upward
or downward, white toward the top, tan below, rind brittle-
tough, the interior spongy; the top of the stem has a rather
flat, subhemispherical head which extends almost through
the cap to the cuticle on top, and which can be separated
easily from the flesh of the cap. Solitary or scattered on
decaying wood, sawdust piles and on the ground.

2. PLUTEUS NANUS.   Cap 2-4 cm. wide, convex, dark
                          brown and appearing velvety when
young, yellowish brown when old, with inconspicuous, irregular ridges radiating out 4-6 mm. from the center of the
cap; when fresh and moist the cap is somewhat translucent
toward the margin and the gills there may be seen from the
top as faint dark striations. Flesh pale brown, thin. Gills
free, 20-25 per cm. at the cap margin, 4-6 mm. wide,
white when young, soon tinged pink. Stem 2-4 cm. long,
3-5 mm. thick, white, curved, striate. Usually singly on
the sides of decayed logs in swamps.

3. PLUTEUS TOMENTOSULUS.   Cap 3-6 cm. wide,
                          slightly convex, or flat
with an umbo, surface covered with short, fine, flat silky
scales or delicate tufts of fine hairs. Flesh 2-4 mm. thick
at the stem, disappearing near the margin, white, soft and
limp. Gills 10-20 per cm. at the cap margin, 4-8 mm.
wide, first white, then salmon colored or reddish tan. Stem
5-8 cm. long, 4-7 mm. thick at the top, enlarged into a
small bulb at the base, white, faintly striate, covered with
short, fine hairs. Solitary or scattered on decayed wood
and on the ground.

Genus VOLVARIA

The genus is characterized by definitely pink spores,
and a thick, tough volva that encloses the entire young plant
and which remains as a torn cup at the base of the stem.
A single species is described here.

1. VOLVARIA BOMBYCINA.   Edible. Cap 8-20 cm.
                          wide, at first conical or
egg-shape, later broad conical to campanulate or convex,
white, covered with dense small tufts or scales of white
mycelium that give it a silky sheen. Flesh thin, white.

Gills 20-25 per cm. at the cap margin, 8-12 mm. wide, free, first white and remaining so for some time, later rather bright pink or flesh color. Stem 5-15 cm. long, 1-1.5 cm. thick at the top, tapering upward, tan at the base, the remainder white, solid. Volva white to tan, tough and leathery, sticky, very obvious. Solitary or scattered in groups of up to a dozen on living trees and logs of hardwoods, principally box elder, maple, and beech.

PURPLE-BROWN SPORED MUSHROOMS

Genus AGARICUS

The genus, in Europe known by the generic name of PSALLIOTA, is characterized by deep purple brown spores, free gills, a ring or annulus on the stem, and the stem easily separable from the cap. All species are edible and of excellent flavor, and one of them, Agaricus campestris, var. bisporiger, or Agaricus bisporiger, is the mushroom raised commercially in Europe and America.

Key to Species of Agaricus

1. Growing in woods and groves - - 2
   Growing in lawns, pastures, and open fields - - 6

2. Flesh turning red when broken - - A. hemorrhodaria
   Flesh not turning red when broken - - 3

3. Cap 2-5 cm. wide - - A. diminutiva
   Cap more than 5 cm. wide - - 4

4. Surface of cap white or nearly so, scales absent or
      very small and inconspicuous - - A. abruptibulba
   Surface of cap brown to black, obviously scaly - - 5

5. Center of cap and the scales dark gray or black
      - - A. placomyces
   Center of cap reddish brown, scales pale brown
      - - A. subrufescens

6. Gills about 1/3 as wide as flesh is thick, ring often
      double, with the upper and lower parts definitely
      separated - - A. rodmani
   Gills 1/2 or more as wide as flesh is thick ring single
      - - 7

7. Entire cap of young specimens and the center of the
      cap of old specimens covered with dark scales
      - - A. placomyces
   Cap not covered with dark scales - - 8

8. Gills white when the cap opens, surface of cap and stem
        becoming yellow where bruised - - A. arvensis
    Gills definitely pink or brown when the cap opens, sur-
        face not becoming yellow where bruised - - A. campes-
        tris

Description of Species of Agaricus

1. AGARICUS ABRUPTIBULBA.   Edible.   Cap 8-15 or 20
                                    cm. wide, at first hemi-
spherical to almost cylindrical, later convex, then flat, surface silky white, becoming pale yellow where bruised.
Flesh 8-15 mm. thick, rather firm, white, turning yellow
where bruised, especially just
beneath the cuticle. Gills 20-
25 per cm. at the margin, 8-
12 mm. wide, free, white
until the cap begins to expand,
then pink, finally dark brown.
Stem 7-12 cm. long, 1-1.5
cm. thick at the top, thicker
toward the base and ending in
an abrupt bulb, at first white,
later yellowish, hollow, with
a rather thick annulus.   In
scattered groups or fairy
rings on the ground in deciduous woods.

2. AGARICUS ARVENSIS.   Edible.   Cap 5-20 cm. wide,
                                convex, or flat with the mar-
gin decurved; surface white when young, pale yellow in age
or when bruised, silky, sometimes with small flat scales.
Flesh 8-15 mm. thick, first white, later yellowish. Gills
20-25 per cm. at the cap margin, 6-12 mm. wide, free, at
first white and remaining so longer than in other species,
pink for a short time, then blackish brown. Stem 5-20 cm.
long, 1-3 cm. thick, white, yellow where bruised, silky
and shiny above the annulus. Annulus prominent, double;
that is, composed of 2 definite layers, the under side
cracked radially into large patches. Solitary or scattered
on the ground in fields, lawns and pastures, or in open
grassy woods.

URPLE-BROWN

3. AGARICUS CAMPESTRIS.   Edible. Cap 4-10 cm.
                                        wide, at first almost
globose, hemispherical when the veil breaks, convex to
nearly flat at maturity; surface white to tan, silky or covered with small flat scales. Flesh 1-2 cm. thick at the
stem, firm, white. Gills 15-20 per cm. at the cap margin,
6-12 mm. wide, free but close to the stem, at first white,
usually pink when the veil breaks, dark purple brown at
maturity. Stem 5-10 cm. long, 1-2 cm. thick, the base
occasionally enlarged slightly. Annulus white, thick, single,
sometimes flaring out like a skirt, sometimes drying and
disappearing quickly. Scattered or in groups or fairy rings
in lawns, grassy fields and on compost heaps.

4. AGARICUS DIMINUTIVA.   Cap 2-5 cm. wide, convex
                                        or almost flat, surface
pale pinkish tan or nearly white, center reddish brown, the
surface layer or cuticle breaking up into numerous small
flat reddish brown scales that are more numerous toward
the center. Flesh white, fragile, 3-5 mm. thick near the
stem. Gills free, first white, then pink, soon gray brown
and finally dark brown, 15-20
per cm. at the cap margin,
5-7 mm. wide. Stem 2.5-5
cm. long, 4-7 mm. thick at
the top, uniform in diameter
or tapering upward slightly,
base sometimes slightly enlarged, white above the annulus, white or yellowish below.
Veil thin, white, forming an
inconspicuous ring that soon
disappears. Scattered on the
ground in woods.

5. AGARICUS HEMORRHODARIA.   Edible. Cap 5-12
                                             cm. wide, at first
oval, later campanulate to flat, surface covered with small
brown flat scales toward the center, white and glabrous
toward the margin. Flesh white, becoming reddish when
broken or bruised. Gills about 20 per cm. at the cap margin, 8-15 mm. wide, free, first white, soon pink, then
dark brown. Stem 5-12 cm. long, 8-15 mm. thick at the
top, tapering slightly upward, white when young, tan when
old, hollow at maturity. Scattered or in groups on the
ground, usually in deciduous or mixed woods.

6. AGARICUS PLACOMYCES. Edible. Cap 5-12 cm. wide, at first oval, later convex to flat, sometimes with a small umbo; surface dark brown to black in the center and covered with rather prominent dark brown scales except at the margin. Flesh white. Gills 20 per cm. at the cap margin, 5-10 mm. wide, free, first white, soon pink, then dark brown. Stem 6-12 cm. long, 4-10 mm. thick at the top, tapering upward, enlarged slightly at the base, white, often yellowish toward the base, hollow when mature.

Annulus prominent, white, in two layers. Solitary or scattered on the ground under trees on lawns, parkways and in the woods.

7. AGARICUS RODMANI. Edible. Cap 4-10 cm. wide, first cylindrical to hemispherical and flattened on top, later convex, then almost flat, the margin at first extending definitely past the ends of the gills; surface white when young, pale yellow when old, silky. Flesh white, thick. Gills 20 per cm. at the cap margin, 4-6 mm. wide, free but almost touching the stem, first white, then pink, later dark brown. Stem 2-7 cm. long, 1-3 cm. thick at the top, usually tapering downward, white, mealy above the annulus. Annulus at or below the middle of the stem, inconspicuous, usually wide, in two layers one of which extends upward and the other downward. Often the cap expands partly while it is still beneath the ground, then the stem elongates, pushing up the cap with soil on top of it; sometimes their presence, as they start to push up, is indicated by a mound of soil raised above them. Solitary or in clumps on the ground in lawns and other grassy places.

8. AGARICUS SUBRUFESCENS. Edible. Cap 5-15 cm. wide, at first hemispherical, then convex, later flat or with a small umbo; surface first uniform silky brown, remaining smooth in the center, toward the margin becoming covered with small flat brown scales, white between the scales. Flesh thin, white. Gills about 20 per cm. at the cap margin, 5-8 mm.

wide, free, first white, then pink, later dark brown. Stem
6-15 cm. long, 1-1.5 cm. thick at the top, tapering slightly
upward, enlarged into a rounded bulb at the base, white,
glabrous above the annulus, scaly below. Annulus prominent, often hanging like a voluminous, flaring skirt around
the stem, white above, brown below. Usually in groups, on
the ground in deciduous woods.

Genus HYPHOLOMA

The genus has violet color to dark purple brown
spores, the veil is thin and breaks at the stem, fragments
of it remain on the margin of the expanding cap for a short
time but soon disappear, the gills are attached to the stem,
and the stem is continuous with and does not separate readily from the flesh of the cap.

Key to Species of Hypholoma

1. Flesh of cap 1-2 mm. thick, cap white or pale tan when
      young, often purplish when old - - H. incertum
   Flesh thicker - - 2

2. Cap reddish brown, glabrous - - H. sublateritium
   Cap yellowish brown, hairy or scaly - - H. velutinum

Description of Species of Hypholoma

1. HYPHOLOMA INCERTUM.

Edible. Cap 2.5-8 cm. wide,
oval when young, broad conical, convex or flat when mature, at first pale tan, later
almost white, when wet the
cap often becomes translucent
and purplish, and sometimes
there are minute white scales
on the cap; margin or the entire cap radially striate. In
newly expanded specimens
pieces of the veil remain attached as scallops to the margin of the cap, but these

usually disappear quickly. Flesh 1-2 mm. thick, white or tan. Gills adnate, then separating from the stem, first white, later pale to dark purple, edge minutely fringed, 20 per cm. at the cap margin, 4-7 mm. wide. Stem 4-11 cm. long, 3-8 mm. thick at the top, tapering upward, white, fibrous, hollow. Sometimes portions of the veil remain attached to the stem as an annulus. Scattered or in dense groups on the ground around decaying stumps or above decaying tree roots. It is common in lawns and boulevards as well as in the woods.

2. HYPHOLOMA SUBLATERITIUM. Edible. Cap 3-11 cm. wide, convex to flat, reddish brown in the center, paler toward the margin. Flesh 4-8 mm. thick near the stem, becoming abruptly thin 1/3 to 1/2 the way to the margin, pale yellow. Gills 20-25 per cm., 2-6 mm. wide, adnate, first pale gray, then grayish brown, purple brown when mature, edge white when seen with a lens. Stem 6-12 cm. long, 3-12 mm. thick, even in diameter, curved, bottom part colored like the cap, the upper part paler, smooth or with flat scales, solid. Scattered or in dense clumps with numerous stems arising from the same place, on decaying stumps and on the ground around them.

3. HYPHOLOMA VELUTINUM. Edible. Cap 3-10 cm. wide, convex to flat, with a broad umbo, yellowish brown, darker in the center, hairy when young, delicately scaly at maturity. Flesh watery tan. Gills 25-30 per cm. at cap margin, 3-8 mm. wide, adnate or sinuate, pale yellow when young, later purple brown, the edge white and in wet weather often beaded with drops of liquid. Stem 2-8 cm. long, 4-10 mm. thick, light brown and delicately scaly up to where the veil is attached, white above. Remnants of the veil remain for a short time on the cap margin. Solitary, scattered or in clumps on low moist ground in woods.

Genus PSATHYRA

The stem is hollow and very brittle, the margin of the young cap is straight, the cap rather watery when fresh and becoming lighter in color as it dries, and the spores deep purple brown. A single species is described.

1. PSATHYRA UMBONATA.   Cap 2-4 cm. wide, first hemispherical, later conical to convex, dark translucent brown when moist, pale tan when dry, the margin slightly paler than the center and with many delicate dark striations (the top edges of the gills seen through the thin cap) extending 2/3 the way to the center.

Flesh 1-2 mm. thick at the center, gradually thinner toward the margin, brown when moist, almost white when dry. Gills about 20 per cm. at the cap margin, 4-6 mm. wide, attached to the stem the full width of the gills at first, later partially separating from the stem, many very short gills at the margin, white or very pale tan when young, later purple brown, the edge sometimes delicately fringed with white. Stem 4-12 cm. long, 2-4 mm. thick, tapering slightly upward, white or nearly so, shiny, usually hollow, fibrous and brittle. Solitary or in clumps on or near very rotten wood in moist places and swamps.

Genus PSILOCYBE

The spores are purple brown, the margin of the young cap incurved, the gills adnexed to short decurrent, the stem rather fragile and brittle and the whole plant small and delicate. Only a single species is included.

1. PSILOCYBE FOENISECII.

Cap 1-2.5 cm. wide, hemispherical or conical when young, later campanulate to convex; surface gray brown when moist, tan when dry and with a metallic luster. Flesh 1-2 mm. thick, pale tan, soft and pliable. Gills 15-20 per cm. at cap margin, 3-5 mm. wide, adnate or sinuate,

mottled dark purple brown, edge white. Stem 4-8 cm. long,
2-3 mm. thick, pale tan or brown, delicately hairy at the
top, otherwise glabrous, hollow, fragile. Scattered or in
dense clumps, sometimes in small fairy rings, on the
ground in lawns, pastures and open grassy woods.

Genus STROPHARIA

The genus has purple brown spores, a ring or annulus, the gills are adnate in young specimens but may break
away from the stem at maturity, the stem is not separable
from the cap, and the cap of most species is sticky when
fresh and moist.

Key to Species of Stropharia

1. Cap green, with white scales toward the margin, very
        sticky - - S. aeruginosa
    Cap pale yellow or white - - 2

2. Ring wide, striate above, edge of cap often scalloped,
        growing on grassy ground - - S. coronilla
    Ring narrow, edge of cap not scalloped, usually grow-
        ing on dung - - 3

3. Cap 1-4 cm. wide, hemispherical to convex - -
        S. semiglobata
    Cap 3-8 cm. wide, convex to nearly flat - - S. stercor-
        aria

Description of Species of Stropharia

1. STROPHARIA AERUGINOSA.   Edible. Cap 3-7 cm.
                                 wide, convex to flat,
surface covered with a sticky, light green layer that can
be peeled off, often with white scales toward the margin;
cuticle beneath the layer of slime yellowish brown or brown,
easily removed. Flesh 3-6 mm. thick, white to gray. Gills
about 20 per cm., 3-7 mm. wide, adnate or sinuate, white
when young, soon grayish brown, later dark purple brown,
edge white. Stem 3-7 cm. long, 5-12 mm. thick, cylindrical, often curved, pale greenish blue, usually covered
with small scales below the ring, smooth above the ring,
soft, hollow. Ring near the top of the stem, usually

inconspicuous, often almost disappearing. Scattered or in groups on the ground or on sawdust piles in woods. Kauffman in "Agaricaceae of Michigan" states that this species is said to be poisonous, but Gussow and Odell, in "Mushrooms and Toadstools" state: " - - one of us (W. S. Odell) has eaten quantities of it with relish and without the slightest inconvenience" and so it apparently is quite edible.

2. STROPHARIA CORONILLA. Cap 2-5 cm. wide, convex, surface slightly sticky when moist, shiny when dry, pale yellow or white, glabrous, remains of veil often hanging from the margin.

Flesh 2-6 mm. thick near the stem, white, soft but firm. Gills about 15-20 per cm. at the cap margin, 3-7 mm. wide, adnexed or sinuate, grayish purple when young, very dark purple brown when mature, edge white. Stem 3-7 cm. long, 2-7 mm. thick, cylindrical or tapering slightly upward, white, fibrous or shiny below the annulus, often delicately scaly above the annulus, hollow when mature. Ring small but persistent, sometimes rather far from the top of the stem, with delicate ridges on the upper side. Solitary or scattered on the ground in lawns, pastures and grassy woods.

3. STROPHARIA SEMIGLOBATA.

Edible. Cap 1-4 cm. wide, hemispherical to convex; surface sticky when fresh and moist, yellow, shiny when dry, glabrous. Flesh 2-4 mm. thick near the stem, becoming gradually thinner toward the margin, white or pale tan, soft. Gills 12-15 per cm. at the cap margin, 3-8 mm. wide, adnate or sinuate, first light gray, then grayish tan, later

dark purple, edge white. Stem 6-10 cm. long, 2-5 mm.
thick, cylindrical or enlarged into an oval bulb at the base,
pale yellow, sticky when young, smooth, brittle, hollow.
Annulus small and inconspicuous, sometimes disappearing
with age. Solitary or scattered on manure and compost
heaps, manured ground, and grassy places.

4. STROPHARIA STERCORARIA.

Cap 3-8 cm. wide, convex with
a broad umbo, pale yellow,
sticky in moist weather. Flesh
almost white, 5-10 mm. thick
near the stem, 1-2 mm. thick
at the margin. Gills about 15
per cm. at cap margin, 7-14
mm. wide, short decurrent or
adnexed, grayish brown or
olivaceous, edge white. Stem
6-10 cm. long, 4-8 mm. thick,
enlarged toward the base, yellowish below the annulus, white
above, fibrous inside. Annulus
inconspicuous, collapsing on
the stem, sometimes striate
on the upper side as the cap expands. Scattered or in groups
on manure and compost piles and on manured ground.

BLACK SPORED MUSHROOMS

Genus COPRINUS

The genus is characterized by black spores and the conversion of cap and gills into liquid as the plants mature. The gills are very close together in young caps, being separated only by microscopic pegs that grow out from the gill surfaces; they liquify from below upwards, and the spores mature and are liberated just ahead of the zone of liquifaction, many of them being trapped in the liquid and giving it the black color.

Key to Species of Coprinus

1. Growing on the ground or on wood - - 2
    Growing on dung - - 6

2. Gills 3-4 mm. wide - - 3
    Gills 8-15 mm. wide - - 4

3. Caespitose, caps at first tan and glabrous
        - - C. micaceus
    Scattered or solitary, cap at first white and scaly
        - - C. stercorarius

4. Cap white, with prominent shaggy brown scales
        - - C. comatus
    Cap gray, striate, delicately or not at all scaly - - 5

5. White rhizomorphs extending from the base of the
        stems into the decayed wood or soil, uncommon
        - - C. quadrifidus
    Without rhizomorphs, common - - C. atramentarius

6. Stem with an inconspicuous volva at the base
        - - C. sterquilinus
    Stem without a volva - - 7

7. Cap 2-6 cm. wide, scaly when young, silky when
        mature - - C. fimetarius
    Cap 0.5-2.0 cm. wide - - 8

8.   Cap with scattered scaly patches of mycelium on the
         surface, growing on fresh horse dung - - C. radiatus
     Cap without scaly patches, growing on partially decom-
         posed horse dung - - C. ephemereus

Description of Species of Coprinus

1.   COPRINUS ATRAMENTARIUS.   Edible.   Cap 2-7 cm.
                                 wide, at first conical
to egg shape, later broadly conical and the margin often
splitting into lobes, surface gray with a darker center, silky

or mealy, sometimes covered
with minute scales, striate or
delicately furrowed. Gills 20
to 30 per cm. at the cap margin, 8-15 mm. wide, free,
first white, soon black. Stem
6-12 cm. long, 8-15 mm.
thick, uniform in diameter,
white and shiny above the faint
annulus, slightly rough or
scaly below. Annulus remaining only as a faint irregular,
narrow ring around the stem,
closer to the base than to the
top of the stem. In dense
clumps on and around decaying
hardwood stumps.

2.   COPRINUS COMATUS.   Edible.   Cap at first cylin-
                              drical or narrow conical, 6-
15 cm. long, 2.5-5 cm. wide, later broadly conical and
radially split; surface of young specimens nearly white,
later tan or purplish tan with prominent scales that some-

times are arranged concentrically, white between the
scales. Flesh 1 mm. or less
thick, white, fragile. Gills
25-30 per cm., 6-15 mm. wide,
free, first white, soon pink,
then black and becoming liquid.
Stem 8-35 cm. long, 6-15 mm.
thick at the top, tapering
slightly upward, white, smooth
or delicately scaly, brittle.

Ring sometimes present, thin, soon disappearing. Solitary, scattered or in clumps of a dozen or more specimens on the ground in lawns, parks, open fields and along roadsides.

3. COPRINUS EPHEMEREUS.

Cap 1-2 cm. wide, first elongate oval, later campanulate to nearly flat, striate or delicately furrowed when young, with narrow prominent folds when old, tan to reddish brown in the center, paler toward the margin. Gills so narrow as to appear only as raised lines, first white, later black and liquifying. Stem 3-6 cm. long, 1-2 mm. wide, white, hollow, very fragile. On manure heaps and manured ground.

4. COPRINUS FIMETARIUS.

Cap 2-5 cm. wide when expanded, first elongate oval, then broadly conical with the margin curved upward and split, brown in the center, gray elsewhere, at first covered with white scales, later naked, radiately furrowed. Gills free, very narrow, becoming wavy, black before the cap expands, liquifying quickly. Stem 10-15 cm. long, 4-6 mm. thick, hollow, fragile, white, scaly, slightly enlarged at the base. Solitary or in groups on manure heaps, the caps usually appearing in the evening and maturing before morning.

5. COPRINUS MICACEUS.

Edible. Cap 2-6 cm. wide, first oval, then conical to campanulate with margin curved upward, with narrow striations or prominent furrows from the edge 2/3 the way to the center, often covered with tiny glistening particles. Gills about 20 per cm. at cap margin, 3-4 mm. wide, first white, then tan, later black and liquifying. Stem 5-10 cm. long, 4-8 mm. thick, white, silky, brittle, with a narrow hollow. In dense clumps on the ground at the base of living trees or around decaying stumps. Often clumps appear several times a year around the same stump, and may continue to do so for many years.

6. COPRINUS QUADRIFIDUS.   Cap 2-5 cm. long before expanding and almost cylindrical, broad conical to campanulate when expanded, surface covered with a layer of mycelium that breaks up into scales and falls off, 4-8 cm. wide when expanded, white or gray, finely striate. Gills 20-30 per cm., 8-15 mm. wide, free, white when young, soon black. Stem 6-12 cm. long, 8-12 mm. thick, hollow, white, brittle, at first scaly like the cap and with a ring that soon disappears. Conspicuous white cords of mycelium, rhizomorphs, extend from the base of the stems into the wood or ground on which it grows. In dense clumps on or near decaying hardwood logs and stumps.

7. COPRINUS RADIATUS.   Cap 5-15 cm. wide, at first elongate oval, later campanulate to flat, the margin upraised; surface with deep radial furrows, covered with scattered scaly patches of mycelium, brown in the center, gray toward the margin, with sparse short hairs. Gills 6-10 per cm., up to 1 mm. wide, free, first white, soon black and liquifying. Stem 2-6 cm. long, 1-2 mm. wide, white, hollow, very fragile, sparsely covered with short hairs. Common on dung of horses and some other herbivores. It can be raised, even in winter, by obtaining fresh horse dung, putting it in a container where it will remain moderately moist, and keeping it for a couple weeks, and thus serves as good classroom material.

8. COPRINUS STERCORARIUS.   Cap at first cylindrical, 1.5-2.5 cm. high, 1-1.5 cm. wide, later conical, then campanulate, surface white and covered with small white scales that disappear

within a few hours, then grayish tan with a tan umbo, finely
striate from margin to umbo, margin splitting as cap expands.   Flesh 1 mm. or less thick, gray. Gills 15-20 per
cm. at cap margin, 2-3 mm. wide, narrowly adnexed, first
white, soon black and liquifying. Stem 5-10 cm. long, 2-3
mm. wide at the top, tapering upward, usually with a small
bulb at the base, white, shiny, hollow, fragile. Scattered
on the ground, decaying wood and manure.

9. COPRINUS STERQUILINUS.   Edible. Cap 4-6 cm.
                                  wide when expanded, at
first elongate oval, later narrow to broad conical, finally
flat with the margin recurved, light brown in the center,
otherwise white, surface at first silky, later rather prominently scaly, radial furrows extending 1-2 cm. in from the
margin. Gills free, narrow, soon black and liquifying.
Stem 10-15 cm. long, 4-7 mm. thick, tapering upward, the
base slightly enlarged and surrounded by an inconspicuous
volva. It somewhat resembles a small Coprinus comatus,
but is less scaly. Scattered and in groups on manure heaps,
manured ground, and straw.

Genus PANAEOLUS

The genus has black spores, narrowly adnate gills,
and the margin of the cap is smooth, not striate. Only two
species are common.

Key to Species of Panaeolus

1. Cap 3-8 cm. wide, stem solid, 5-10 mm. thick
      - - P. solidipes
    Cap up to 4 cm. wide, stem hollow - - P. retirugis

Description of Species of Panaeolus

1. PANAEOLUS RETIRUGIS.   Cap 1.5-4 cm. wide, oval
                                to conical when young,
later hemispherical to convex, often with an umbo; surface
dark gray when moist, tan or pale yellowish gray to silvery
when dry, sometimes brown on the umbo and paler toward
the margin, smooth or the center covered with a network
of irregular ridges, occasionally the surface breaking up

into large scales; sometimes remains of the veil hanging
from the margin. Flesh 1-2 mm. thick, pale gray or white.
Gills 16-20 per cm. at the cap margin, 3-6 mm. wide, adnate or almost free, first white, later mottled dark gray or
black, edge white. Stem 5-12 cm. long, 2-5 mm. thick,
cylindrical, pale gray or tinged with red or purple, darker
toward the bottom, when young covered with short hairs that
give it a frosty appearance, hollow, fragile, the base slightly
enlarged and covered with white mycelium. Rarely a narrow
black annulus is present above the middle of the stem. Solitary, scattered or in groups oh manure heaps and manured
lawns and fields. Kauffman in "Agaricaceae of Michigan"
lists it as "suspected", but states that it is not poisonous,
and Thomas, in "Field Book of Common Gilled Mushrooms"
quotes Murril to the effect that it is of good flavor and edible, although an extract of it was found fatal to guinea pigs.

2. PANAEOLUS SOLIDIPES.   Cap 4-8 cm. wide, hemi-
                               spherical to convex, white
or pale yellow, smooth when young and fresh, the surface
layer of some specimens cracked concentrically or cracked
into irregular polygonal areas from a few millimeters to a
centimeter across, slightly sticky when moist. Flesh 3-4
mm. thick, becoming gradually thinner toward the margin,
white or nearly so, soft, brittle. Gills 8-14 mm. wide,
about 15 per cm. at the margin of large caps and 25 per cm.
at the margin of small caps, gray when young, becoming
variegated black, edge white, in mature specimens becoming soft and almost liquid. The gills of mature specimens
split into two readily from where they are attached to the
cap down to the lower edge. Stem 10-15 cm. long, 5-10
mm. thick at the top, white, solid, brittle, striate or
ridged toward the top. In young specimens droplets of liquid about 1/2 mm. in diameter are exuded on the upper part
of the stem. Scattered or in groups of several dozen specimens on manure heaps, manured ground, and straw.

Genus PSATHYRELLA

The genus closely resembles Psathyra, but differs
in the spores being definitely black and the margin of the
cap of young specimens being straight. Only a single species is described here.

1.   PSATHYRELLA DISSEMINATA.   Cap 5-12 mm. wide,
                                     oval when young,
later campanulate to convex with an umbo, surface prominently furrowed from the margin to the umbo, first white,
then gray or grayish brown, the umbo pale brown.   Flesh
less than 1 mm. thick, tough.   Gills about 15 per cm. at
the cap margin, 2 mm. wide, tapered toward both ends, adnate, white when young, gray to black when mature.   Stem
2-3 cm. long, slender, white, first delicately hairy, later
glabrous, hollow, fragile.   Scattered or in groups or clumps
on the ground in woods, around stumps, and on compost
heaps.

SHAPE AND METHOD OF
ATTACHMENT OF PORE FUNGI

(see page 141)

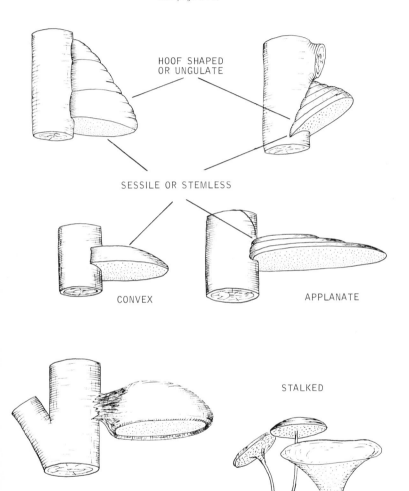

HOOF SHAPED
OR UNGULATE

SESSILE OR STEMLESS

CONVEX

APPLANATE

STALKED

STEM
LATERAL

STEM
CENTRAL

PLATE 8

GROWTH AND STRUCTURE
OF PORE FUNGI

(see page 141)

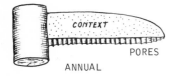

ANNUAL

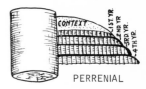

PERRENIAL

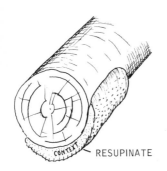

RESUPINATE

EFFUSED-
REFLEXED

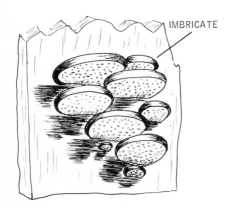

IMBRICATE

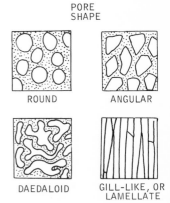

PORE
SHAPE

ROUND

ANGULAR

DAEDALOID

GILL-LIKE, OR
LAMELLATE

PLATE 9

FAMILY POLYPORACEAE

PORE FUNGI

The family includes those pore fungi in which the fruit bodies are tough, leathery, or woody, and in which the pore layer usually can not be separated easily from the context or flesh, as it can be in the Boletaceae. Those interested in pursuing this group in more detail are referred to "The Polyporaceae of the United States, Alaska and Canada" by L. O. Overholts, purblished by the University of Michigan Press, Ann Arbor, 1953, which describes 235 species, and to "The Polyporaceae of New York State" by Josiah L. Lowe, a bulletin published by the New York State College of Forestry in 1942, which describes 146 species. The present work contains 57 species.

Key to the Genera of Polyporaceae

1. Fruit bodies perennial; usually very hard and woody
   - - Fomes
   Fruit bodies annual - - 2

2. Fruit bodies soft and fleshy - - 3
   Fruit bodies tough, leathery, or hard - - 4

3. Fruit body 8-16 cm. wide, 1.5-3 cm. thick, semicircular or kidney shaped, with a lateral stem; surface liver colored or brown, flesh soft, white with red streaks; pores 3-7 mm. long, about 10 per cm., each pore separate and distinct from its neighbor. On hardwood stumps - - Fistulina hepatica - Page 144.

4. Pores meeting the context in an irregular, uneven line
   - - Trametes
   Pores meeting the context in an even line - - 5

5. Pores diamond shaped, fruit body kidney shaped, 3-5 cm. wide, reddish brown to tan or white, with a lateral stem - - Favolus canadensis - Page 144.

Pores very daedaloid - - Daedalia
Pores round, angular, or irregular - - Polyporus

The characters which have been used for more than a
century to separate Favolus, Polyporus, Daedalia, and
Trametes are unsatisfactory because they vary so much
from species to species. Polyporus schweinitzii, for ex-
ample, often has pores as daedaloid as those of Daedalia,
and the character used to separate Trametes from the other
genera with annual fruit bodies is a rather subtle one. For
these reasons, an unknown, annual fruit body should first
be compared with Fistulina hepatica, page 154 and Favolus
canadensis, page 154. If it does not fit these, it should be
tried in the genus Trametes, of which only 2 species are
included, then in the genus Daedalia, of which only 3 species
are included. If it does not agree with any of these, it is
almost sure to be a species of Polyporus.

Key to the Species of Daedalia

1. Pileus hoof shaped, thickness of walls between the
       pores equal to or greater than the diameter of the
       pores - - D. quercina
    Pileus applanate, walls of pores thin - - 2

2. Surface hairy, context about 1 mm. thick, pores break-
       ing up into teeth - - D. unicolor
    Surface glabrous, concentrically zoned, context 5-10
       mm. thick, pores, often elongated radially and some-
       times quite gill like - - D. confragosa

Description of Species of Daedalia

1. DAEDALIA CONFRAGOSA.

Pileus sessile, sometimes
with an effused portion, the
shelf 4-15 cm. wide, projecting 3-10 cm.; surface when
fresh deep rich brown or with
narrow zones of brown and
white, delicately pubescent,
later pale brown, glabrous;
margin thin, with the pores
extending to the margin.

Context 4-10 mm. thick, at first almost white, later tan to brown, tough, firm. Pores 5-15 mm. long, 5-20 per cm., usually elongated radially, especially toward the margin, or poroid near the point of attachment and gill like elsewhere, at first white, later brown. Solitary, scattered or in imbricate groups on decaying wood of deciduous trees.

2. DAEDALIA QUERCINA.   Pileus sessile, ungulate, usually solitary, 3-15 cm. wide, projecting 3-12 cm., 3-8 cm. thick at the base, the upper surface straight, the pore surface slanting upward to the margin, surface gray to black with inconspicuous concentric ridges. Context 0.5-2 cm. thick at the base, becoming rapidly thinner toward the margin, tan or light brown, in rather definite horizontal layers, firm and woody. Pores 1-5 cm. long, 5-10 per cm. measured parallel to the margin, usually radially elongate and daedaloid, the walls between the pores about 1 mm. thick, rounded on the lower edge, pale tan. On deciduous wood.

3. DAEDALIA UNICOLOR.   Pileus effused reflexed or sessile, rarely entirely resupinate, imbricate, each shelf 2-8 cm. wide, projecting 1-5 cm. Surface buff near the base, white toward the margin, later dark gray toward the base or becoming green from the growth of algae, woolly, with 4-8 concentric ridges. The margin thin and with a poreless band on the under side from 1-3 mm. wide. Context up to 1 mm. thick, white or pale tan, tough, pliable but firm. Pores 0.5-1 mm. wide across the narrowest portion, 1-5 mm. long, at first sinuate and very irregular in shape, later the walls breaking up to form teeth (on the vertical, effused portion the pores often are toothlike from the first, at first white, later pale tan or gray.) On deciduous wood, often with a single effused portion extending for several feet along a log.

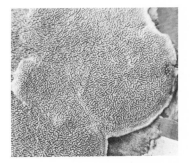

Genus FAVOLUS

1. FAVOLUS CANADENSIS.   (Also known as Favolus
                          alveolaris). Cap circular
to reniform, 3-6 cm. across, shallow funnel shape, with a
short lateral or central stem or tapering to a stemlike base,
surface first reddish brown, later pale tan to nearly white,
usually with flat darker scales. Context up to 2 mm. thick,
white to pale tan, tough when fresh, brittle when dry. Pores

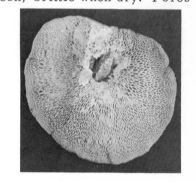

5-15 per cm. , 2-5 mm. long,
white, the pore walls becoming rather prominently toothed
at the lower end, usually diamond shape, sometimes hexa-
gonal, somewhat longer in a
radial than tangential direction. On dead branches and
logs of deciduous trees. There
is no good reason, other than
custom, for not including this
fungus in the genus Polyporus.

Genus FISTULINA

1. FISTULINA HEPATICA.   Cap 8-16 cm. wide, 1.5-3
                          cm. thick, slightly convex
to flat or with the margin raised slightly, semicircular or
kidney shape, with a lateral stem; surface red, liver colored
or brown, usually with darker radial streaks, slightly sticky
when young and moist. Flesh 1-2.5 cm. thick, white,
streaked with red, soft and watery. Pores 3-7 mm. long,
about 10 per cm. , each pore with the walls distinct and
separate from the walls of the neighboring pores, red or
brown. Stem lateral, 2-4 cm. thick, 2-10 cm. long. Solitary or in groups on stumps and logs of hardwoods, rarely
on living trees. The fungus is edible, and in America is
known as the "beefsteak fungus", in France as "beef tongue."
Hard in "The Mushroom" states that "when properly pre-
pared it is equal to any kind of meat"; he obviously was not
well acquainted with very good meat. Atkinson, in "Mushrooms", is more conservative and says that it "is highly
recommended by some, while others are not pleased with
it as an article of food". Regardless of its meaty appearance, like other mushrooms that grow on wood it probably
is not very nutritious.

Genus FOMES

This genus is distinguished by the perennial habit of the fruit bodies, some of them living and continuing to produce a new layer of pores each year for more than 50 years, although such longevity is relatively unusual among even the Fomes. The fruit bodies are in nearly all species very firm, hard, and woody.

Key to Species of Fomes

1. Context pink - - F. roseus (see T. subrosea, p. 170)
   Context white or pale tan - - 2
   Context dark brown - - 5

2. Pileus less than 3 cm. in diameter, usually on alder
       - - F. scutellatus
   Pileus larger - - 3

3. Surface white or yellow, coarsely hairy, often covered
       with green moss - - F. connatus
   Surface of old growth gray or black, margin white or
       red - - 4

4. Pores 5-10 mm. long each season, those of one year
       usually separated by a layer of mycelium from those
       of the next - - F. pinicola
   Pores 2-5 mm. long each season, successive pore
       layers not separated by a layer of mycelium, usually
       on ash - - F. fraxinophilous

5. Successive layers of pores separated by a distinct layer
       of dark brown mycelium, pore surface white but be-
       coming brown when scratched - - F. applanatus
   Successive layers of pores not separated by a layer of
       mycelium - - 6

6. Pores white or straw colored, usually on ash
       - - F. fraxinophilous
   Pores grayish brown to dark brown - - 7

7. Growing on coniferous trees or wood, fruit bodies re-
       supinate, effused-reflexed, conch shaped, or hoof
       shaped, pores irregular in size and shape - - F. pini
   Growing on deciduous trees or wood - - 8

8. Surface not cracked - - 9
   Surface with obvious radial and tangential cracks - - 11

9.   Fruit body resupinate, effused reflexed, or plane, sur-
        face dark brown to black, radially furrowed and con-
        centrically ridged - - F. conchatus
     Fruit body ungulate, surface hard, gray or light brown
        - - 10

10. Surface not ridged, pores dark brown, 50-70 per cm.,
        growing only on Prunus - - F. pomaceus
     Surface with many narrow concentric ridges, pores
        grayish brown, 30-40 per cm., common on birch and
        sugar maple - - F. fomentarius

11. Old pores, and usually the context, filled with white
        flecks, fruit body plane to ungulate - - F. igniarius
     Flecks inconspicuous or absent, fruit body ungulate,
        only on oak - - F. everhartii

Description of Species of Fomes

1. FOMES APPLANATUS.   Pileus sessile, applanate,
                           semicircular to spathulate,
on living oak sometimes ungulate, each shelf from 4-40 cm.
wide, projecting 4-30 cm., surface gray, brown, or nearly
black, usually smooth and with a hard outer layer, with
prominent concentric ridges, margin usually rounded and
with a narrow band free of pores on the under side. Context dark brown, firm, woolly when broken, often with
faint growth zones. Pores 50 per cm., 5-15 mm. long,
angular in cross section, the pore layers formed in successive years separated from one another by a layer of brown
mycelium 2-3 mm. thick. The pore surface, or mouth, is
at first white, and if this surface is scratched, even lightly,
the brown mycelium beneath is exposed. Solitary and in
groups on hardwood stumps and logs. This fungus sheds
spores for some months each year, from the time the pores
of the current year begin to grow in the spring until they
cease to grow in the fall; the spores are produced in such
quantity that on a still, humid day they can be seen issuing
from the under side of a fruit body and floating away like a
thin cloud of smoke. A. H. R. Buller in his "Researches
on Fungi" computed that a large specimen might liberate
30 billion spores a day for a period of 6 months, producing
a total of 5,460,000,000,000 spores, a rather astounding
total, although, as he pointed out, this involves the discharge of only 1 spore from each pore every six seconds

throughout this period. This figure was no mere guess, but was arrived at by counting fairly large samples of spores discharged over a given period. The spores are brown, and often cover the surface of the fruit body from which they are released.

2. FOMES CONCHATUS.   Pileus sessile, effused re-
                       flexed or rarely resupinate,
4-15 cm. wide, projecting 1-10 cm., the resupinate or ef-
fused part often covering an area 1 to 2 meters long; surface brown to black, with many narrow, irregular concentric ridges and a few broad, shallow radial furrows, often partly overgrown with moss; margin rather narrow, on the under side with a narrow band free of pores. Context 1-6 mm. thick, brown, hard and woody. Pores 50-70 per cm., 1-4 mm. long, at first pale tan, later brown, the pore layers of successive years not distinctly separated. On logs of deciduous species, most commonly on ash.

3. FOMES CONNATUS.   Pileus sessile and shelflike
                      to ungulate, often imbricate
in habit, each shelf 4-12 cm. wide, projecting 2-8 cm., surface at first pale yellow and coarsely hairy, later white and nearly glabrous, usually covered with a dense growth of moss and algae; margin either sharp or rounded. Context 5-15 mm. thick, white or pale yellow, rather soft, woolly when broken, soon infested with larvae. Pores 50-60 per cm., 1-5 mm. long, angular, white or pale yellow, old pores often light brown, successive pore layers separated by a thin layer of mycelium the same color as the pores. On living maple, rare on other hardwoods.

4. FOMES EVERHARTII.   Pileus sessile and shelflike
                       to ungulate, 5-25 cm. wide,
projecting 3-15 cm., surface at first smooth and tan to brown, later becoming black and very rough and cracked into irregular portions. Context 0.5-5 cm. thick, brown, hard and woody. Pores 50-60 per cm., 3-8 mm. long, circular or angular, brown, successive layers of pores not separated by a layer of mycelium, older pores partly filled with yellow or brown mycelium. On living hardwoods, especially oaks. It resembles Fomes igniarius, but the surface is rougher; also it has brown spores, while those of Fomes igniarius are white.

5. FOMES FOMENTARIUS.   Pileus sessile, ungulate,
                                        3-12 cm. wide, projecting
2-10 cm. , 3-12 cm. in a vertical direction, surface gray
to tan, with numerous faint concentric bands of color and
several wide or narrow long concentric ridges, hard, glabrous, smooth and often shiny; margin rounded and free of
pores below. Context 1-3 cm. thick at the base, becoming
rapidly thinner toward the margin, dark brown, firm but

rather woolly when broken,
with faint growth zones. Pores
30-35 per cm. , 0.5-2 cm.
long each season, those of
successive years continuous
with each other and not filled
with mycelium, so that it is
not possible to determine
where the pores of one year
end and those of the next year
begin. On dead hardwood
trees and logs, especially
common on birch.

6. FOMES FRAXINOPHILOUS.   Pileus applanate to un-
                                          gulate, 5-20 cm. wide,
projecting 4-15 cm. , 3-10 cm. thick, surface of present
year's growth (the margin) white, older portion dark gray
or black and usually cracked into irregular squares, margin rounded. Context 0.5-1.5 cm. thick, pale tan to brown,
hard and woody. Pores 2-4 mm. long each year, 20-30 per
cm. , the walls rather thin, pale tan, the old pores colored
like the context but filled with pale tan mycelium, the successive layers of pores indistinctly separated visually, but
capable of being peeled apart. On living or dead hardwoods,
especially ash.

7. FOMES IGNIARIUS.

Pileus sessile and ungulate,
rarely resupinate, on birch
often applanate, each shelf 4-
20 cm. wide, projecting 1-15
cm. surface dark gray to
black, divided by fine cracks
into irregular squares, with
many concentric ridges, rarely
brown and not at all or only

slightly cracked. Context dark brown, woody, brittle,
flecked with white. Pores 40-70 per cm., 2-5 mm. long,
at first grayish tan, later brown, pore layers of successive
years not distinctly separated but the old pores filled with
mycelium and flecked with white, walls of pores often twice
as thick as the pore openings. Common on living and dead
trees of deciduous species. There are numerous forms of
this species, some of which seem very distinct.

8. FOMES PINI.   Pileus sessile, effused reflexed or
                  shelflike, rarely resupinate, the indi-
vidual shelves 3-12 cm. wide, projecting 1-8 cm., surface
first reddish brown and pubescent, later almost black and
glabrous, with many narrow, definite, concentric ridges,
and irregular radial ridges or folds. Context 1-10 mm.
thick at the base, first yellow
brown, later reddish brown,
hard, woody. Pores 6-40 per
cm., 1-5 mm. long, often
very irregular in shape and
size, first yellowish brown,
later dark reddish brown,
often the successive layers of
pores indistinctly separated.
Common on living trees, less
common on logs, of coniferous
species. This species probably causes more decay in
living conifer trees throughout
the northern hemisphere than
any other single fungus.

9. FOMES PINICOLA.   Pileus sessile, applanate or
                     considerably thicker at the base
than at the margin, sometimes almost spherical when
young, 6-40 cm. wide, projecting 5-30 cm., surface variable in color, the current year's growth pale tan at first,
soon becoming deep red, the older part black; sometimes
the current season's growth is white to pale tan, last year's
growth bright red, and the older portion black; with rather
wide rounded concentric ridges. Context 0.5-3 cm. thick,
pale tan, tough but rather woolly when broken. Pores 40-
50 per cm., 5-10 mm. long, round, regular in size and
shape, at first white to pale yellow, later pale tan or brown,
layers of successive years separated by a layer of mycelium 1-3 mm. thick and of the same color as the pores.

On dead trees and logs of coniferous and deciduous species;
it is more common on conifers than on hardwoods, but has
been found on more than 100 species of trees.

10. FOMES POMACEUS.   Fruit body sessile and ungulate
                          or pendulous, 2-6 cm. wide,
projecting 1-3 cm., surface of present year's growth brown
and pubescent, the older portion gray to black and glabrous,
occasionally slightly cracked. Context 5-10 mm. thick,
dark brown, hard, sometimes with faint growth zones.
Pores 50-70 per cm., 2-5 mm. long, brown like the context, the layers formed in successive years not distinctly
separated from each other. On dead branches of pome-fruit
trees, and on the trunks of dead trees.

11. FOMES ROSEUS.   Pileus sessile, ungulate to appla-
                        nate, 3-10 cm. wide, projecting
2-8 cm., surface with narrow concentric ridges, the older
part cracked, pale pink near the margin, otherwise black.
Context 5-10 mm. thick, pale pink, with faint growth zones,
firm, woolly when broken. Pores 30-50 cm., 1-3 mm.
long, at first pale pink, later tan to brown, layers of successive seasons not separated by a layer of mycelium, the
older pores filled with mycelium. On conifer logs.

12. FOMES SCUTELLATUS.   Pileus sessile or attached
                            by a narrow base and then
pendulous, 0.5-2.5 cm. wide, projecting 0.3-2 cm., surface at first almost white, becoming tan, then brown to

black, usually remaining paler at the margin, with narrow concentric ridges. Context 1-2 cm. thick, tan to brown, firm. Pores 1-3 mm. long, 35-45 per cm. toward the center and 50-60 per cm. at the margin, tan to brown, the successive annual pore layers not distinctly separated, old pores filled with mycelium. Common on dead alder and witch hazel. Because of its small size this Fomes can easily be confused with a Polyporus, especially when only 1 year old.

Key to the Species of Polyporus

1. Fruit body with a central or lateral stem - - 2
   Fruit body without a stem - - 16

2. Context very pale tan or white - - 3
   Context brown - - 12

3. Base of stem or entire stem black - - 4
   Stem not black - - 7

4. Surface of cap white, scaly - - 5
   Surface yellow to brown or black, not scaly - - 6

5. Scales large, pores 3-10 per cm., stem lateral or sub-
      lateral, growing on wood - - P. squamosus
   Scales minute, pores 20-30 per cm. stem central,
      growing on ground - - P. melanopus

6. Pileus 1.5-6.0 cm. wide, stem 1-6 cm. long, 2-6 mm.
      thick, pores 40-50 per cm. - - P. elegans
   Pileus 5-25 cm. wide, stem 1-6 cm. long, 0.5-2.0 cm.
      thick, pores 60-80 per cm. - - P. picipes

7. Stem unbranched - - 8
   Stem repeatedly branched - - 11

8. Stem lateral, short - - 9
   Stem central, length more than several times the diam-
      eter - - 10

9. On birch, cap rounded above, context 1 cm. or more
      thick, margin rounded and projecting beyond the
      pores - - P. betulinus
   On elm, cap depressed at the point of attachment, con-
      text about 1 mm. thick - - P. conchifer

10. Pores elongated radially, somewhat diamond shaped,
      10-20 per cm. - - P. arcularius
    Pores usually not elongated radially, 20-30 per cm.
      - - P. brumalis

11. Caps attached centrally - - P. umbellatus
     Caps attached laterally - - P. frondosus

12. Cap with a shiny crust, stem usually lateral, rarely
        central - - 13
     Cap without a shiny crust, stem usually central, rarely
        lateral - - 14

13. Surface uniformly dark reddish brown, on coniferous
        wood - - P. tsugae
     Surface reddish brown near the stem, paler toward the
        margin, on hardwoods - - P. lucidus

14. Cap thin, context less than 3 mm. thick, almost gla-
        brous, with narrow concentric bands of light and
        dark brown - - P. perennis
     Cap thin, context less than 3 mm. thick, silky, shiny
        yellowish brown or reddish brown - - P. cinnamomeu
     Cap fleshy, context 5 mm. or more thick, surface
        hairy - - 15

15. Context in two layers, the upper one soft and spongy,
        the lower one fibrous and firm - - P. circinatus
     Context uniform, pores of fresh specimens often
        daedaloid - - P. schweinitzii

16. Context white or nearly so - - 17
     Context brown - - 31
     Context orange, red or yellow - - 35

17. Pore surface enclosed by a tough layer of mycelium
        that covers the entire lower surface of the fruit body
        - - P. volvatus
     Pore surface exposed - - 18

18. Entire fruit body sulphur yellow to orange
        - - P. sulphureus
     Fruit body not yellow - - 19

19. Pores red, 1 mm. or less long, pore layer elastic
        when fresh, easily separated from the context
        - - P. dichrous
     Pores gray to black - - P. adustus
     Pores violet tinted - - 20
     Pores white, tan or brown - - 21

20. Pores becoming tooth-like, common on the wood of
        deciduous trees - - P. pargamenus
     Pores often radially elongated, on coniferous wood
        - - P. abietinus

21. Pileus white - - 22
     Pileus gray, yellow, or brown - - 27

22. Context 1-3 mm. thick - - 23
     Context 5 mm. or more thick - - 24

23. Pileus sessile, attached by a narrow base, growing
         only on elm - - P. conchifer
     Pileus effused-reflexed, pores large, the walls soon
         becoming toothlike - - P. tulipiferus

24. On the wood of deciduous trees - - 25
     On coniferous trees and wood - - 26

25. Fruit body resupinate, convex, only on oak
         - - P. compactus
     Fruit bodies usually effused-reflexed, imbricate, on
         hardwoods - - P. albellus

26. Fruit body attached to the wood throughout the entire
         width of the base, each shelf projecting 1-3 cm.
         - - P. anceps
     Fruit body attached only by a narrow stemlike base,
         each shelf projecting 6-12 cm. - - P. guttulatus

27. Context 1 mm. or less thick, fruit bodies 0.5-3.0 cm.
         wide, upper surface brown or black, sometimes
         with alternate zones of brown and black
         - - P. planellus
     Context 1 cm. or more thick - - 28
     Context 1-8 mm. thick - - 29

28. Pileus applanate, surface brown, velvety
         - - P. resinosus
     Pileus ungulate, surface yellow to gray, coarsely
         hairy - - P. obtusus

29. Surface with many narrow zones of light and dark
         brown, gray, or black - - P. versicolor
     Surface inconspicuously or not at all zonate - - 30

30. Surface at first pale yellow, later pale brown or buff,
         covered with fine hair, inconspicuously zonate with
         faint bands of tan and yellow - - P. zonatus
     Surface gray to brown, covered with long coarse hair
         - - P. hirsutus

31. Context with a granular core - - P. dryophilus
     Context uniform in texture - - 32

32. Pores white or tan, surface brown and velvety, incon-
         spicuously zonate - - P. resinosus
     Pores brown - - 33

33. On conifer trees, logs, and stumps, pores 10-30 per
        cm. irregular or daedaloid - - P. schweinitzii
     On hardwood logs, pores 40-80 per cm. , round - - 34

⌄4. Surface when fresh with alternate, narrow, shining
        golden and brown zones, covered with short hair,
        pores toward the margin 40-50 per cm. - - P. radiatu
     Surface when fresh buff to brown, azonate, glabrous or
        nearly so, pores toward the margin 50-80 per cm.
        - - P. gilvus
     Pileus shelflike, cinnamon brown throughout, glabrous,
        soft - - P. nidulans (P. rutilans)

35. Entire fruit body sulphur yellow or reddish yellow,
        usually many fruit bodies arising from a common
        base - - P. sulphureus
     Entire body orange or red, solitary or scattered, never
        in clumps arising from a common base - - 36

36. Surface hairy, pores 10-20 per cm. - - P. fibrillosus
     Surface glabrous or nearly so, pores 30-40 per cm.
        - - P. cinnabarinus

Description of Species of Polyporus

1. POLYPORUS ABIETINUS.   Pileus sessile, effused
                                reflexed, or rarely re-
supinate, imbricate, the shelves 1-8 cm. wide, projecting
1-3 cm. , 2-4 mm. thick, sometimes the base narrowed,
surface covered with rather coarse hair, with many narrow concentric ridges, gray to brown or black at the base,
paler toward the margin, sometimes green from algae
growing upon it, margin thin, pores extending to the margin. Context 1 mm. or less thick, white, tough, limp.
Pores at first round to angular or daedaloid, usually elongated radially, at first deep purple and either remaining
so or fading to tan, 20-30 per cm. parallel to the margin,
1-3 mm. long. On conifer logs and wood. It resembles
Polyporus pargamenus in color, but the radially elongate
pores usually serve to distinguish it.

2. POLYPORUS ADUSTUS.   Pileus effused reflexed or
                                sessile, rarely resupinate,
imbricate, the effused portion often covering an area a
foot or more in length and several inches wide, each shelf
3-20 cm. wide, projecting 1-4 cm.; surface gray to tan,
sometimes with several broad, indistinct zones, finely

pubescent to glabrous; margin thin, with a poreless white band 1-2 mm. wide on the under side in fresh specimens, the band in older specimens often turning black. Context 2-3 mm. thick, white to gray, tough; in some specimens there is a narrow dark line between the pores and the white context, but this is not always present. Pores dark gray to black, 0.5-2 mm. long, 60-80 per cm. On dead trees and logs of deciduous species.

3. POLYPORUS ALBELLUS.

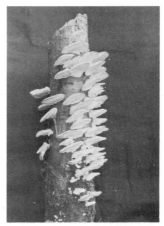

Pileus 2-10 cm. wide, project-ing 2-7 cm., 1-5 cm. thick at the base, sessile and shelflike, imbricate but not densely so, white when fresh, becoming pale yellow when dried. Con-text 0.5-2 cm. thick at the base, very thin at the margin, white with faint curved growth zones, soft and watery when fresh, brittle and easily crumbled when dry. Pores 2-8 mm. long, 30-40 per cm., an occasional large pore among the smaller ones, round to angular, white when fresh, pale yellow when dry. On deciduous trees. Lowe, in "The Polyporaceae of New York State" considers that this species and Polyporus lac-teus are only extreme forms of the same fungus.

4. POLYPORUS ANCEPS.

Pileus white or pale cream, resupinate, effused reflexed, or rarely sessile, the resup-inate part up to 10 cm. long; individual shelves 3-6 cm. wide, projecting 1-3 cm., 5-15 mm. thick, the surface rough and irregularly pitted. Context white, tough, not zoned. Pores 4-10 mm. long, 40-50 per cm., slightly angu-lar, white when fresh, often pale yellow when dry or where bruised. Solitary or scattered

on conifer posts and logs. It causes a rather important rot
of the heartwood of western yellow pine and possibly some
related pines, but fruits only on dead and down material.

5. POLYPORUS ARCULARIUS.   Cap 2-6 cm. wide, 2-4
                                mm. thick, circular,
depressed in the center, glabrous, or sometimes hairy or
scaly, brown when fresh and moist, pale tan when dry.   Context white or pale tan, up to 2 mm. thick, tough and flexible
when moist, brittle when dry.
Pores 1-2 mm. long, 10-20
per cm. , radially elongated
and usually diamond shape,
edges thin and slightly toothed,
white to pale brown.   Stem
central, 2-7 cm. long, 2-5
mm. thick, tan to dark brown,
usually slightly hairy or scaly,
especially toward the base.
Solitary or in groups on stumps,
logs and wood of deciduous
trees.

6. POLYPORUS BETULINUS.   Pileus usually convex,
                                rarely pendulous, circular
to reniform, often with a short lateral stem, 5-25 cm. wide,
projecting 5-15 cm. , surface white to brown, at first smooth,
later cracked; margin thick
and rounded, forming a band
up to 1 cm. wide around the
pore surface.   Context 1-3
cm. thick, white, firm. Pores
30-40 per cm. , 5-15 mm.
long, at first white, later yellow or tan, walls between the
pores at first thick but later
becoming thin and toothed.
In fresh specimens the entire
pore layer can be peeled from
the fruit body.   The pore
layer does not begin to form
until the fruit body has attained
its maximum size, and so
rather large fruit bodies can
be found with very short pores
or none at all.   On dead trees,
logs and branches of birch.

7. POLYPORUS BRUMALIS.   Cap 2-6 cm. wide, 2-5
mm. thick, circular, de-
pressed in the center, dark brown when moist, tan when dry,

velvety when young but later
glabrous, sometimes with indistinct concentric zones.
Context 1-3 mm. thick, nearly
white, tough and elastic when
fresh, brittle when dry. Pores
1-3 mm. long, 20-30 per cm.,
angular, sometimes longer
radially, almost white when
fresh, later pale brown. Solitary or scattered on logs and
stumps of deciduous trees.

8. POLYPORUS CINNABARINUS.   Pileus sessile, rarely
effused reflexed, each
shelf 3-14 cm. wide, projecting 2-6 cm., 7-20 mm. thick
at the base, surface bright orange red when fresh, fading
to tan when old, at first pubescent, later glabrous. Context
orange red when fresh, fading to tan in old specimens, 5-15
mm. thick, spongy, with definite curved growth zones that
sometimes can be separated from each other. Pores 20-40
per cm., often large and irregular near the base and small
twoard the margin, 2-5 mm. long, slightly angular, orange
red and remaining so much longer than the upper surface.
Solitary or scattered on stumps and logs of deciduous trees.

9. POLYPORUS CINNAMOMEUS.   Pileus 1-4 cm. wide,
almost flat, with a
narrow central depression, shiny, reddish or yellowish
brown, with faint concentric zones, often the caps of two or
more adjacent fruit bodies grown together. Context 0.5 mm.
or less thick, pliable, rather tough, reddish brown, when
fresh and moist somewhat elastic. Pores about 20-30 per
cm. at the margin, sometimes larger toward the stem,
angular, dark reddish brown, walls between the pores thin
and toothed. Stem 2-5 cm. long, 2-4 mm. thick, reddish
brown, tough and flexible, velvety. Scattered or in groups
on the ground in woods.

10. POLYPORUS CIRCINATUS.   Pileus 5-15 cm. wide,
circular or irregularly
circular, flat to shallow funnel shape, one or more fruit
bodies often growing out from the top of another one, some-

times two or more adjacent fruit bodies grown together; surface buff to dark brown, hairy, usually with concentric ridges and faint concentric zones of color; margin thin, usually decurved. Context 5-13 mm. thick at the stem, tan to brown, made up of two rather distinct layers, the upper one soft and spongy, the lower one fibrous and more firm. Pores 30-40 per cm., 2-4 mm. long, irregular in shape and size, walls thin, very light tan to dark brown, sometimes decurrent but usually ending abruptly near the stem. Stem 2-5 cm. long, 1-2 cm. thick, buff to brown, hairy, made up of two layers like the cap, the outer layer spongy, the inner one fibrous. Solitary, in groups, or in small clumps under conifer trees in which it causes a white pocket rot of the roots and base of the trunk.

11. POLYPORUS COMPACTUS.

Pileus resupinate, rarely with a narrow shelf, convex, 3-20 cm. long, 2-10 cm. wide, 8-20 mm. thick, irregular in outline. Context white or nearly so, with definite growth zones, 6-17 mm. thick, firm, tough. Pores often indistinct, 1-3 mm. long, 30-40 per cm., white, pale tan when old or where bruised. Solitary or scattered on stumps and logs of oak. The fungus causes decay in living trees, but fruits only after the trees have been blown or cut down.

12. POLYPORUS CONCHIFER.

Pileus circular to reniform, sessile or with a short stem-like base, 1-8 cm. wide, surface white to pale tan, faintly zoned, often with faint radial furrows, frequently with a small cuplike structure in the center or at the place of attachment; margin thin. Context up to 1 mm. thick, white,

firm, and pliable. Pores 30-40 per cm. , 05. -3 mm. long,
the walls thin and toothed, white to pale tan.   Common on
the upper sides of dead branches of elms and related hardwoods.

13. POLYPORUS DICHROUS.   Fruit body resupinate to
                                effused reflexed, rarely
shelflike and sessile, the resupinate portion 3-20 cm. long,
2-7 cm. wide, the shelves 2-10 cm. wide, projecting 0. 5-
4 cm.   Upper side white, velvety when fresh, glabrous
when old.   Context white, 1-3 mm. thick.   Pores red to
reddish tan, lighter in color toward the margin, 60 per cm. ,
irregular in shape and size, up to 1 mm. long.   Pore layer
elastic when moist, and easily peeled from the context.   On
logs and stumps.

14. POLYPORUS DRYOPHILUS.   Pileus sessile, applan-
                                ate with a thick base to
ungulate, 3-12 cm. wide, projecting 3-8 cm. , 3-8 cm.
thick at the base, tapering to a sharp or rounded margin;
surface tan to reddish brown,
usually faintly zonate, first
thickly covered with coarse
hair, later almost glabrous,
at least toward the margin.
Context dark brown, the outer
part rather soft and woolly,
with faint growth zones, the
base with a hard, granular
core that is flecked with
streaks of white.   Pores 35-
45 per cm. , 8-12 mm. long,
pore ends first gray, later
dark brown.   Occasional on
living and dead hardwoods.

15.   POLYPORUS ELEGANS.·

Pileus 1. 5-6 cm. in diameter,
round to irregular, flat or depressed in the center, tan to
light reddish brown, glabrous.
Margin thin, the under side
with a narrow band free of
pores.   Context 2-3 mm. thick,
tan, tough when fresh, brittle

when dry. Pores 1-2 mm. long, 50-60 per cm., angular, decurrent, walls thin. Stem central or eccentric, rarely lateral, 1-6 cm. long, 2-6 mm. in diameter, glabrous, black from the base almost to the pores, upper part tan. Solitary or scattered on decaying hardwood stumps and logs.

16. POLYPORUS FIBRILLOSUS.   Pileus sessile or ef-
                                   fused reflexed, 3-6
cm. long, projecting 2-4 cm., 0.5-2 cm. thick at the base, surface orange red, coarsely hairy, sometimes with a few faint zones. Context the same color as the surface or paler, 3-15 mm. thick, tough, when squeezed exuding a watery liquid colored like the context. Pores 2-5 mm. long, 10-20 per cm., colored like the context, angular, the walls thin and becoming toothed. Solitary or scattered on decaying logs and stumps.

17. POLYPORUS FRONDOSUS.   Fruit body compound,
                                   the entire structure
arising from one large stem and comprising a mass from 30-50 cm. wide, made up of 20 to 100 or more lateral stemmed, branching caps, each cap 3-10 cm. wide, surface brown to tan, pubescent, faintly zoned, radially striate, the margin even or wavy, thin or thick, with pores extending to the edge. Stem lateral, 1-3 cm. thick, 1-4 cm. long, repeatedly and irregularly branched. Pores 10-30 per cm., 1-3 mm. long, white, round or irregular, edges becoming thin and toothed, extending all the way down the stem. On the ground near stumps of deciduous trees.

18. POLYPORUS GILVUS.   Pileus sessile and shelflike
                               or effused reflexed, 3-10 cm.
long, projecting 2-6 cm., 1-2.5 cm. thick at the base; surface yellowish brown to reddish brown, slightly pubescent when young, glabrous when mature, margin sharply acute, the under side with a narrow band free of pores. Context 5-15 mm. thick, golden brown, with faint growth zones, tough when fresh, firm when dry. Pores brown, 3-7 mm. long, 50-80 per cm., slightly angular, walls about as thick as the diameter of the pores. Scattered on wood of deciduous trees, especially on the sapwood of oak.

19. POLYPORUS GUTTULATUS.   Fruit bodies sessile,
                                   6-15 cm. wide, pro-
jecting 6-12 cm., 1.5-4 cm. thick at the base, with a narrow, lateral, stemlike attachment, rarely almost circular

and with a central stemlike attachment, often sloping downward from the margin to the base.   Surface white when
young, reddish brown when old, with several broad, inconspicuous ridges.   Context 1-4 cm. thick at the stemlike
base, 2-3 mm. thick at the margin, white, fibrous.   Pores
4-9 mm. long where longest,
tapering to nothing at the margin, 40-50 per cm., circular
or irregular, pale yellow inside, becoming reddish when
bruised.   Sometimes the pores
are in 2 or 3 rather distinct
layers.   When young, and
growing in humid weather, the
fruit bodies exude drops of
clear liquid all over the upper
surface, and fresh fruit bodies
have a faint but definite and
rather sweet odor.   Solitary,
scattered or in clumps on
stumps, logs and the bases of
dead conifer trees, especially
spruce and firs.

20. POLYPORUS HIRSUTUS.   Pileus sessile or effused
                                reflexed, the reflexed
portion of each shelf remaining distinct from those adjacent
to it and not fused to form one large reflexed portion as in
so many Polypores, sometimes imbricate, when growing
from the top of a log the pileus may be circular, shallow
funnel shape and have a stemlike base; the shelf 1-8 cm.
wide, projecting 1-5 cm., surface faintly zoned, densely
hairy, the hairs long and coarse, gray to light brown, margin usually thin and with a narrow pore free band on the
under side.   Context 1-4 mm. thick, white, tough and pliable when fresh, but stiff and brittle when dry.   Pores 25-
40 per cm., 1-3 mm. long, usually round, rarely irregular
or daedaloid, scattered pores 0.5-1 mm. in diameter, first
white, soon yellowish or tan.   On stumps and logs of hardwoods, rare on conifers.

21. POLYPORUS LUCIDUS.   Pileus almost circular or
                              irregularly semicircular,
3-25 cm. in diameter, 1-3 cm. thick, surface shiny reddish brown near the stem, pale brown toward the margin,

often concentrically ridged,
margin pale tan, thick and
rounded. Context light brown,
firm, fibrous, 5-15 mm.
thick. Pores 30-50 per cm.,
5-15 mm. long, tan to brown.
Stem 2-5 cm. long, 1.5-3
cm. thick, central, eccentric,
or lateral, shiny reddish
brown. On stumps and logs,
and on the ground near decaying stumps.

22. POLYPORUS MELANOPUS.   Pileus 3-15 cm. wide,
                                circular, shallow fun-
nel shape, surface tan to dark brown, minutely scaly. Context white to pale tan, 3-15 mm. thick, spongy when fresh,
brittle when dry. Pores 20-30 per cm., 1-5 mm. long,
white when fresh, pale brown when dry, walls thin and
toothed. Stem central, rarely branched, 5-10 cm. long,
0.5-2 cm. thick, black and velvety toward the base, extending several cm. into the ground.

23. POLYPORUS NIDULANS. (also known as Polyporus
                        rutilans). Pileus sessile
and shelflike, 3-8 cm. wide, projecting 2-5 cm., 1-2 cm.
thick at the base, tapering to a thin margin, surface uniform
yellowish brown or cinnamon color. Context and pores
same color as the surface, soft and spongy when fresh,
brittle and easily crumbled when dry. Pores 3-8 mm. long,
30-40 per cm., circular to angular or irregular. Solitary
or scattered on decaying branches of hardwood trees.

24. POLYPORUS OBTUSUS.   Pileus sessile, usually
                              ungulate, 4-12 cm. wide,
projecting 3-10 cm., 3-8 cm. thick, the surface white or
yellow when fresh, densely covered with coarse hair that
may disappear with weathering. Context white to tan, 1.5-
4 cm. thick, soft and spongy. Pores 1.5-5 cm. long, 5-15
per cm., white when fresh, tan or light brown when old,
irregular in shape and diameter, the walls thin and the
lower edges becoming toothed. On living deciduous trees,
especially oaks.

25. POLYPORUS PARGAMENUS.

Pileus sessile and shelflike or effused reflexed, imbricate, the effused portion sometimes covering an area of several square feet and the shelves arising from it irregularly or in rows; each shelf 1-5 cm. wide, projecting 1-4 cm. , 2-6 mm. thick, the base often narrowed so that the shelf is fan shape; surface with different colored zones, usually yellow to brown when fresh, fading to almost white in age, densely pubescent when young, often almost glabrous when old; margin thin, with a narrow band free of pores on the under side. Context white, up to 1 mm. thick, tough and flexible. Pores 1-6 mm. long, 30-40 per cm. , at first deep violet, later fading to pale straw color or white, at first round to slightly angular, the lower edges of the walls be-

coming toothed so that the typical pore structure may disappear altogether except near the margin. Sometimes a new pore layer will form on the fruit body produced the preceding year, but the fungus is not truly perennial.

26. POLYPORUS PERENNIS.

Pileus 2-6 cm. wide, circular, flat or shallow funnel shape, surface with several to many circular, narrow, sharply delimited zones of color, the narrower zones reddish brown and the broader zones gray, sparsely pubescent, margin thin, slightly wavy. Context up to 1 mm. thick, dark brown, tough and pliable. Pores 20-35 per cm. , 1-2 mm. long, gray to brown, short decurrent, walls at first equal in thickness to the diameter of the pores, later thin and the edge toothed. Stem 2-5 cm. long, 2-5 mm. thick, central, brown, velvety, uniform in diameter or tapering upward, solid, firm but flexible. Solitary or scattered on the ground.

27. POLYPORUS PICIPES.   Pileus with a central or eccentric stem, top 5-25 cm.
wide, circular to reniform, surface glabrous, dark reddish
brown in the center, tan toward the margin; margin wavy,
often decurved, very thin, pores extending to the edge.
Context white or pale tan, 4-10 mm. thick at the stem, very
thin at the margin, tough and pliable when fresh, brittle
when dry. Pores 60-80 per
cm. , 1-4 mm. long, first
white, later tan, circular in
young specimens but becoming irregular with maturity,
slightly decurrent. Stem 1-6
cm. long, 0.5-2 cm. thick,
enlarged at the base, black at
the base or all the way up to
the pores, the black portion
velvety. Solitary, scattered,
or in groups on decaying hardwood logs, rare on conifers.

28. POLYPORUS PLANELLUS.   Fruit bodies typically
on twigs 0.5 cm. or less
in diameter, shelflike, the shelf often extending across the
under side of the twig, sometimes resupinate on the under
sides of twigs. Each shelf 0.5-3 cm. wide, projecting 1-2
cm. , 1-2 mm. thick, some-
times narrowed to a stemlike
base. Upper surface when
fresh and moist dark brown
or nearly black, when dry
with alternating zones of
brown and black, and radially
wrinkled. The margin of
fresh, growing specimens
nearly white. Context 1 mm.
or less thick, tough and pliable. Pores about 40-50 per
cm. , 1 mm. or less long,
nearly white or with a tinge
of pale red, round to angular
or daedaloid, the lower ends
of the walls often toothed and sometimes covered with a
delicate fuzz of mycelium. This delicate little Polypore
has been said to be rare, but in the writer's experience it
is relatively common, growing on fallen twigs of deciduous
trees.

29. POLYPORUS RADIATUS.

Pileus 2-5 cm. wide, projecting 1-4 cm., 8-15 mm. thick
at the base and tapering toward the rounded margin; surface golden yellow to brown
when fresh, usually with alternate narrow zones of yellow and brown, covered with
short silky hairs, shiny.
Context yellowish brown and
firm when fresh, soon dark
brown and woody, with narrow
growth zones. Pores 3-6 mm.
long, 40-50 per cm., almost
circular or angular, pore
surface light grayish brown
when fresh and remaining so
unless bruised to expose the
dark brown mycelium beneath.

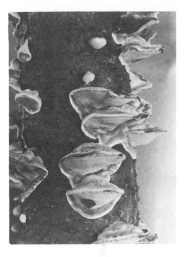

Usually in imbricate groups
on dead branches and small trees of deciduous species.

30. POLYPORUS RESINOSUS.

Pileus sessile and shelf-
like or effused reflexed,
rarely resupinate, each shelf 5-40 cm. wide, projecting
5-30 cm., the reflexed or resupinate portion on the under
side of logs sometimes extending a meter or more. Surface at first dark brown to reddish brown, velvety, often
concentrically zoned, with
definite radial ridges. Margin round and thick. Context
1-4 cm. thick, light tan, soft
and watery but tough when
fresh, brittle when dry.
Pores 40 per cm., 3-8 mm.
long, pale tan when fresh,
pale brown when dry, round
to angular, lower edges often
becoming toothed. Common-
ly in groups and clusters on
decaying hardwood logs.

31. POLYPORUS SCHWEINITZII.

Pileus circular,
shallow funnel shape
and with a central stem when growing from roots, sessile
and shelflike when growing from stumps or the ends of cut

logs, 6-25 cm. wide, surface first yellowish brown, soon
dark reddish brown, usually with concentric ridges, at
first densely hairy. Context yellow to dark brown, 2-10
mm. thick, spongy when fresh, brittle and fragile when dry.
Pores 2-6 mm. long, 10-30 per cm. usually very daedaloid
in young specimens and tinged with green, when old dark
brown and the walls becoming toothed at the lower ends.
Stem usually central, up to 6 cm. long, 1-4 cm. thick,
tough, yellow when fresh, later brown, hairy or glabrous.
Near coniferous trees, and on conifer logs and stumps.

32. POLYPORUS SQUAMOSUS.   Cap 8-30 cm. wide,
                             reniform to nearly cir-
cular, shallow funnel shape, surface pale tan to brown,
with many large, flat, pointed scales, margin thin and
usually turned down. Context white, 1-3 cm. thick near
the stem, soft or tough when fresh, brittle when dry. Pores
4-10 per cm., 2-6 mm. long, white or pale tan, irregular
in size and shape, walls thin, the bottom edge toothed when
old, decurrent and ending in a network on the stem. Stem
lateral to nearly central, 1-6 cm. long, 1-4 cm. thick,
black at the base, pale tan or white toward the top. On
stumps, logs, and living hardwood trees. If a fresh, mature fruit body is placed in a covered glass container it will
shed spores copiously for a week or more, and the falling
spores can be seen readily by shining a light through the
glass. A. H. Reginald Buller, famous mycologist at the
University of Manitoba, estimated that a single fruit body
of this fungus produced about 50 billion spores, illustrating
the prolificacy of these fungi. The fungus is said to be edible, but one man who tested it was moved to write to me,
stating, "So tough when fried it couldn't be cut with a steak
knife!"

33. POLYPORUS SULPHUREUS.   Pileus sessile and
                                      shelflike or effused re-
flexed, narrowed at the base, each shelf 5-30 cm. wide,
projecting 3-25 cm., on standing trees the effused portion
extending as much as a meter up and down the trunk, on the
upper side of logs often forming a rosette of many shelves,
many of them narrow and tongue shape; surface yellow to
bright golden orange when fresh, with few to many zones of
slightly contrasting color, fading to pale tan in age, finely
pubescent or glabrous, radially ridged and furrowed, the
margin usually thick and rounded, often wavy. Context 0.5-
2 cm. thick, white or pale yellow, firm but easily broken
when fresh, brittle when dry. Pores 30-40 per cm., 1-5
mm. long, angular, golden yellow when fresh, pale tan
when dry, the walls at first thick, later thin. Common on
stumps, logs and living trees of hardwoods, rare on conifers. This is one of the few Polypores succulent enough
to be edible - cut in thin slices and fried it often is delicious.

34. POLYPORUS TSUGAE.   Pileus reniform, semicircu-
                                 lar or rarely circular, 10-
30 cm. wide, projecting 8-20 cm., 1-3 cm. thick; surface
uniform reddish brown and shiny as if varnished, concentrically zoned. Context tan to almost white, spongy, 2-10 mm.
thick. Pores 55-65 per cm., 8-15 mm. long, circular to
angular, tan, pore layer ending very abruptly on the stem.
Stem usually lateral, occasionally central, 3-10 cm. long,
2-8 cm. wide, rarely branched, colored like the cap. On
logs and dead trees of hemlock, rarely on wood of other
coniferous species.

35. POLYPORUS TULIPIFERUS.

Pileus usually effused reflexed,
sometimes resupinate, imbricate, shelves numerous, up to
3 cm. wide and projecting as
much as 1 cm.; surface white,
pubescent when fresh, faintly
zoned, margin thin. Context
0.5-3 mm. thick at the base,
white, tough and pliable.
Pores 1-8 mm. long, 10-20
per cm., the walls soon forming long, irregular, pointed
teeth; usually shallow pores can be distinguished at the margin. Common on dead trees and branches of hardwood species.

36. POLYPORUS UMBELLATUS.   Fruit body compound,
                              made up of many cen-
trally stemmed caps, each cap 1-4 cm. wide, convex but
with a narrow depression in the center, surface almost
white to pale brown, glabrous or fibrous, the margin thin.
Context white, 1 mm. thick, tough when fresh, brittle when
dry. Pores 20-40 per cm. , 1-2 mm. long, white when
fresh, later pale brown. Stems central, repeatedly branched. At the base of deciduous trees and stumps.

37. POLYPORUS VERSICOLOR.   Pileus 2-6 cm. wide,
                              projecting 1-4 cm. , 2-
3 mm. thick, often narrowed toward the base, sessile and
shelflike or effused reflexed, usually densely imbricate;
surface with many narrow
concentric bands of gray,
brown, white and black, some
of the narrower bands usually
glabrous and shiny but the
wider ones covered with thick
short hair. Context 1 mm. or
less thick, white, flexible
when fresh, tough when dry.
Pores 40-60 per cm. , 1-2
mm. long, very white when
fresh and remaining nearly so
when dry, round or slightly
angular. Common on stumps
and logs of deciduous trees.

38. POLYPORUS VOLVATUS.

Pileus 1-3 cm. wide, projecting 1-3 cm. , 1-3 cm. thick
at the base, ungulate or globose, usually sessile but sometimes with a stemlike base;
surface glabrous, shiny, tan
to brown when fresh, paler
when old; the pore surface
covered by a tough layer of
mycelium. Context white or
pale tan, spongy when fresh,
firm and hard when dry, 5-15
mm. thick at the base, thinner
toward the margin. Pores

4-10 mm. long, 40-50 per cm., tan to brown, walls at first
very thick and rounded, later thin. On logs and standing
dead conifer trees.

39. POLYPORUS ZONATUS.   Pileus 3-8 cm. wide, pro-
                              jecting 2-5 cm., 3-6 mm.
thick at the base, sessile and shelflike; surface at first pale
tan, later becoming dark tan or with alternate zones of yellowish tan and brown, densely covered with short hair.
Context white, firm, 2-3 mm. thick. Pores white when
young, later yellowish, 30-40 per cm., 1-3 mm. long, angular, the bottom edges becoming somewhat toothed when old.
Scattered or in dense clumps, often imbricate, on logs and
stumps of hardwoods.

Key to the Genus Trametes

1. Fruit bodies imbricate in clusters of 3 to 20 fruit bodies,
        each shelf 3 to 8 cm. wide, 5 to 10 mm. thick at the
        base, surface covered with long, coarse yellowish or
        brown hair, pores 5-10 mm. long, 8-15 per cm.,
        angular or daedaloid - - T. hispida
    Fruit bodies imbricate or scattered, each shelf 2 to 8
        cm. wide, 5 to 10 mm. thick at the base, pores 2-4
        mm. long, 30-50 per cm., entire fruit body pale rose
        colored inside and out when fresh, the top later fading
        to pinkish tan - - T. subroseus or Fomes subrosea

Description of Species of Trametes

1. TRAMETES HISPIDA.   Pileus sessile or effused re-
                          flexed, each shelf 3-8 cm.
wide, projecting 2-5 cm., 1-2 cm. thick at the base, tapering to the margin, surface gray, yellowish, or brown, covered with long coarse hair when young but weathering to
almost smooth, context pale brown, firm, 5-10 mm. thick.
Pores 5-10 mm. long, 8-15 per cm., angular, sometimes
daedaloid, usually varying greatly in shape and size in each
fruit body, grayish brown. Usually in imbricate clusters
containing 3 to 20 fruit bodies, sometimes solitary, on living and dead hardwoods.

2. TRAMETES SUBROSEA.   Pileus sessile or effused
reflexed, each shelf 2-8 cm.
wide, projecting 1-4 cm. , 5-10 mm. thick at the base, tapering to a thin margin, surface pale rose colored and
delicately hairy when young, grayish brown and glabrous
when old, smooth, without definite zones. Context 2-6 mm.
thick near the base, pale rose colored, firm, rather woolly
where broken. Pores 2-4 mm. long, 30-50 per cm., pale
pink or grayish pink, sometimes a new pore layer is formed
on a fruit body of the previous year, but the fungus is not
truly perennial. Usually imbricate on conifer logs and
stumps.

FAMILY HYDNACEAE

TOOTH FUNGI

All of the species included here are placed in the genus HYDNUM, following the usage in many of the reference books to which a beginning student might have ready access. For a more detailed account of the family Hydnaceae, in which the group is divided into 13 genera, see "The Hydnaceae of Iowa" by L. W. Miller and J. S. Boyle, University of Iowa Studies in Natural History, Vol. 18, No. 2, 1943. Also "The Stipitate Hydnums of the Eastern United States" by W. C. Coker and Alma H. Beers, University of North Carolina Press, Chapel Hill, North Carolina, 1951. Below each specific name listed in the key is given in parentheses the name applied by Miller and Boyle.

Key to Species of Hydnaceae

1. Growing on wood - - 2
    Growing on the ground, or from pine cones buried in
        the ground - - 5

2. Fruit bodies shelflike or with a short lateral stem - - 3
    Fruit bodies of many divided branches - - 4

3. Fruit bodies white, usually in a clump of several, one
        above the other, each shelf from 10 to 30 cm. wide,
        on living hard maple
        - - H. septentrionale
    (Steccherinum septentrionale)

    Fruit bodies tan to brown, up to 10 cm.
        wide, on decaying hardwood logs
        - - H. adustum (Steccherinum adustum)

4.   Fruit bodies forming a coralloid clump
       up to 20 cm. in diameter, teeth small
       and delicate, 3-8 mm. long
       - - H. coralloides
     (Hericium coralloides)

     Fruit bodies a dense clump of pendant,
       tapering teeth up to 2 cm. long, that
       conceal the branches - - H. caput-ursi
       (The work cited above considers
       that this species grades into
       H. coralloides, although no such
       intergrades have been seen by the writer)

5.   Growing from buried pine cones (the writer
       has found it only on cones of red pine,
       Pinus resinosa - - H. aurisclapium
     (Aurisclapium vulgare)
     Growing in soil - - 6

6.   Flesh of cap in 2 distinct layers, the
       upper one soft, the lower one, which
       continues down into the stem, firm
       and almost woody - - 7
     Flesh of cap not obviously in two
       layers - - 9

7.   Spore print brown - - H. velutinum
     (Calodon velutinus)
     Spore print white - - 8

8.   Hard interior portion of cap dark blue-black
       - - H. albonigrum
     (Calodon alboniger)
     Hard interior portion of cap light in color - - H. amicum
     (Calodon amicus)

9.   Cap, teeth and stem tan to yellow
       - - H. repandum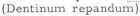
     (Dentinum repandum)
     Cap, teeth and stem tan to brown, cap
       usually dark in center, paler toward
       the margin, sometimes zoned, often
       shallow or deep funnel shape
       - - H. cyathiforme
     (in the publication cited above this is divided into 3 spe-
     cies, Calodon zonatus, C. ferrugineus, and C. scrobi-
     culatus)

Description of Species of Hydnum

1. HYDNUM ADUSTUM.   Fruit bodies shelflike, 3-8 cm.
                    wide, projecting 2-4 cm. , 1-3
cm. thick, often reniform in outline and with a short lateral
stem, usually several shelves together in imbricate fashion;
surface tan to cinnamon brown, pubescent, faint concentric
zones near the margin. Teeth 1-4 mm. long, first white,
later pink, reddish brown when dry. On, hardwood logs and
stumps.

2. HYDNUM ALBIGONER.   Cap 4-8 cm. wide, convex
                    to shallow funnel shape,
hairy, grayish, the interior of the cap dark blue-black and
solid, the color and texture of this interior portion extending down into the stem. Stem 1-2 cm. thick, 3-6 cm. long,
gray. Solitary on the ground.

3. HYDNUM AMICUM.   Cap 6-12 cm. wide, convex to
                    shallow funnel shape, covered
with coarse hair, brown toward the center, white toward
the margin. Teeth 2-4 cm. long, nearly white when young
and fresh, gray or pale brown when dry. Stem 1-2 cm.
thick, 2-4 cm. long, pale brown. Solitary or scattered on
the ground.

4. HYDNUM AURISCLAPIUM.   Cap 1-2 cm. in diameter,
                    almost circular to reni-
form, the stem attached at one side, surface flat or convex,
brown to nearly black, faintly zoned, hairy. Teeth 1-2 mm.
long, paler than the cap. Stem 3-5 cm. long, 2-3 mm.
thick, brown, tough, hairy. The plant grows singly from
cones to pine trees that have become buried an inch or so
beneath the surface of the ground. It will shrivel and become almost invisible in dry weather, but revive again
when moistened, and so may endure for some weeks.

5. HYDNUM CAPUTURSI.   Fruit body formed of one or
                    more clumps of teeth, the
teeth in each clump arising from a common, solid, stemlike base, usually 10-30 teeth in each clump and 10-25
clumps in a fruit body; each tooth 3-10 cm. long, 2-4 mm.
thick at the upper portion, narrowed downward to a fine
point, entirely white when fresh, tan when old. On hardwood logs.

6. HYDNUM CORALLOIDES.   Fruit body originating
                            from a single stem that
branches repeatedly to form an irregularly spherical or
hemispherical cluster 4-30 cm. wide, the teeth 3-6 mm.
long, tapering to a point, borne on the under sides of the
branches, white when fresh, tan when old.   On decayed
hardwood logs.

7. HYDNUM CYATHIFORME.   Cap 4-8 cm. wide, tan to
                            brown, darker in the cen-
ter, often zoned toward the margin; teeth 1-3 mm. long,
brown; stem 1-2 cm. thick, 2-3 cm. long, brown like the
cap.   Solitary, scattered or in groups on the ground.

8. HYDNUM REPANDUM.

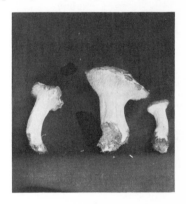

Cap 3-8 cm. wide, convex or
nearly plane, surface yellow,
tan or reddish tan, smooth.
Flesh white, 5-10 mm. thick
near the stem, spongy. Teeth
4-8 mm. long, pointed, pale
yellow, decurrent. Stem 3-6
cm. long, 1-2 cm. thick, at
first solid, later hollow,
usually central but sometimes
eccentric. On the ground in
woods.

9. HYDNUM SEPTENTRIONALE.   Fruit body shelflike
                            and sessile, a number
of shelves growing out in imbricate fashion from a common
base, each shelf 8-30 cm. wide, projecting 5-15 cm., 2-3

cm. thick, surface white, slightly hairy or glabrous, margin rounded. Flesh 1-2 cm. thick, white, firm and tough. Teeth 1-2 cm. long, fine, not tapering to a point. In clumps on living hardwood trees.

10. HYDNUM VELUTINUM.   Cap convex, flat or shallow funnel shape, pale tan to brown, surface pubescent. The context is divided into 2 portions, the upper soft and spongy, the lower firm and solid, and this solid layer extends down into the stem. The plants are irregular in shape and size, up to 10 cm. in diameter, often with several caps grown together. Stem 1-2 cm. thick, 2-8 cm. long, bulbous at the base, the outside soft and spongy, the interior hard. On ground in woods.

FAMILY BOLETACEAE

According to "A Dictionary of the Fungi", by G. C. Ainsworth and G. R. Bisby, published by the Imperial Mycological Institute, Kew, Surrey, England, the family Boletaceae includes 220 species, 200 of them in the genus Boletus. The group as it occurs in the eastern U. S. is taken up in detail in "The Boletaceae of North Carolina", by Coker and Beers, whose thorough and excellent account includes keys, descriptions and illustrations of probably most of the species that occur in eastern North America.

Many species of Boletus can be distinguished from one another only by microscopic characters, and even with the aid of the microscope it is difficult to identify some of them with any degree of certainty. The present key includes only some of the more common species supposedly identifiable by characters visible to the naked eye, although the writer himself has some doubts as to the certainty of identification of some of those included. This is merely a recognition of the fact, very obvious to anyone who has studied the genus Boletus, that many of the species are not readily identifiable.

Key to Genera of Boletaceae

1. Caps covered with large woolly tufts,
       entire plant dark brown to blue-
       black, stem 12-20 cm. long, cap
       10-15 cm. in diameter
       - - Strobilomyces strobilaceus
    Caps smooth, scaly, or mucilaginous,
       but not covered with prominent
       tufts - - 2

2. Pores shallow, pore layer not
       easily peeled from flesh of
       the cap - - Boletinus

Pores deep, pore layer easily
  peeled from flesh of cap
  - - Boletus

Key to Species of Boletinus

1. Pores very shallow, the pore walls
      made up of thick, irregular
      veins, stems often eccentric
      or lateral, cap red-brown
      - - B. porosus

Pores 2-3 mm. long, cap covered
  with red scales between which
  the yellow flesh of the cap is
  exposed, with a definite veil
  when young - - B. pictus

Description of Species of Boletinus

1. BOLETINUS PICTUS.   Edible. Cap convex to almost
                              flat, 4-12 cm. wide, dark
red, often yellowish toward the margin, surface usually
with scattered yellow scales.
Flesh yellow, becoming reddish when broken, 0.5-1 cm.
thick. Pores yellow, 3-5
mm. long, 5-20 per cm. , angular or irregular. Stem 1-2
cm. thick, 4-7 cm. long,
colored like the cap. Young
specimens have a rather thick
white veil which remains as a
ring on the stem when the cap
expands. Scattered on the
ground from swamps to up-
lands in woods.

2. BOLETINUS POROSUS.   (also known as Boletinus
                              merulioides). Edible.
Caps 5-12 cm. wide, convex to flat or shallow funnel shape,
irregular in outline, sometimes reniform or strongly in-
dented where the stem is attached, olive brown to reddish

brown. Flesh 0.5-1 cm. thick near the stem, pale yellow
or greenish yellow. Pores very irregular in shape and size,
and only 1-3 mm. deep, the walls between the pores frequently being no more than veins, continuing down the stem
a short distance, lighter in color than the cap. Stem lateral
or very eccentric, 1-2 cm. thick at the top, tapering toward
the base, 2-4 cm. long, colored like the cap surface. In
groups or dense clumps around decaying hardwood stumps.

Key to Species of Boletus

1. Definite veil between margin
   of cap and upper stem on
   young plants, which remains
   as a ring on the stem of
   mature plants - - 2
   Plants without veil or ring - - 3

2. Caps pores and stems chrome yellow - - B. luteus
   Caps red-brown, veil usually tough and persistent
      - - B. sphaerosporus

3. Flesh of cap not changing color when broken or bruised
      - - 4
   Flesh of cap changing color when broken or bruised
      - - 5

4. Cap surface red-brown, sticky when fresh, flesh of cap
      white or pale yellow, stem without markings
      - - B. granulatus
   Cap surface yellow to brown, sticky when fresh, flesh
      of cap yellow, stem covered with a network of
      markings - - B. retipes and B. edulis

5. Surface of cap of fresh specimens covered with a thick
      layer of slime, flesh of cap pale yellow, turning faint
      pink or violet when broken - - B. subaureus
   Surface of cap of fresh specimens not covered with a
      layer of slime - - 6

6. Cap surface smooth, sometimes somewhat sticky, flesh
      of cap turns red when broken - - B. scaber
   Cap surface tan, brown, reddish or mottled tan and
      reddish, flesh of cap turns pale pink when broken
      - - B. felleus

Description of Species of Boletus

1. BOLETUS EDULIS.   Edible. Cap 10-20 cm. wide,
convex, reddish tan to brown,
smooth, slightly sticky when fresh and moist.   Flesh white
and remaining so when broken, 1-2 cm. thick.   Pores
white, 20-30 per cm., 1.5-2 cm. long, the pore surface
curving upward near the stem.   Stem 6-12 cm. long, 1-2
cm. in diameter, colored like the cap or nearly white.

2. BOLETUS FELLEUS.   Edible. Cap 12-20 cm. wide,
convex, smooth, light to dark
brown.   Flesh 2-3 cm. thick, first white, pale pink where
broken.   Pores white when young, flesh color or almost
rosy when old or where bruised, 1-2 cm. long, 10-20 per
cm.   Stem 6-15 cm. long, 1-2 cm. thick at the top, often
bulbous at the base, colored like the cap or paler, sometimes with a network of ridges near the top or most of the
way down.

3. BOLETUS GRANULATUS.   Edible. Cap 6-12 cm. wide,
convex, smooth, sticky
when young and moist, covered with a thin transparent
cuticle than can be peeled off easily, reddish tan to reddish
brown.   Flesh 1-1.5 cm. thick near the stem, white or pale
yellow.   Pores first pale yellow, later reddish brown, 15-
20 per cm., 3-5 mm. long.   Stem 4-6 cm. long, 1-1.5 cm.
thick, white to pale yellow but covered with specks or dots
that first are red and later reddish brown.

4. BOLETUS LUTEUS.   Edible. Cap 6-12 cm. wide,
convex, yellow to yellowish
brown, smooth, the cuticle rather thick and easily peeled
off.   Flesh white to pale yel-
low, 1-1.5 cm. thick at the
stem.   Pores pale yellow to
yellowish brown, 5-10 mm.
long, 15-20 per cm.   Stem
4-8 cm. long, about 1 cm.
thick, colored like the cap.
Young specimens have a
rather thick, tough, sticky
veil that remains as a prominent annulus near the top of
the stem.

5. BOLETUS RETIPES.

Edible. Cap 8-16 cm. wide,
convex, smooth, yellow to
brown. Flesh pale yellow, becoming deep yellow when brok-
en. Pores pale to deep yellow,
10-20 per cm., 8-10 mm. long,
the pore surface curved upward near the stem. Stem 7-
10 cm. long, 1.5-2 cm. thick,
yellow, covered with a network
of ridges.

6. BOLETUS SPHAEROSPORUS.   Edible. Cap 6-12 cm.
wide, convex, light
brown when young, dark reddish brown when mature,
smooth. Flesh pale yellow to pale brown, 1-1.5 cm. thick
near the stem. Pores pale yellow, 2-6 mm. long, the lower
edges becoming toothed when old, irregular or angular in
outline. Stem 4-6 cm. long, 2-3 cm. thick. Young specimens have a thick white or tan veil that when the cap expands
remains as a persistent and prominent annulus near the base
of the stem.

7. BOLETUS SUBAUREUS.   Edible. Cap 6-10 cm. wide,
convex to flat, sticky when
young and moist, pale yellow or with spots of reddish brown.
Flesh pale yellow, becoming faint reddish brown when brok-
en,1-1.5 cm. thick at the stem. Pores 8-12 mm. long, 10-
20 per cm., yellow or yellowish brown. Stem 5-8 cm. long,
1-1.5 cm. thick at the top, yellow or dotted with reddish
brown specks.

Genus STROBILOMYCES

So far as is known this genus contains only a single
species. Strobilomyces strobilaceus. Edible. Cap 6-12
cm. wide, spherical when young and covered with a thick
layer of woolly, dark brown mycelium that breaks up into
soft tufts or pyramidal scales as the cap expands, exposing
the pale brown under layer; hemispherical or convex when
mature. Flesh 1-2 cm. thick near the stem, disappearing
near the margin, soft and dark, pale tan when first broken,
becoming reddish brown within a few minutes; often exuding

a reddish brown juice, slowly becoming dark blue or blue-
black. Pores 1.5-2.5 cm. long, 10 per cm. near the stem,
20 per cm. near the margin, dark brown, soft, each pore
not separable as a unit. Stem 8-12 cm. long, 1-2 cm. thick
at the top, enlarged at the base, dark brown outside, with a
tough and fibrous outer layer, the interior firm but not
tough, differing in texture from the flesh of the cap and easily removed from the cap; colored like the flesh of the cap
and exuding a red juice when cut, usually with a peculiar
square cavity in the interior near the top. Young specimens
have a veil which as the cap expands forms a ring on the
stem, but this disappears quickly. The spore print is dark
brown. Scattered on the ground in deciduous woods.

FAMILY CLAVARIACEAE

CLUB FUNGI

This family of fungi, commonly called the Club Fungi, includes about 200 species. The family is taken up in detail in "The Clavarias of the United States and Canada", by W. C. Coker, published by the University of North Carolina Press in 1923. Many of the species are identifiable only by microscopic characters and some of them are by no means easily identified even with this aid. Only those are included here which the writer has found commonly and which he feels can be identified with at least reasonable certainty in the field. As with the Family BOLETACEAE, the writer is of the opinion that this group of fungi is not yet well enough known throughout the country to enable us to identify even some of the more common kinds with a high degree of certainty with or without recourse to the microscope. All of the species included in the present key are in the genus Clavaria.

Key to Species of Clavaria

1. Plants repeatedly branched
    - - 2

    Plants not branched - - 5

2. Growing on decayed wood - - C. stricta
    Growing on the ground - - 3

3. Fruit body pale violet - - C. amethystina
    Fruit body ash gray - - C. cinerea
    Fruit body yellow - - 4

4. Flesh of stems and branches turning red when bruised
    - - C. flava
    Flesh not turning red when bruised - - C. aurea

5. Fruit bodies 6-15 cm. high, tan in color, often thick at
    the top and tapering downward - - C. pistillaris
    Fruit bodies 0.5 to 1.0 cm. high, on decaying hardwood
    logs covered with the green alga Chlorococcus
    - - C. mucida

Description of Species of Clavaria

1. CLAVARIA AMETHYSTINA.   Edible. Fruit bodies
                                 2-8 cm. tall, composed
of numerous rather fine main branches that rebranch near
the top, the entire plant violet colored toward the top, paler
toward the base.

2. CLAVARIA AUREA.

Edible. Fruit bodies 8-12
cm. high, composed of many
main branches that branch
repeatedly, golden yellow to
tan. Usually in scattered
clumps on the ground under
conifers.

3. CLAVARIA FLAVA.   Edible. Fruit bodies essentially
                          identical with those of Clavaria
aurea, but the flesh when broken becomes reddish brown.

4. CLAVARIA MUCIDA.   Fruit bodies consisting of a
                          single unbranched (or rarely
branched once) upright stalk that tapers to a point at the
top, about 1 cm. high, 1-2 mm. in diameter, golden yellow
to pale yellow, tough. Growing in groups of dozens to hundreds of plants on decaying hardwood logs covered with
the alga Chlorococcus.

5. CLAVARIA PISTILLARIS.

Edible. Fruit bodies consisting
of an unbranched or rarely
branched upright stalk up to 10
cm. tall, 1-2 cm. in diameter
at the top, tapering downward,

pale yellow to light brown, often with irregular vertical
ridges, flesh white. Scattered or in groups, often of hundreds of specimens, on the ground under pine trees.

6. CLAVARIA STRICTA.

Edible. Fruit bodies consisting of a mass of main branches
arising from a common point,
up to 10 cm. high and sometimes 15-20 cm. wide, the
branches usually flat or irregular, the topmost branchlets
terminating in 2 or 3 delicate
teeth, tan to yellowish brown
in color. In clumps on decaying logs and at the base of trees.

FAMILY THELEPHORACEAE

The fungi in this family are characterized by fruit
bodies with a more or less smooth hymenial surface; that
is, the hymenium is not distributed over gills, pores, or
teeth, although in some species there is at least a sugges-
tion of gills. According to "A Dictionary of the Fungi" by
Ainsworth and Bisby, the family includes 900 species in 33
genera. The genera, and many of the species within genera,
are distinguished from one another on a basis of microscopic
characters, and, because of this, any attempt to present
them without including the essential microscopic details is
of limited value. While recognizing this obvious limitation,
it still is thought worthwhile to include some of the more
prevalent, abundant, and easily recognized species. Those
interested in studying the group further are referred to the
following publications.

Lentz, P. L. Stereum and Allied Genera of Fungi in the
Upper Mississippi Valley. USDA Agriculture Monograph
24. 1955. For sale by Supt. of Documents, Government
Printing Office, Washington 25, D. C. 35¢. The author
cites nearly 150 papers dealing with Thelephoraceae.
Burt, E. A. "The Thelephoraceae of North America I-XII.
Annals of the Missouri Botanic Garden 1-7, 1914-1920.

Key to the Genera of Thelephoraceae

1. Fruit bodies growing on the ground - - 2
    Fruit bodies growing on wood - - 4

2. Fruit bodies a mass of short, upright, flat white
        branches - - Tremellodendron pallidum
    Fruit bodies vase shaped, tapering downward to a stem
    or stemlike base - - 3

3. Fruit body fleshy or brittle in texture - - Craterellus
    Fruit body tough, flexible, leathery - - Thelephora

4. On the bark of living trees, fruit body white or gray,
    flat, circular, 3-8 mm. in diameter, resembling a
    flat cupfungus - - Aleurodiscus
    On branches or trunks of dead trees, logs, timbers
    - - 5

5. Fruit body red, soft, cushion-shaped or hemispherical,
    5-10 mm. in diameter, on twigs and branches of
    Populus, especially aspen - - Cryptochaete rufa
    Fruit body resupinate, effused-reflexed, shelflike or
    (in Stereum frustulatum) consisting of many small gray
    cushions or lumps - - Corticium, Cytidia, Hymeno-
    chaete, Laxitextum, Peniophora, Stereum

Genus ALEURODISCUS

According to Burt (cited above) the genus Aleurodiscus
includes 25 described species, of which 14 occur in North
America, and of these 14 only 3 have a wide range in the
United States - A. acerinus, A. candidus, and A. nivosus -
to which might be added A. oakesii. Macroscopically these
look very much alike, and a single description will serve
here for all 4.

Fruit body flat, circular
or somewhat irregular in outline, up to 1 cm. in diameter,
less than 1 mm. thick, white
or pale gray, usually in groups
on the dead bark of living
trees, where the fungus may
cause the outer bark to scale
off, but evidently causes no
other harm to the tree.   A.
candidus, A. acerinus, and
A. oakesii occur on the bark
of various hardwoods, especially white oaks, while A.
nivosus is found on the bark of
red cedars and Chamaecyparis.
The fruit bodies have a superficial resemblance to those of
cup fungi, and indeed they
were first described as a species of Peziza, before microscopic examination revealed

that they were Basidiomycetes.   They are worth examining
microscopically, since some of them have unusual para-
physes in the hymenium, and nearly all of them have very
large basidia and basidiospores.   The fruit bodies shrink
and shrivel in dry weather and become inconspicuous, but
in moist weather they expand and become readily visible.
They persist for some time, and can be found during the
winter; this ready availability and their rather showy microscopic features make them excellent classroom material.

Genus CORTICIUM

About 150 species have been described in this genus,
nearly all of them with resupinate fruit bodies on wood.
Some of the species are fairly common, several are widely
distributed, and nearly all are difficult for even an expert
to identify with any certainty.   The one species described
here probably is sufficiently distinctive to be recognized on
sight.

CORTICIUM INCARNATUM.   Fruit body flat, thin, rather
                            bright reddish brown, the
margin pale or nearly white, circular or irregular in outline, 5-15 cm. in diameter, or adjacent ones grown together
to form a single crust that extends for 30 cm. or more
along the under side of a branch or log. On dead, decaying
hardwoods that still retain their bark, especially common
on aspen.

Key to Species of Craterellus

1. Upper surface of cap brown, stem tan, hollow
        - - C. cornucopioides
    Entire fruit body yellow to tan, vase shaped, stem
        solid - - 2

2. Fruit body eggyolk yellow - - C. cantharellus
    Fruit body tan to light brown - - C. pistillaris

Description of Species of Craterellus

1. CRATERELLUS CANTHARELLUS.   Edible.   Fruit
                                body 6-9 cm. high,
    4-6 cm. wide at the top, tapering downward into a stem that

is 5-10 mm. in diameter at the base, the hymenial surface
often slightly ridged, suggesting gills, entire plant bright
eggyolk yellow, stem solid but soft and spongy. Except for
lack of definite gills, this species closely resembles Cantharellus cibarius. Singly or in groups on the ground in woods.

2. CRATERELLUS CORNU-COPIOIDES.

Edible. Fruit body 5-8 cm.
tall, the cap 2-4 cm. wide,
upper surface of the cap dark
brown, the margin lobed and
curved downward, depression
in the center of the cap extending down into the hollow stem,
hymenial surface tan to light
brown, smooth or slightly
rough. Solitary or scattered
on the ground in woods.

3. CRATERELLUS PISTILLARIS.

Fruit body 8-12 cm. tall, cap
2-4 cm. wide, flat or convex
on top, slightly rough, tapering downward into a solid stem
5-10 mm. in diameter at the
base. Burt, cited above, says,
"It is a vexed question with
mycologists whether Craterellus pistillaris Fr. is Clavaria
pistillaris L.", but goes on to
say that in his opinion the two
species are distinct. Single
or in scattered groups on the
ground in woods.

Genus CRYPTOCHAETE

CRYPTOCHAETE RUFA.   Fruit bodies hemispherical or
                         cushion shaped, circular or
nearly so in outline, 4-8 mm. in diameter, 3-5 mm. thick,
dull red and somewhat wrinkled when dry, bright scarlet
and plump when fresh and moist, in groups of many fruit
bodies on decaying twigs and branches of Populus, especially

aspen, that still retain their bark. Often the fruit bodies
are so numerous as to cover the twigs and branches on
which they occur. The fungus often has been described
under the name of <u>Stereum</u> <u>rufum</u>. The fungus evidently is
specialized to inhabit the smaller branches and twigs of dead
aspen trees, since it almost never is found on branches or
trunks more than a few inches in diameter, and never has
been reported on any host or substrate other than poplar.

Genus CYTIDIA

About 10 species have been described in this genus,
but of these only the one described here is common.

CYTIDIA SALICINA.

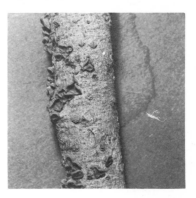

Fruit bodies 4-8 mm. in
diameter, 1-2 mm. thick,
irregular or circular with a
stemlike base, bright red to
reddish brown, gelatinous-
tough when moist and in texture resembling some of the
jelly fungi, hard when dry,
in dense clusters that extend
for 10-20 cm. or more along
branches and twigs of dead
alders, poplars, and willows.

Genus HYMENOCHAETE

The fungi in this genus have resupinate, effused-
reflexed, or stalked fruit bodies, like many other members
of the Thelephoraceae, and they can be distinguished from
their near relatives only by the presence of microscopically
prominent, pointed brown setae in the hymenium. Only 1
common species is described here.

HYMENOCHAETE TABACINA.

Fruit bodies resupinate
or effused-reflexed, the
appressed portion often extending for 20-30 cm. or more
along a twig or branch, with many small and imbricately
arranged shelves, each of which extends for 1-2 cm. along

the twig or branch and proj-
ects up to 1 cm. from it,
dark brown, thin, pliable and
leathery. On dead branches
and twigs of hardwood trees.
Burt, cited above, states:
"H. tabacina is the commonest species of its genus in the
northern United States and
may be recognized by its reflexed fructifications tobacco-
colored with bright golden
yellow margin and intermediate layer, and by having the
hymenium deeply cracked in
resupinate portions into radiating systems, one system
for about each centimeter of
area."

Genus LAXITEXTUM

This genus was erected or first described by Lentz,
in the publication cited above, to include several species
that previously had been placed in Stereum, Corticium,
Hymenochaete, or Thelephora (a given fungus may have been
placed, by different students - experts all - in each of these
several genera, as well as in Peniophora, which illustrates
the taxonomic difficulties encountered in the Thelephoraceae.
According to Lentz (pg. 18) "This genus differs from Corticium and Peniophora by having a more complex organiza-
tion of the basidiocarp than is found in most species of
those genera and by always having some individuals that are
not totally resupinate. It differs from Stereum by lacking
a cuticular layer, by not having a horizontally parallel arrangement of the context hyphae, and thus by having a much
more loosely arranged context than is found in Stereum."

LAXITEXTUM BICOLOR.   Fruit bodies effused reflexed,
                                          with a mass of densely im-
bricate, irregularly arranged shelves 5-20 cm. long, each
shelf projecting 1-3 cm., often adjacent shelves grown together haphazardly, upper surface very dark brown, fuzzy,
with faint concentric ridges and prominent radial folds,

hymenial surface light tan.
On logs and stumps of hardwood trees. The dark brown
upper surface and light colored hymenium serve to distinguish this fungus from its
close relatives. Like most
common and widely distributed fungi it has been described
under a variety of names at
one time or another, among
them Thelephora bicolor,
T. fusca, Stereum bicolor,
S. fuscum, S. coffeatum,
S. pannosum, and S. laxum.

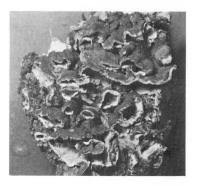

Genus PENIOPHORA

Approximately 100 species have been described in
this genus, many of them probably identifiable only by those
who named and described them. Only a single common
species is included here.

PENIOPHORA GIGANTEA.   Fruit body a thin, entirely re-
                            supinate crust on the under
side of logs of conifer trees that still retain their bark, especially common on logs of red pine (Pinus resinosa), circular or oval, 5-15 cm. in diameter, 2 mm. or less thick,
light tan color, easily peeled from the bark.

Genus THELEPHORA

Some 75 species have been described in the genus,
many of them widely distributed and a few of them uncom-
mon.

Key to Species of Thelephora

1.   Fruit body with short stem or stemlike base and a thin
        spreading cap shaped like a shallow, much-torn-and-
        slashed funnel - - T. anthocephala.
     Fruit body with partly circular shelves arising one above
        the other from a thick central portion - - 2

2.   Fruit body 1-3 cm. high with few shelves
     - - T. fimbriata
     Fruit body 3-8 cm. high, with several to many shelves
     - - T. terrestris.

Description of Species of Thelephora

1.   THELEPHORA ANTHO-
     CEPHALA.

Fruit body 2-4 cm. wide, 3-
5 cm. high, with short central
stem, the cap consisting of
repeatedly divided flat strips
or branches, light to medium
brown in color, the tips of
the branches lighter or almost white, the whole plant
rather tough, but pliable.

2.   THELEPHORA FIMBRIATA.   Fruit bodies 1-3 cm.
                                high, growing up around
the stems of small plants or of twigs, with a few irregular
flat branches growing out from the central portion, medium
to dark brown.

3.   THELEPHORA TERRES-
     TRIS.

Fruit body irregular vase-
shaped, with concentrically
arranged shelves growing out
one above the other, 2-5 cm.
wide, 3-8 cm. high, reddish
brown to dark brown, tough
and pliable in texture.
Usually in groups on sandy
ground in conifer woods.

Genus TREMELLODENDRON

     The genus includes 8 or 9 species, all restricted to
North America; the single species here described is widely
distributed and common.

TREMELLODENDRON PALLIDUM.

Fruit body a dense mass of
rather flat upright branches,
the entire mass 2-5 cm. in
diameter and 3-4 cm. high,
white, individual branches 3-
8 mm. wide at the widest
portion, some of them
branched at least once, fleshy
tough in texture. On the
ground in woods. Superficially
this fungus resembles members of the Clavariaceae, and it
is a common error to try to find a description of it among
species of that family.

Genus STEREUM

According to "A Dictionary of the Fungi" by Ainsworth
and Bisby, 100 species have been described in the genus
Stereum.   Sixteen species are included in the monograph by
Lentz, cited above.

Key to Species of Stereum

1. Fruit bodies small, flat, gray, round or polygonal lumps
       on oak wood - - S. frustulatum
    Fruit bodies effused-reflexed or shelflike - - 2

2. On branches, trunks, or logs of conifers
       - - S. sanguinolentum
    On hardwoods - - 3

3. Fruit body mostly resupinate, shelves narrow, rather
       thick, surface dark brown - - S. murraii
    Fruit body effused reflexed or shelflike, shelves thin,
       surface gray to yellow brown - - 4

4. Surface of shelves gray, covered with coarse hair,
       shelves usually not densely imbricate - - S. hirsutum
    Surface of shelves yellow to brown, not coarsely hairy,
       shelves usually densely imbricate - - 5

5. Upper surface of shelves zoned, fuzzy, hymenial surface
        light tan - - S. gausapatum
    Upper surface of shelves not zoned, hymenial surface
        with tinge of lavender - - S. purpureum

Description of Species of Stereum

STEREUM FRUSTULATUM.

Fruit bodies small, flat, round
or polygonal grayish lumps,
2-5 mm. in diameter and 1-2
mm. thick, very hard in texture, usually in groups of
from several dozen to several
hundred, on the surface of
wood (never on bark) of stumps
and logs mainly of oak, in
which it causes a white pocket
rot.

STEREUM GAUSAPATUM.

Fruit bodies usually effused
reflexed or of shelves nar-
rowed to a stemlike base, imbricate with several to many
fruit bodies in a clump, the margins of the shelves very
wavy, upper surface definitely zoned, fuzzy or hairy, tan
to yellowish brown, hymenial surface light tan. On logs,
stumps, posts and timbers of trees, especially oaks. This
species is one of the major causes of heartrot of living oaks
in stands where the trees have grown up as sprouts from the
stumps of a previous stand.

STEREUM HIRSUTUM.

Fruit body shelflike or effused
reflexed, the appressed or re-
supinate portion 5-10 cm. or more long, the shelves projecting 2-3 cm., upper surface gray to yellowish brown,
covered with dense and rather coarse hair, with several
broad concentric zones or ridges, the margin wavy, sometimes extremely so, hymenial surface tan, often darker
toward the margin. On logs of hardwood trees.

STEREUM MURRAYI.

Fruit bodies mostly resupinate but with a reflexed margin projecting as much as 1
cm. , individual fruit bodies
2-10 cm. long, but adjacent
ones may coalesce to form a
crust of greater length, 2-3
mm. thick, the hymenial surface light tan in color, the upper side of the reflexed shelves
dark brown, often with irregular concentric ridges and
radial folds, sometimes overgrown with moss. On logs of
hardwoods, especially birch.

STEREUM PURPUREUM.   Fruit body effused-reflexed,
the resupinate portion 4-6
cm. wide, the shelves often imbricate, each shelf 1-3 cm.
wide and projecting 1-1.5 cm. , the upper surface light yellowish brown or slightly darker, the hymenial surface tan
with a lavender or purple tinge, smooth, and with a waxy
appearance when fresh. On logs and wood of hardwoods; it
sometimes invades living trees of apples, plums, and their
relatives and causes a fatal disease known as "silver leaf",
so named from the silvery appearance of the leaves of af-
fected trees.

STEREUM SANGUINOLENTUM.   Fruit body effused-re-
flexed, the resupinate
or appressed portion 5-10 cm. long, although adjacent
fruit bodies may coalesce to form a still larger crust, the
reflexed portion projecting 1-1.5 cm. , the shelves sometimes imbricate, the upper surface covered with fine hairs
toward the margin and with coarse hairs toward the base,
with indistinct zones, yellowish brown, the hymenial surface medium brown. On the wood of conifers, especially
balsam fir and white pine; the fungus invades living trees
of these species through pruning or other wounds that expose the heartwood, and causes a rather distinctive decay
known as "redheart" which has been responsible for heavy
losses in some forests, especially those carefully managed,
in which branches large enough to have heartwood have been
pruned off, exposing heartwood through which this fungus
invades the trunk of the tree.

GASTROMYCETALES

PUFFBALLS AND RELATIVES

The name Gastromycetales means "stomach fungi", and was given to this group because some of the common puffballs suggest the shape of a stomach. The puffballs are among the best of the edible fungi, and some of them are among the easiest fungi to recognize. At one time the spore mass of ripe puffballs was used to stop bleeding, and while it had none of the efficacy of a modern hemostatic it probably was of some good by virtue of its powdery nature which exposed a large surface area and caused quick clotting, and at least the spores of a fresh puffball would be relatively free of filth and bacteria, which is probably more than can be said of many medical materials of a few hundred years ago. There is a common superstition that the spores from puffballs will cause blindness if got into the eyes in quantity, but this has no basis in fact. Those who wish to explore the group more thoroughly are referred to "The Gastromycetes of Iowa" by Paul E. Kambly and Robert E. Lee, published by the University of Iowa, Iowa City, Iowa, as Studies in Natural History, Vol. 17, No. 4; and to "The Gastromycetes of the Eastern United States and Canada" by W. C. Coker and John N. Couch, published in 1928 by the University of North Carolina Press, Chapel Hill, North Carolina.

Keys to the Families of Gastromycetales

1. Fruit body consisting of a stalk with a slimy, evil smelling mass of spores at the top - - Phallaceae (Stink Horns)
   Fruit bodies small, usually not more than 1 cm. in diameter and 2 cm. high, shaped like a cup or the flaring mouth of a trumpet, containing several tiny egg like bodies - - Nidulariaceae (Birds Nest Fungi)

Fruit body spherical or pear shaped, solid and white
inside when young, at maturity the interior filled with
a brown or purple mass of spores - - 2

2. Fruit body with a stalk extending through the interior
from bottom to top - - Secotiaceae
Fruit body without a stalk extending through the interior
- - 3 (Puffballs)

3. Fruit body at first subterranean, very hard and firm
when young with a thick, leathery outer rind
- - Sclerodermataceae
Fruit body firm but soft, with a thin outer wall
- - Lycoperdaceae

FAMILY LYCOPERDACEAE

Keys to the Genera of the Family Lycoperdaceae

1. Wall of the upper part of the fruit body breaking up and
disappearing at maturity, exposing the spore mass
- - Calvatia
Spores escaping through a pore formed at the top of the
fruit body at maturity - - 2

2. Outer wall at maturity splitting into star like rays and
folding back - - Geaster
Outer wall not splitting into rays - - 3

3. Fruit body tapering toward the base, base composed of
spongy mycelium that does not form spores
- - Lycoperdon
Fruit body spherical and without a sterile base
- - Bovista

Genus BOVISTA

Key to Species of Bovista

1. Fruit bodies 2-4 cm. in diameter - - B. plumbea
Fruit bodies 5-10 cm. in diameter - - B. pila

Description of Species of Bovista

1. BOVISTA PILA.   Edible. Fruit body globose or nearly so, 4-12 cm. in diameter, outer layer at first white and smooth, at maturity scaling off and exposing the inner wall that is smooth, shiny, rather firm, brown with inconspicuous mottled gray patches. It opens at first by a small irregular pore at the top, and this may be enlarged further by cracking or tearing of the wall so that the opening finally is irregular. The spore mass at maturity is deep brown. The fruit bodies are attached to the ground by a small cord of mycelium that usually breaks at maturity and if the fruit bodies are in exposed places they may be rolled about by the wind, shedding their spores as they roll. Solitary or scattered on the ground in pastures and grassy places. The fruit bodies are rather durable, and may be found in good condition nearly a year after they appear.

2. BOVISTA PLUMBEA.   Edible. Fruit body spherical or nearly so, 2-3 cm. in diameter, surface first white and mealy, later the outer layer cracks off and exposes the inner wall which is firm, shiny and gray to gray brown. An almost circular, regular pore is formed at the top. The base is attached to a clump of fibrous mycelium and usually does not break away, as does Bovista pila. Spore mass at maturity dark brown. Scattered on the ground in grassy places.

Genus CALVATIA

Key to Species of Calvatia

1. Fruit body almost spherical, sterile base inconspicuous or absent, mature spore mass greenish yellow, plants 15 cm. or more in diameter - - C. maxima
    Fruit body with a thick, tapering base composed of spongy mycelium, distinct from the spore bearing part above - - 2

2. Spore mass at maturity dark purple - - C. cyathiformis
    Spore mass at maturity dark brown - - C. elata
    Spore mass olive yellow - - 3

3. Irregular polygonal warty patches formed on the outer
        wall toward maturity - - C. caelata
    Outer wall smooth - - C. craniformis

Description of Species of Calvatia

1. CALVATIA CAELATA.   Edible.   Fruit bodies 5-12
                            cm. wide, 6-14 cm. tall,
typically with an almost spherical top and a cylindrical or
tapering stalk.   Surface white when young, later pale yellow
or brown, divided on top into regular patches formed, in

some specimens, by the tips of spines being united, and, in
other specimens, merely by cracks in the superficial layer.
Interior at first white, the spore bearing portion distinct
from the sterile base even while both still are white, because the base is spongy with small but obvious chambers,
while the portion in which the spores later will be formed
is uniform in texture and quite smooth.   Spore mass becoming first yellow, then chocolate brown.   The odor of
recently mature specimens is somewhat aromatic, and is
characteristic of the species.   The cup shaped base often
remains on the ground over winter.   Solitary or scattered
on the ground in pastures, grassy places and open woods,
sometimes in cultivated fields.

2. CALVATIA CRANIFORMIS.   Edible. Fruit body
rounded or spherical at
the top, usually with a definite, tapering, stalklike base, 5-
14 cm. in diameter at the top, surface at first smooth and
pale tan or grayish, becoming inconspicuously scaly at maturity, the entire upper part breaking away in flakes at maturity. Spore mass yellowish green at maturity. The
stalklike base is composed of spongy mycelium and has a
structure suggesting that of a honeycomb. It may remain
in place for a long time after the spores have been blown
away, in the manner of Calvatia cyathiformis, from which
it may be distinguished by the greenish yellow spores. On
the ground in grassy places and open woods.

3. CALVATIA CYATHIFORMIS.   Edible. Fruit bodies
6-15 cm. in diameter,
varying from nearly spherical to flattened or irregularly
puckered, usually with a tapering stemlike base. The surface of the upper portion is typically brown, but varies
from tan to brown, and often has a tint of lilac or purple.
As the fruit body grows this outermost layer cracks, forming a multitude of small, irregular thin patches separated
from each other by the slightly paler under layer. At maturity the spores are dark purple brown. Most of the wall
of the upper part of the fruit body breaks away irregularly,
leaving the cup shaped base. In groups and often in fairy
rings in grassy places and fields.

4. CALVATIA ELATA.   Fruit body with a spherical or
flattened head 3-6 cm. wide
upon a tapering stemlike base 4-8 cm. long and 2-4 cm.
thick at the top; surface of head white when young, tan to
brown when old, the wall of the upper part cracking into
fragments and falling away at maturity, exposing the brown
spores. Solitary or scattered on the ground.

5. CALVATIA MAXIMA.   Edible. Fruit body globose or
nearly so, sometimes greater
in height than width, 15-60 cm. wide, surface smooth,
white when fresh, becoming tan to brown in age, wall breaking up irregularly and falling away at maturity, exposing the
brown spores. Interior white and solid when young, changing to yellowish green, then olive brown. Sometimes there
is an inconspicuous sterile portion at the base. In grassy
places, pastures, and fields. Specimens of this fungus
weighing 45 pounds have been found, and the writer has seen
one approximately 2 feet in diameter.

Genus GEASTER

Key to Species of Geaster

1. Rays folding up over the spore sack when dry
    - - G. mammosus
    Rays remaining curved down when dry - - 2

2. Base of mature plant cup shaped and enclosing the lower
    half of the spore bearing sack - - G. fimbriatus (In
    G. triplex the inner part of the outer wall often re-
    mains as a cup about the base of the sack)
    Base of mature plant not cup shaped - - 3

3. Base of mature plant hollow, formed by the expansion
    of a double wall - - 4
    Base not hollow - - 5

4. Area around the pore distinct in texture and often in
    color - - G. limbatus
    Area around the pore not distinct - - G. rufescens

5. Area around the pore outlined by a groove or ridge,
    spore sack with a narrow stalk - - G. coronatus
    Area around the pore not outlined by a groove or ridge,
    spore sack not stalked - - G. triplex

Description of Species of Geaster

1. GEASTER CORONATUS.   Spore sac 6-12 mm. wide,
                               10-15 mm. high, elongate
oval, pointed above, tan to brown, with a short but definite
stalk 1-2 mm. long and about 2 mm. in diameter, the mouth
area grayish, silky, outlined
by a narrow ridge. The outer
wall splits to the base into 4-
8 (usually 4-5) long, narrow
rays that at maturity extend
almost straight down, lifting
the spore sac above the leaf
mold on which it is borne.
The exposed surface of the
recurved rays at first is nearly white, but becomes brown
when old. Often leaves or
other debris between the tips
of the recurved rays are bound

together by a delicate weft of mycelium that formed the outer covering of the unexpanded plant. Solitary or in groups of 2 or 3 on the ground in woods.

2. GEASTER FIMBRIATUS.   Fruit body 2-3 cm. wide when expanded, spore sac 1-1.5 cm. wide, almost spherical, pale brown when fresh, darker when old, the mouth elevated, area surrounding the mouth slightly paler than the rest of the surface but without a distinct border. Outer wall splitting 1/2 the way to the bottom into 5-8 rays, the points of which curl under and remain so, the exposed surface of the recurved rays pale tan. In spite of the specific name, the mouth is no more fringed or fimbriate than in other species. Usually in groups on the ground or leaf mold in forests.

3. GEASTER LIMBATUS.   Fruit body at first rounded below and somewhat pointed above, 2-3 cm. in diameter, outer surface grayish brown or brown, splitting into 5-8 pointed rays that fold back as in Geaster triplex. Spore chamber grayish brown or brown, smooth, shiny, with a definite round pore, the base often stalklike. The base of the plant, below the spore sac or chamber, is hollow and the walls expand to form a bladder-like structure that serves to raise the spore chamber off the ground. Spore mass dark brown. Scattered or in groups on the ground in moist woods.

4. GEASTER MAMMOSUS.   Spore chamber almost spherical, 1-2 cm. wide, grayish brown when fresh, darker when old, the mouth area silky and paler than the rest of the surface. Outer wall splitting into 7-10 rays of unequal size, the rays recurved when moist, returning to their original position about the spore chamber when dry, grayish brown when fresh, dark brown when old. The hygroscopic character of the rays serves to distinguish this species readily, but moist specimens must be dried somewhat before this becomes evident. Solitary or scattered on the ground in woods and fields.

5. GEASTER RUFESCENS.   Fruit body at first subterranean, spherical or nearly so, not pointed at the top, appearing above the surface of the soil only after the outer layer has split into sections, outer wall up to 5 mm. thick, splitting only half way to the bottom into 7-10 rays which curve downward. The unsplit

portion of the base forms a hollow structure below the spore chamber, as in Geaster Limbatus. Spore chamber gray or brown, delicately granular, often with a short stalklike base. Spore mass dark brown. Solitary or scattered on the ground. The very thick outer wall should serve to distinguish it from closely related species.

6. GEASTER TRIPLEX. Spore chamber almost spherical, 2-4 cm. in diameter, pale grayish brown when fresh, brown to reddish brown when old, the pore or opening in the top surrounded by a light colored, silky shining area 5-12 mm. in diameter, the margin of the pore projecting upward and fringed. Outer wall splitting almost to the base into 6-8 rays that in wet weather or when moistened curl down so that the points meet or are inrolled beneath the center of the fruit body. Sometimes an inner part of the wall remains as a cup around the lower part of the spore chamber. Outer surface of the wall dark brown, usually splitting or cracking longitudinally. When fresh the exposed part of the recurved rays is pale brown and smooth or concentrically cracked. In groups on the ground in woods, often around old stumps.

Genus LYCOPERDON

Key to Species of Lycoperdon

1. Growing on stumps and logs, usually in clumps, surface
       at first covered with scattered spines - - L. pyriforme
     Growing on the ground, surface at first densely spiny
       - - 2

2. Tips of numerous spines united with each other - - 3
     Tips of spines not united - - 4

3. Spore mass at maturity olive brown, spines 1-1.5 mm.
   long - - L. peckii
   Spore mass dark purple brown, spines 2-5 mm. long
   - - L. pulcherrimum

4. Spines minute, of uniform size - - L. umbrinum
   Spines of various sizes intermixed with warts
   - - L. gemmatum

Description of Species of Lycoperdon

1. LYCOPERDON GEMMATUM.   Edible. Fruit body
                            with a spherical or
rounded top, tapering gradually or sharply to a definite,
stalklike base, 3-6 cm. wide, 4-7 cm. high, surface first
white, later brown, top at first densely covered with a mix-
ture of numerous short spines and warts and less numerous
long spines which are smaller toward the base of the plant.
The longer spines usually are shed at maturity, leaving
characteristic smooth patches on the top of the fruit body;
the short spines usually persist. Spore mass at maturity
yellowish olive brown or dark brown with a purple tinge.
Singly or scattered on the ground or on very rotten wood.

2. LYCOPERDON PECKII.

Edible. Fruit body with an
almost spherical head 2-4 cm.
in diameter and a tapering base
1-2 cm. long, surface covered
with fine white tapering spines
1-1.5 mm. long, the tips of
adjacent spines united. At
maturity the spines become
tan to brown and fall off, leaving a smooth brown inner wall.
The spore mass is first white, then greenish yellow, finally
olive brown. On the ground in woods.

3. LYCOPERDON PULCHERRIMUM.   Edible. Fruit
                                body spherical or
with a tapering stalklike base, 2-5 cm. in diameter, surface first densely covered with tapering spines up to 8 mm.
long, the tips of which are united, white when young, later
pale tan. When the fruit bodies are mature this coating of
spines is shed from the rounded upper part, exposing the

smooth, shiny, brown or purple brown wall of the spore
chamber. Spores at maturity olive brown or dark purple
brown. Almost mature plants, when broken, have a distinct
aromatic odor. Usually solitary, on the ground in woods
and fields.

4. LYCOPERDON PYRIFORME.   Edible. Fruit body
                             pear shape, with a
rounded top and tapering stem, 2-4 cm. wide, 3-5 cm. high,
surface white when young, later tan, then dark grayish
brown, at first covered with very short spines and warts
which later disappear. Spore mass dark olive brown at maturity. White strands of mycelium extend from the base of
the fruit bodies into the decaying wood on which they grow.
Usually in dense clumps on decaying wood and at the base
of decaying trees.

5. LYCOPERDON UMBRINUM.   Fruit body with a globose
                            or flattened top that ta-
pers rather abruptly to the stem, 2-4 cm. wide, 3-5 cm.
high, stem 1-2 cm. long, surface of top covered with spines
1-2 mm. long that first are white and later become brown.
Spore mass at maturity golden brown or dark brown, rarely
with a tinge of purple. Solitary or scattered on the ground
in woods.

FAMILY SCLERODERMATACEAE

Only a single genus and species is here considered,
Scleroderma vulgare. Fruit bodies spherical, 2-5 cm. in
diameter, at first white, later brown, the wall thick and
leathery. The interior is first white, very firm and hard,
and when young the numerous spore producing chambers
are definitely outlined; at maturity the interior is filled
with a mass of purple black spores; there is no regular
opening, the fungus apparently depending on insects or ani-
mals to distribute the spores. Often the fruit bodies are at
first formed just beneath the surface of the soil, and become visible only as they enlarge. The fruit body is attached
to the soil by a rather dense tuft of coarse mycelium. There
are several closely related species of Scleroderma, some
of which are said to be poisonous. The present species is
found most frequently under oaks, and may be rather common in lawns where oak trees grow.

FAMILY SECOTIACEAE

This family contains a single genus, Secotium, of which there is only a single species, Secotium agaricoides. Fruit body irregularly conical or somewhat heart shaped, 3-6 cm. in diameter at the base, 4-10 cm. high, surface at first silky white toward maturity becoming pale tan, the outer layer breaking up to form rectangular, concentrically arranged, flat scales that gradually disappear toward the top. The wall is 2-3 mm. thick and rather firm. Stem short and pointed, terminating in a strand of mycelium 2-3 mm. thick. The stem extends up through the interior of the fruit body and is continuous with the outer wall at the top; stem 6-12 mm. in diameter near the top, larger toward the base, soft and fibrous. At maturity the wall splits away from the stem at the base, thus allowing the spores to fall out. The spore mass at first is white, later becomes yellow and finally dark yellowish brown. The spore chamber contains many plate-like walls that are most apparent when the plants are mature. Odor of ripe specimens rather sweet and pleasant. Usually in groups or dense clumps in pastures. At least one of the older mushroom books states that this fungus is suspected of being poisonous, but one of the writer's correspondents who had sent in a number of them for identification stated, "If they are poisonous we have all been dead for 6 weeks." They had been eating them in quantity for some time, and from this evidence it seems likely that the species is edible.

FAMILY NIDULARIACEAE

Key to the Genera of Nidulariaceae

1. Fruit body cup shaped, or cylindrical with a rounded base - - Crucibulum vulgare
    Fruit body narrowed toward the base, the top flaring, like the mouth of a trumpet - - Cyathus

Genus CRUCIBULUM

CRUCIBULUM VULGARE.   Fruit body cupshaped or almost cylindrical with a rounded base, 8-12 mm. high, 4-8 mm. wide, outer surface at first covered with velvety, light brown hair, later glabrous or nearly so, pale brown or gray. The top at first covered with velvety, light brown hair, later glabrous or nearly so, pale brown or gray.

The top at first is rounded and as this expands a hairy, pale brown membrane is exposed, which covers the spore masses. This membrane soon ruptures and exposes another, very delicate, white membrane which also soon breaks and disappears. The inner wall of the cup is smooth, sometimes shiny, pale silvery gray. Spore chambers 1-2 mm. across, at first white, later often brown. Usually scattered or in fairly dense groups on rotten wood, twigs, or plant debris, rarely on the dead outer bark of living trees.

Key to Species of Cyathus

1. Interior of the fruit body longitudinally striate
        - - C. striatus
    Interior not striate, outer wall covered with coarse hair
        when specimens are young, later it becomes almost
        smooth - - C. stercoreus and C. vernicosus

Description of Species of Cyathus

1. CYATHUS STERCOREUS AND CYATHUS VERNICOSUS.

Fruit body shaped like an inverted cone with a flaring mouth, 5-12 mm. high, 4-8 mm. wide at the top, tapering down to a narrow stalk, outer surface tan or grayish brown and covered with coarse hair when young, almost black and sometimes glabrous when old, inner surface pale or dark gray, smooth, top at first rounded and closed, expanding to expose a delicate membrane stretched across the opening; this membrane soon breaks, exposing a cluster of black, flattened spore balls, most of which are attached to the base of the cup by an elastic strand of mycelium, although some may be quite loose. In groups, often of several dozen to several hundred specimens, on manured ground, plant debris and rotten wood. The two species here described together can be separated with certainty only by the use of microscopic characters.

2. CYATHUS STRIATUS.   Fruit body shaped like an inverted, flaring cone, 8-16 mm. high, 6-10 mm. wide at the top, narrowed at the base to a stem. Outer surface brown or blackish brown, at first covered with coarse hair, later glabrous; inner surface gray to dark grayish brown, with distinct, regular striations running downward from the mouth. Spore chambers 1.5-2 mm. in diameter, round, flattened, grayish brown, each one attached to the base of the cup by an elastic strand of mycelium that, when moist, will stretch for several centimeters. The young plant, like that of the species described above, has a rounded top that, as it expands, exposes a white

membrane covering the spore balls. Auxiliary spores, conidia, are formed on the surface of this membrane and dispersed by the wind before the membrane breaks and disappears. Scattered or in groups on twigs, plant debris and wood.

FAMILY PHALLACEAE - STINK HORNS

The stink horns and some closely related fungi produce spherical or oval eggshaped structures beneath the surface of the soil; the plant develops within this structure, protected from drying out and from injury by the thick outer wall of the "egg" and a thick layer of gelatinous material just inside the wall. When the spores are almost mature, the stem elongates rapidly, rupturing the tough wall of the egg, and the cap, covered with a mass of gooey, ill smelling material in which the spores are borne, is raised up into the air.   The evil odor of the material in which the spores are imbedded is very attractive to some kinds of flies, especially those associated with carrion.   These flies wallow about in this material, and presumably carry the spores to places where the fungus can survive and grow.

Key to the Family Phallaceae

1. Spores borne on the narrowed tip of the stalk, not on a
        special cap like structure - - Mutinus revenelii
    Spores borne on a definite cap like structure at the top
        of the stalk - - 2

2. A flaring, pendulous, netted veil extending below the
        edge of the cap - - Dictyophora duplicata
    Veil not extending below the edge of the cap - - 3

3. Surface of the cap chambered - - Ithyphallus impudicus
    Surface of cap smooth or granular
        - - Ithyphallus ravenelii

Description of Species of Phallaceae

1. DICTYOPHORA DUPLICATA.   Stalk 10-15 cm. long,
                                 3-4 cm. thick, cylin-
drical or nearly so, tapering at the tip and the base, white, hollow and with an opening at the tip into the hollow; cap conical to almost globose, 3-5 cm. high, surface of the cap covered with angular, shallow, thinwalled chambers each 4-6 mm. in diameter, covered with olive brown, very evil smelling slime, joined to the top of the stem by a rounded collar.   A netlike veil is attached to the tip of the stalk beneath the cap and hangs down against the stem or flares out below the lower edge of the cap for 3-4 cm.   Solitary or more often in groups above decaying roots of trees.

2. ITHYPHALLUS IMPUDICUS.   Stalk 10-15 cm. long,
                                 2-3 cm. in diameter,
white, brittle, hollow, tapering almost to a point at both the upper and lower ends, cap attached to the tip and hanging down about 3 cm., the surface with conspicuous polygonal chambers from 4-10 mm. in diameter.   Spore mass dark olive brown and very evil smelling.   The species is

distinguished from Dictyophora duppicata by its lack of a
veil beneath the cap, and from Ithyphallus revenelii by the
chambered surface of the cap.

3.   ITHYPHALLUS RAVENELII.   Stalk 10-15 cm. long,
                                 2-3 cm. in diameter,
white, brittle, hollow, composed of several layers of chambers, tapering at the tip and base, the cap conical, 2-3 cm.
long, surface of the cap rough but not chambered.   Spore
mass dark olive brown and evil smelling.   A thin veil is
present beneath the cap but does not extend beyond the lower
margin of the cap.   Solitary or scattered above decaying
wood and rotten roots of trees, common in lawns and gardens, occasional on sawdust piles.   This stinkhorn sometimes is so abundant in lawns and gardens as to constitute
a minor nuisance, especially to those who think that every-
thing strange is to be feared.

4.   M. RAVENELII.   Stalk 1 - 1.5 cm. in diameter, 8-12
                        cm. tall, fragile, rather bright red
just below the cap, paler toward the bottom, top tapered to
a point and covered with a brown, very ill-smelling mass
of spores.   Scattered on the ground in lawns and gardens,
but not common.

TREMELLALES

JELLY FUNGI

This group of fungi were so named because some of them, when moist, have a consistency suggesting jelly, although it frequently is a decidedly tough jelly. Most of them grow on wood and only one of them, so far as is known, is good to eat. They are taken up in detail in "Revision of the North Central Tremellales" by G. W. Martin, University of Iowa Studies in Natural History Vol. 19, No. 3, 1952; available from the Dept. of Publications, University of Iowa, Iowa City.

Key to Tremellales

1. Fruit body black, tough-gelatinous, irregularly convoluted, 1-2 cm. in diameter - - Exidia glandulosa
   Fruit body pear-shaped, tough, 3-5 cm. wide, common on old logs - - Hirneola auricula-judae
   Fruit body yellow, very gelatinous, translucent, 1-5 cm. in diameter, hemispherical or irregular - - Tremella lutescens
   Fruit body white, gelatinous, 1-5 cm. in diameter, hemispherical or irregular - - Tremella albida
   Fruit bodies golden yellow, upright, pointed stalks - - Calocera cornea

Description of Species of Tremellales

1. CALOCERA CORNEA.

Fruit bodies consisting of upright unbranched or rarely branched stalks, each 8-15 mm. high, 2-4 mm. thick, golden yellow, hard and brittle when dry, firm gelatinous

when moist.   In groups or clusters on the bark or wood of
fallen trees.

2. EXIDIA GLANDULOSA.   Fruit body 1-2 cm. wide,
                             irregularly circular in out-
line, lying flat on the surface of branches or trunks of fallen
trees, convex above, the surface convoluted with narrow
ridges, jet black, shrinking to a flat membrane when dry.
Usually in groups on hardwoods.

3. HIRNEOLA AURICULA-JUDAE.   Edible.   Fruit body
                             3-7 cm. wide, al-
most flat or shallow cup shape or like an ear, the surface
often with several rounded ridges, tan to brown, hard and
leathery when dry, flexible when moist.   On branches and
trunks of fallen trees, often in groups.

4. TREMELLA LUTESCENS.   Fruit bodies 1-3 cm. wide,
                             irregularly hemispherical,
convoluted, translucent golden yellow when fresh and moist,
paler when old.   Solitary or scattered on branches and
trunks of dead trees.

ASCOMYCETES

CUP FUNGI AND RELATIVES

There are a considerable number of genera of fleshy Ascomycetes, and some of these contain a large number of species, of which only the more common are included here. For a more detailed account of these fungi the reader is referred to the two books by F. J. Seaver, "The North American Cup Fungi", one volume dealing with the "Operculates" and the other with the "Inoperculates".

Keys to Families, Genera, and Species of Ascomycetes

1. Fruit bodies fleshy or leathery - - 2
   Fruit bodies hard and woody, solid, black when mature, growing on the branches, trunks, or roots or living or recently dead trees, or black or colored and growing from scale insects or insect larvae - - 4

2. Fruit body cup or disc shaped, stalked or sessile - - Pezizaceae

   Fruit body bell or saddle shaped or conical, stem distinct from the cap - - Helvellaceae
   Fruit body spathulate - - 3

3. Entire fruit body black - - Geoglossum

   Top of fruit body yellow, stem tan or white - - Spathularia

   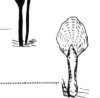

4. Fruit bodies stalked, slender,
   finger like - - Xylaria
   polymorpha (on wood)..

   Cordyceps (on insects)..

5. Fruit bodies hemispherical, the interior divided into concentric
   zones, on dead trees and wood
   - - Daldinia concentrica ....

   Fruit bodies irregular, on the
   branches of living cherries
   and plums
   - - Dibotryon morbosum ....

Genera of the Family Helvellaceae

1. Surface of the pileus with prominent irregular ridges that
   give a sponge like appearance
   to the cap - - Morchella.............................

   Surface of the pileus smooth or
   with slight convolutions
   - - Verpa...

   Pileus saddle shaped or irregularly
   globose, smooth or convoluted
   - - Helvella ....

Descriptions of Genera and Species of Ascomycetes

MISCELLANEOUS ASCOMYCETES

1. CORDYCEPS.   Fruit bodies various colors, but the
                 common species bright orange red,
3-5 cm. high, up to 5 mm. in diameter near the top, club
shape with a tapering stem, the entire surface of the club

covered with pimple like
projections, which are the
snouts of the cavities in
which the spores are borne
and from which the spores
are forcibly expelled. Singly
or in clumps of 2 to 5, arising from insects in ground or
decayed wood.

2. DALDINIA CONCENTRICA.

Fruit body hemispherical to
almost spherical, 1-4 cm. in
diameter, first brown, later
black, the interior composed
of a series of concentric
zones and very brittle in texture. Solitary or scattered
on decaying wood. Fruit bodies of this fungus taken into
the laboratory and kept in a
moderately humid air will
discharge its black spores in
quantity, usually only at
night, every night for a week
or more.

3. DIBOTRYON MORBOSUM.

Fruit body surrounding the
twigs of Prunus, black, up
to 20 cm. long, 1-2 cm.
thick, first brown, later
black, the interior brittle.

4. GEOGLOSSUM.

Fruit body consisting of a
stem 2-4 cm. long, 2-4 mm.
thick, and a flattened oval
head pointed or rounded at
the top, black, flexible and
rather tough in texture. In
groups on decaying stumps
of trees.

5. LEOTIA LUBRICA.

Cap irregularly hemispherical, translucent yellow or yellowish green, surface covered with wartlike humps, 2-12 mm. wide, sticky or slimy; stem 2-5 cm. long, 2-5 mm. thick, cylindrical, hollow, continuous with and colored like the cap. In dense clumps of up to 50 or more specimens on the ground or on very rotten wood.

6. SPATHULARIA FLAVIDA.

Fruit body shaped somewhat like a broad tipped, narrow handled spatula, cap rather fan shaped, 2-3 cm. wide, 3-5 mm. thick, yellow and fleshy; stem white or tan, 2-3 cm. long, 3-6 mm. thick, solid. Usually in groups under conifer trees.

7. XYLARIA POLYMORPHA.

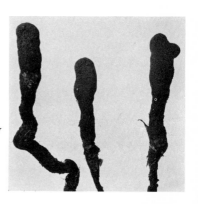

Fruit body with an irregularly cylindrical or fingerlike head that tapers gradually into a stem, the head 4-8 cm. long, 0.5-2 cm. thick, often flattened, grayish and somewhat fleshy when young, soon woody and black, the surface roughened by the tips of the spore-producing cavities which can be easily seen if the surface is cut off with a sharp knife. Stem 4-8 cm. long, 5-10 mm. thick, tapering downward, sometimes branched. Usually in groups of several on decaying wood.

Genus HELVELLA
Key to Species of Helvella

1. Stem ridged - - 2
   Stem even or pitted - - 3

2.   Cap and stem white or pale tan - - H. crispa
     Cap dark brown, stem paler - - H. mitra

3.   Stem 1 cm. or more in diameter, surface of cap very
        much convoluted - - H. infula
     Stem not over 7 mm. in diameter, surface of cap smooth
        or nearly so - - 4

4.   Cap and stem black - - H. atra
     Cap tan to black, stem paler - - H. elastica

Description of Species of Helvella

1. HELVELLA ATRA.   Cap irregularly saddle shape,
                                surface even, black or nearly so,
margin lobed, under surface dark brown. Stem 3-5 cm.
long, 3-4 mm. thick, whitish at the base, otherwise black,
enlarged at the base. Solitary or scattered on the ground
in woods.

2. HELVELLA CRISPA.

Cup saddle shape, smooth or
irregularly wrinkled and
lobed, 2-5 cm. wide, white
or pale tan, margin entirely
free. Stem 3-6 cm. long,
1-2 cm. thick, with prominent
branched ridges, straight or
slightly curved. Usually in
groups of 2-6 on moist ground
in woods.

3.   HELVELLA ELASTICA.   Cap irregularly saddle
                                shape, surface even, brown
to black, margin free from the stem, sometimes lobed.
Stem 4-8 cm. long, 3-7 mm. thick, tan, smooth. Scattered or solitary on the ground in woods.

4. HELVELLA INFULA.   Cap 5-10 cm. wide, irregu-
                                larly spherical or somewhat
saddle shaped, very much convoluted, reddish brown or
dark brown. Stem 4-8 cm. long, 2-4 cm. thick, white or
tan, pitted but not ridged, hollow except at the base, very
brittle and fragile. Solitary or scattered on the ground in

woods. Seaver, in "North
American Cup Fungi (Oper-
culates)" considers Gyromitra
esculenta merely a form of
this species; by many it is
thought to be a very desirable
edible fungus, but it also has
been responsible for some
cases of fatal poisoning, and
therefore should not be eaten.

5. HELVELLA MITRA.   Cap irregularly saddle shape
                     and convoluted, 2-5 cm. wide,
dark brown, margin usually curved in and attached to the
stem in several places. Stem 5-10 cm. long, 1-2 cm.
thick, with prominent twisted and branched ridges, tan or
brown. Scattered on the ground in woods.

Genus MORCHELLA

All of the species of this genus are edible and many
consider them to be the choicest of the edible wild fungi.
Attempts have been made to cultivate them, so far without
success - the mycelium grows very readily in culture, but
fruit bodies are not produced.

Key to Species of Morchella

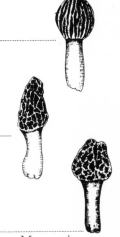

1. Margin of the cap free from
       the stem - - M. hybrida
    Margin of the cap attached
       to the stem - - 2

2. Ribs of cap thin, pits large
       and shallow, stem consider-
       ably enlarged at the base
       - - M. crassipes
    Ribs thick, pits small and
       deep, stem slightly or not
       at all enlarged - - 3

3. Cap subglobose or cylindrical,
       with a rounded top
       - - M. esculenta
       Cap conical, with a pointed top - - M. conica

Description of Species of Morchella

1. MORCHELLA CONICA.

Edible. Cap more or less
conical in shape, 4-8 cm.
high, 2-4 cm. wide at the
base, ridges and pits often
extending longitudinally, at
least more so than those of
Morchella esculenta, which
it most resembles. Stem 4-8
cm. long, 1-3 cm. thick,
white, cylindircal, hollow,
brittle. Scattered on the
ground in woods. This species grades into Morchella
esculenta and some authors
consider it to be only a variety of that species.

2. MORCHELLA CRASSIPES.

Edible. Cap irregularly
cylindrical or narrow
conical, 5-8 cm. high, 3-5 cm. wide at the base, tan or
pale brown, ribs irregularly branched, narrow, pits large
and shallow. Stem 5-10 cm. long, 2-3 cm. thick at the
top, enlarged at the base, white or pale tan, hollow, brittle. Scattered on the ground in woods.

3. MORCHELLA ESCULENTA.

Edible. Cap almost spher-
ical to irregularly oval,
usually rounded at the top,
not pointed as are those of
the other species, 4-8 cm.
high, 3-5 cm. wide at the
base, ridges irregularly
branched, pits rounded or
irregular, 5-10 mm. wide,
5-10 mm. deep, tan or brown.
Stem 4-8 cm. long, 1-3 cm.
thick, white, hollow, fragile.
Scattered on the ground in
woods, grassy places and
orchards.

4. MORCHELLA HYBRIDA.   Edible. Cap bell shape or
                                almost spherical, 2-3 cm.
vertically and horizontally, with longitudinal, branched
ridges, tan, margin of cap free from the stem. Stem 4-10
cm. long, 1-2 cm. thick, white, hollow, brittle, often enlarged at the base, attached to the inside of the cap half way
up from the margin to the top. Scattered on the ground in
woods.

Genus VERPA

Key to Species of Verpa

1. Cap with shallow vertical ribs
        - - V. bohemica ....

    Cap smooth or pitted
        - - V. conica ....

Description of Species of Verpa

1. VERPA BOHEMICA.   Edible. Cap 2-3 cm. long, 1-2
                                cm. wide, free from the stem,
tan or brown, conical or almost cylindrical, margin
slightly flaring and wavy, surface with low branched ridges
and shallow, irregular furrows, inside of cap white. Stem
4-8 cm. long, 10-15 mm. thick, white, smooth, cylindrical, hollow or filled with loose mycelium. Scattered on the
ground in woods.

2. VERPA CONICA.

Edible. Cap 1.5-2.5 cm.
high, 1-2 cm. wide, cylindrical with a rounded top or
conical, tan to brown, at first
smooth, soon with delicate
netlike ridges, the under side
of the cap white, margin often
flaring slightly and upturned
to show the white under side.
Stem 4-6 cm. long, 10-15

mm. thick, cylindrical, smooth or with scales arranged in partial circles around it. Scattered on the ground in woods.

FAMILY PEZIZACEAE

Key to the Genera of the Family Pezizaceae

1. Outer wall of fruit body thick and gelatinous
    - - Bulgaria inquinans
    Outer wall leathery or brittle, thin - - 2

2. Outer wall hairy - - 3
    Outer wall glabrous - - Peziza

3. Fruit body deep cut shaped, tapering to a stalk at the
    base - - 4
    Fruit body usually disc like, without a stalk - - 6

4. Growing attached to branches and twigs on the ground
    - - 5
    Growing on the ground, tan or
    brown in color - - Paxina

5. Inner surface red, outer sur-
    face white and hairy
    - - Sarcoscypha coccinea
    Entire fruit body dark brown
    - - Urnula craterium

6. Outer surface white, hairy - - Aleuria aurantia
    Outer surface dark brown, hairy - - Patella

ALEURIA AND PHAEOBULGARIA

1. ALEURIA AURANTIA.   Fruit body at first spherical, then becoming saucer shape, irregular in outline when old and often distorted by mutual pressure of adjacent specimens when many grow together, each fruit body 1-5 cm. wide, outer surface nearly white, covered with fine hair, inner surface bright orange when fresh, fading to pale yellowish orange. Usually in clusters on the ground in woods, fields, and lawns. Seaver, in "North American Cup Fungi (Operculates)" states, "- - it is one of the commonest and most widely distributed of the larger cup fungi, occurring from the Atlantic to the Pacific and probably throughout temperate North America as well as abroad."

2. PHAEOBULGARIA INQUINANS.   Fruit body at first
                                cup shape, later al-
most flat, 2-3 cm. in diameter, jet black, the outer wall
2-4 mm. thick, tough and elastic, gelatinous when moist,
thinner and pliable when dry, attached to the bark on which
it grows by a short stemlike base. When placed in a moist
chamber it will deposit an abundance of spores that are
black in mass. With only casual examination it could easily
be confused with a jelly fungus. On the bark of living trees
and on partially decayed wood.

Genus PATELLA

Key to Species of Patella

1. Inner surface white to brown - - Patella albida
    Inner surface red - - P. scutellata

Description of Species of Patella

1. PATELLA ALBIDA.   Fruit body at first spherical,
                        later deep or shallow cup shape,
1-3 cm. wide, 5-15 mm. deep, circular or irregular in
outline, outer surface brown and covered with bristlelike
hairs up to half a mm. long that form a fringe at the margin, inner surface at first white or nearly so, later becoming pale tan. Usually in groups on the ground or on very
rotten wood.

2. PATELLA SCUTELLATA.   Fruit body globose when
                           young, soon flat with an
upturned margin, 3-10 mm. wide, upper surface bright
orange red when fresh, fading to pale red or yellowish red
when old, lower surface dark brown, covered with bristly
hairs that reach a length of 1 mm. on the margin and form
a visible fringe. Commonly in groups on very decayed wood.

Genus PAXINA

Key to Species of Paxina

1. Outside of fruit body veined
        - - P. acetabulum ....
    Outside not veined - - 2

2.   Stem 3-4 cm. long, slender
       - - P. hispida
     Stem not over 1 cm. long,
        thick - - P. semitosta

Description of Species of Paxina

1. PAXINA ACETABULUM.

Fruit body cup shape, 2-5 cm.
wide, the cup 1-3 cm. deep,
outer surface grayish tan or
brown, with prominent, branching, connected ribs that arise
from ridges on the stem and
become smaller toward the
margin of the cup, delicately
hairy; inner surface brown or
blackish brown; stem 1-4 cm.
long, 1-2 cm. thick, with
large, irregular ridges, colored like the outside of the
cap. Solitary or a few together
on the ground in woods and open
places.

2. PAXINA HISPIDA.   Fruit body cup shape, 2-3 cm.
                        wide, 8-12 mm. deep, regular in
outline, outer surface grayish brown and densely covered
with short hairs, inner surface brown; stem 2-5 cm. long,
2-4 mm. thick at the top, tapering upward slightly, smooth
or faintly ridged, pubescent, colored like the outside of the
cup, solid and somewhat flexible. Solitary or scattered on
the ground or on very rotten wood in the forest.

3. PAXINA SEMITOSTA.   Fruit bodies, 2-5 cm. wide,
                         2-5 cm. high, deep cup shape
and tapering gradually to a thick stem, larger below the
top than at the top itself, margin incurved, irregular; outer
surface brown, delicately hairy, inner surface pale tan
when young and fresh, brown when old, stem up to 1 cm.
long, 1-2 cm. thick, ridged, hairy, colored like the outside of the cap, partly or entirely submerged. In groups
on the ground and on rotten wood.

Genus PEZIZA & RELATIVES

Key to Species of Peziza

1. Inner surface of fruit bodies violet - - P. violacea
    Inner surface tan to brown - - 2

2. Fruit body nearly flat at maturity - - P. repanda
    Fruit body cup shaped at maturity - - 3

3. Outer surface rough or coarsely granular near the base
        - - P. vesiculosa
    Outer surface smooth - - P. badia

Description of Species of Peziza

1. PEZIZA BADIA.

Fruit body at first nearly
spherical, later cup shape
with incurved margin or flattened and the margin irregularly circular in outline, 3-6
cm. in diameter, outer surface
pale tan or white when young,
later brown, smooth, inner
surface dark brown.   Usually
several specimens grow to-
gether so closely that they are somewhat distorted by mutual pressure.   On the ground in woods.

2. PEZIZA REPANDA.   Fruit body 3-12 cm. wide, first
                        cup shape, later nearly flat,
margin irregularly circular, notched or lobed; outer surface pale tan or white, inner surface pale brown when young,
darker when old, stem 2-3 cm. long or lacking. Usually in
groups on decaying wood, sometimes on the ground.

3. PEZIZA VESICULOSA.   Fruit body 2-6 cm. wide,
                        irregularly cup shape, usual-
ly much contorted from mutual pressure, sessile or tapering to a stemlike base, margin wavy and often split, outer
surface white or gray, coarsely roughened or granular toward the base, inner surface pale translucent brown.   In
clumps on manure piles, recently manured ground, compost heaps and sometimes on soil.

4. PEZIZA VIOLACEA.   Fruit body 2-5 cm. wide, cup
shape or nearly flat, margin irregularly lobed and split, outer surface almost white when young, pale violet when old, inner surface at first pale violet, later deep violet brown. Scattered or in groups on the ground, especially in areas recently burned over.

5. SARCOSCYPHA COCCINEA.   Fruit body cup shape, 1-2 cm. wide, with a stem 1-3 cm. long and 3-5 mm. thick, outside of cup and stem covered with white woolly hair, inner surface of cup bright scarlet. In groups and colonies on decaying twigs on the ground in the spring.

6. URNULA CRATERIUM.

Fruit body 2-4 cm. wide, 3-6 cm. deep, dark brown or almost black, spherical when young, later irregularly cup shape, the margin notched or lobed; outer surface of cup densely covered with short black hair, wall pliable but breaking rather easily; inner surface brown. The cup tapers to a stem 1-4 cm. long, 4-8 mm. thick, black, covered with woolly black mycelium at the base. In clumps of several on the ground.

REFERENCES

Atkinson, George F., Mushrooms. Andrus & Church, Ithaca, New York. 1901.

Christensen, Clyde M., Common Edible Mushrooms. Univ. of Minnesota Press, Minneapolis, Minn. 1943.

Christensen, Clyde M. Molds and Man. University of Minnesota Press, Minneapolis 14, Minnesota. 1951.

Clements, Frederic E., Minnesota Mushrooms. University of Minnesota Plant Studies. No. IV. 1910.

Coker, W. C. The Clavarias of the United States and Canada. Univ. of North Carolina Press, Chapel Hill, N. C. 1923.

Coker, W. C. and Alma Holland Beers. The Boletaceae of North Carolina. Univ. of North Carolina Press, Chapel Hill, N. C. 1943.

Coker, W. C. and Alma Holland Beers. The Stipitate Hydnums of the Eastern United States. University of North Carolina Press, Chapel Hill, North Carolina. 1951.

Coker, W. C., and John N. Couch. The Gastromycetes of the Eastern United States and Canada. Univ. of North Carolina Press, Chapel Hill, N. C. 1928.

Cooke, M. C. British Edible Fungi. Kegan Paul, Trench, Trübner & Co., London, England. 1891.

Graham, V. O. Mushrooms of the Great Lakes Region. Chicago Academy of Science, Chicago, Ill. 1944.

Groves, J. Walton. Edible and Poisonous Mushrooms of of Canada, Dept. of Agriculture, Ottawa, Canada. 1962.

Güssow, H. T. & W. S. Odell. Mushrooms and Toadstools. Division of Botany, Dominion Experimental Farms, Ottawa, Canada. 1928.

Hard, M. E. The Mushroom. Mushroom Publishing Company, Columbus, Ohio. 1908.

Hay, W. DeLisle. The Fungus-Hunter's Guide. Swan Sonnenschein, Lowry and Co. London, England. 1887.

Kauffman, C. H., Agaricaceae of Michigan. 2 volumes. Michigan Geological and Biological Survey Publication No. 26. Lansing, Michigan. 1918.

Krieger, Louis C. C. A Popular Guide to the Higher Fungi
(Mushrooms) of New York State. New York State Museum
Handbook No. 11. University of the State of New York,
Albany, N. Y. 1935.

Lowe, Josiah L. The Polyporaceae of New York State.
New York State College of Forestry, Syracuse, N. Y.
1942.

McIlvaine, Charles, and Robert K. MacAdam. One Thou-
sand American Fungi. Bowen-Merrill Company, Indian-
apolis, Indiana. 1902.

Overholts, L. O. The Polyporaceae of the United States,
Alaska and Canada. University of Michigan Press, Ann
Arbor, Michigan. 1953.

Ramsbottom, John. Mushrooms and Toadstools - A Study
of the Activities of Fungi. Collins, 14 St. James's
Place, London, England. 1953.

Seaver, F. J., The North American Cup-fungi. Published
by the Author. (New York Botanic Garden), 1942.

Smith. The Mushroom Hunter's Field Guide. University
of Michigan Press, Ann Arbor. 1963.

Step, Edward. Toadstools and Mushrooms of the Country-
side. Hutchinson & Co., London, England. 1913.

Swanton, E. W. Fungi and How to Know Them. Methuen
and Company, London, England. 1909.

Thomas, William S. Field Book of Common Gilled Mushrooms. G. P. Putnam's Sons. 1928. 2nd Edition, 1935.

GLOSSARY

ABORTIVE - - imperfectly formed

ACUTE - - tapering to a very narrow or sharp edge

ADNATE - - gills joined to the stem their entire width

AGARIC - - any gill fungus

ANASTOMOSING - - branching so as to form a network

ANNULUS - - the ring around the stem of a mushroom that is formed by the broken veil

APPLANATE - - flat (see plate 8, page 139)

APPRESSED - - flat, not raised

AZONATE - - without zones

CAESPITOSE - - in dense bunches or tufts

CAMPANULATE - - (see plate 7, page 9)

CARTILAGINOUS - - resembling cartilage in texture, rather tough and stringy

CONCENTRIC - - successive circles of increasing size around a common center

CONTEXT - - that portion of the fruit body above the pores or gills

CONVOLUTE - - with irregular, curved furrows

CRENULATE - - with tiny scallops

DAEDALOID - - pores that are very irregular in shape (see plate 9, page 150)

DECURRENT - - gills that run down the stem

DECURVED - - curved downward

DENTATE - - edge irregular, suggesting teeth

DICHOTOMOUS - - forked into two branches

ECCENTRIC - - attached off center

ECHINULATE - - covered with minute spines

EFFUSED REFLEXED - - partly flat on the surface, partly shelving (see plate 9, page 140)

FARINACEOUS - - an odor resembling that of freshly crushed wheat

FIMBRIATE - - fringed

FLOCCOSE - - covered with coarse woolly hairs

FREE - - gills that do not touch the stem

GLABROUS - - naked, not covered with hair

GRANULAR - - slightly rough, covered with tiny grains

GREGARIOUS - - numerous individuals near each other, but not in tufts

HYGROSCOPIC - - taking up water

IMBRICATE - - overlapping, something like shingles on a roof (see plate 9, page 140)

INTERVENOSE - - with veins between, said of gills having, on their sides, branched ridges that resemble veins

INVOLUTE - - rolled inward

LATERAL - - stem attached at one side of the cap

LOBED - - having rounded divisions on the margin

LONGITUDINAL - - lengthwise

OBTUSE - - rounded, not tapering to a sharp edge

PELLICLE - - the cuticle or thin skin forming the surface of a mushroom cap

PILEUS - - the cap of a mushroom; the entire fruit body of any stalkless fleshy fungus

POROID - - resembling pores

PUBESCENT - - covered with fine hairs

RECURVED - - curved upward and inward

RENIFORM - - shaped like a kidney bean

RETICULATE - - covered with a network of raised ridges

SECEDING - - gills that at first are attached to the stem but separate from it later

SEPARABLE - - easily removed

SERRATE - - with pointed teeth, like the edge of a saw

SESSILE - - without a stem, shelf-like

SHEATH - - a membrane of mycelium enclosing the stem of a mushroom

SINUATE - - gills notched at the stem (see plate 7, page 9)

SPATHULATE - - shaped like the blade of a spatula

STRIATE - - marked with tiny streaks, furrows or lines

STRIATIONS - - delicate lines or furrows

UMBILICATE - - a small depression in the center of the cap

UMBONATE - - having a raised portion in the center of the cap

UNDULATE - - wavy

UNGULATE - - hoof shaped (see plate 8, page 139)

VOLVA - - the cup shaped structure surrounding the base of the stem of some mushrooms

INDEX
GENERA AND SPECIES

GENUS
  species   Page   Page

AGARICUS   122   BOLETINUS   177
  abruptibulba   123   pictus   177
  arvensis   123   porosus   177
  campestris   124
  diminutiva   124   BOLETUS   178
  hemorrhodaria   124   edulis   179
  placomyces   125   felleus   179
  rodmani   125   granulatus   179
  subrufescens   125   leteus   179
                                   retipes   180
ALEURIA   sphaerosporus   180
  aurantia   221   subaureus   180

ALEURODISCUS   186   BOVISTA   197
                                   pila   198
AMANITA   17   plumbea   198
  flavoconia   18
  frostiana   18   CALOCERA
  mappa   19   cornea   211
  muscaria   19
  phalloides   20   CALVATIA   198
  rubescens   20   caelata   199
  russuloides   21   craniformis   200
  solitaria   21   cyathiformis   200
  verna   22   elata   200
                                   maxima   200
AMANITOPSIS   22
  vaginata   23   CANTHARELLUS   24
                                   aurantiacus   25
ARMILLARIA   23   cibarius   25
  mellea   23   floccosus   25
                                   infundibuliformis   26
BOLBITIUS
  tener   89

	Page		Page
CLAUDOPUS	113	confluens	38
nidulans	113	dryophila	39
variabilis	114	familia	39
		hariolarum	40
CLAVARIA	183	longipes	40
amethystina	183	maculata	41
aurea	183	myriadophylla	41
flava	183	platyphylla	41
mucida	183	radicata	42
pistillaris	183	stipitaria	43
stricta	184	velutipes	43
CLITOCYBE	26	COPRINUS	132
albissima	28	atramentarius	133
caespitosa	29	comatus	133
candida	29	ephemereus	134
cartilaginea	29	fimetarius	134
dealbata	30	micaceus	134
eccentrica	30	quadrifidus	135
ectypoides	31	radiatus	135
gigantea	31	stercorarius	135
infundibuliformis	33	sterquilinus	136
illudens	32		
laccata	33	CORDYCEPS	214
maxima	34		
multiceps	34	CORTICIUM	187
ochropurpurea	34	incarnatum	187
parilis	35		
sinopica	35	CORTINARIUS	89
truncicola	35	alboviolaceus	91
		annulatus	91
CLITOPILUS	114	armillatus	91
abortivus	114	cinnabarinus	92
caespitosus	115	cylindripes	92
micropus	115	deceptivus	92
novaboracensis	116	distans	92
orcella	116	mucifluus	93
prunulus	116	semisanguineus	93
subvilis	117	violaceus	93
COLLYBIA	36	CRATERELLUS	187
abundans	37	cantharellus	187
aquosa	37	cornucopioides	188
butyracea	38	pistillaris	188

	Page		Page
CREPIDOTUS	94	EXIDIA	
fulvotomentosus	94	glandulosa	212
haerens	95		
herbarum	95	FAVOLUS	
malachius	95	canadensis	144
mollis	95		
putrigenus	96	FISTULINA	
versutus	96	hepatica	144
CRUCIBULUM		FLAMMULA	96
vulgare	206	alnicola	97
		polychroa	97
CRYPTOCHAETE	188	sapinea	97
rufa	188	spumosa	98
CYATHUS	207	FOMES	145
stercorius	207	applanatus	146
striatus	208	conchatus	147
vernicosus	207	connatus	147
		everhartii	147
CYTIDIA	189	fomentarius	148
salicina	189	fraxinophilus	148
		igniarius	148
DAEDALIA	142	pini	149
confragosa	142	pinicola	149
quercina	143	pomaceus	150
unicolor	143	roseus	150
		scutellatus	150
DALDINIA			
concentrica	215	GALERA	98
		antipus	99
DIBOTRYON		hypnorum	99
morbosum	215	tenera	99
DICTYOPHORA		GEASTER	201
duplicata	209	coronatus	201
impudicus	209	fimbriatus	202
		limbatus	202
ENTOLOMA	117	mammosus	202
clypeatum	117	rufescens	202
rhodopolium	118	triplex	203
sericatum	118		
		GEOGLOSSUM	215

	Page		Page
HELVELLA	216	INOCYBE	99
atra	217	caesariata	100
crispa	217	calospora	100
elastica	217	destricta	101
infula	217	fastigiata	101
mitra	218	fibrosa	101
		geophylla	102
HIRNEOLA		rimosa	102
auricula-judae	212		
		ITHYPHALLUS	
HYDNUM	171	impudicus	210
adustum	173	ravenelli	210
albigoner	173		
amicum	173	LACTARIUS	49
aurisclapium	173	affinis	49
caputursi	173	clicoides	50
coralloides	174	chrysoreus	50
cyathiforme	174	controversus	50
repandum	174	deceptivus	51
septentrionale	174	deliciosus	51
velutinum	175	indigo	51
		insulsus	52
HYGROPHORUS	43	piperatus	52
cerasus	44	subdulcis	52
chrysodon	45	torminosus	53
conicus	45	trivialis	53
eburneus	45	uvidus	53
miniatus	46	velerius	54
pratensis	46	volemus	54
psitticinus	47		
pudorinus	47	LAXITEXTUM	190
puniceus	47	bicolor	190
russula	47		
		LENTINUS	55
HYMENOCHAETE	189	cochleatus	56
tabacina	189	lepideus	56
		tigrinus	57
HYPHOLOMA	126	vulpinus	57
incertum	126		
sublateritium	127	LENZITES	58
velutinum	127	betulina	58
		sepiaria	58
HYPOMYCES		trabea	59
lactifluorum	54		

Page   Page

LEOTIA   MYCENA   70
  lubrica   216   atroalba   71
                                      corticola   71
LEPIOTA   60   galericulata   71
  acutesquamosa   61   haematopa   72
  americana   61   immaculata   72
  asperula   62   leajana   73
  cepaestipes   62   pura   73
  clypeolaria   63   subincarnata   73
  cristata   63
  glioderma   64   NAUCORIA   102
  granulosa   64   platysperma   103
  morgani   64   semiorbicularis   103
  naucina   65
  procera   65   OMPHALIA   74
  rachodes   66   campanella   74
  rubrotincta   66   epichysium   74

LYCOPERDON   203   PANAEOLUS   136
  gemmatum   204   retirugis   136
  peckii   204   solidipes   137
  pulcherrimum   204
  pyriforme   205   PANUS   75
  umbrinum   205   rudis   75
                                     stipticus   75
MARASMIUS   66   strigosus   76
  cohaerans   67
  delectans   67   PATELLA   222
  olneyi   68   albida   222
  oreades   68   scutellata   222
  resinosus   69
  rotula   69   PAXILLUS   103
  siccus   69   atrotomentosus   104
  urens   70   involutus   104
                                     rhodoxanthus   105
MORCHELLA   218
  conica   219   PAXINA   222
  crassipes   219   acetabulum   223
  esculenta   219   hispida   223
  hybrida   220   semitosta   223

MUTINUS   PENIOPHORA   191
  ravenellii   210   gigantea   191

	Page		Page
PEZIZA	224	circinatus	157
badia	224	compactus	158
repanda	224	conchifer	158
vesiculosa	224	dichrous	159
violacea	225	dryophilus	159
		elegans	159
PHAEOBULGARIA	221	fibrillosus	160
inquinans	222	frondosus	160
		gilvus	160
PHOLIOTA	105	guttulatus	160
adiposa	106	hirsutus	161
albocrenulata	107	lucidus	161
caperata	107	melanopus	162
confragosa	108	nidulans	162
destruens	108	obtusus	162
discolor	109	pargamenus	163
erinaceela	109	perennis	163
marginata	110	picipes	164
muricata	110	planellus	164
praecox	110	radiatus	165
rugosa	111	resinosus	165
squarrosa	111	schweinitzii	165
squarrosoides	112	squamosus	166
		sulphureus	167
PLEUROTUS	76	tsugae	167
ostreatus	77	tulipiferus	167
sapidus	77	umbellatus	168
ulmarius	78	versicolor	168
		volvatus	168
PLUTEUS	119	zonatus	169
cervinus	119		
nanus	120	PSATHYRA	127
tomentosulus	120	umbonata	128
POLYPORUS	151	PSATHYRELLA	137
abietinus	154	disseminata	138
adustus	154		
albellus	155	PSILOCYBE	
anceps	155	foenisecii	128
arcularius	156		
betulinus	156	RUSSULA	78
brumalis	157	aeruginea	79
cinnabarinus	157	amygdaloides	80
cinnamomeus	157	atropurpurea	80

	Page
aurantialutea	80
borealis	81
delica	81
emetica	82
foetans	82
nigricans	83
roseipes	83
rubescens	83
virescens	84

SARCOSCYPHA
| coccinea | 225 |

SCHIZOPHYLLUM
| commune | 84 |

SCLERODERMA
| vulgare | 205 |

SECOTIUM
| agaricoides | 206 |

SPATHULARIA
| flavida | 216 |

STEREUM | 193 |
frustulatum	194
gausapatum	194
hirsutum	194
murrayi	195
purpureum	195
sanguinolentum	195

STROBILOMYCES
| strobilaceus | 180 |

STROPHARIA | 129 |
aeruginosa	129
coronilla	130
semiglobata	130
stercoraria	131

	Page
THELEPHORA	191
anthocephala	192
fimbriata	192
terrestris	192

TRAMETES | 169 |
| hispida | 169 |
| subrosea | 170 |

TREMELLA
| lutescens | 212 |

TREMELLODENDRON | 192 |
| pallidum | 193 |

TRICHOLOMA | 85 |
flavobrunnea	85
melaleucum	86
personatum	87
sulphureum	87
terreum	87

TROGIA
| crispa | 88 |

URNULA
| craterium | 225 |

VERPA
| bohemica | 220 |
| conica | 220 |

VOLVARIA
| bombycina | 120 |

XYLARIA
| polymorpha | 216 |